System Change

for a Liveable Future

Terry Leahy

Published by Mayfly Books. Available in paperback
and free online at www.mayflybooks.org in 2025.

ISBN (Print)   978-1-906948-80-1
ISBN (PDF)   978-1-906948-81-8

Cover art work by Brenna Quinlan who retains the image copyright.

may fly

System Change

for a Liveable Future

Terry Leahy

Contents

Introduction: System Change for a Liveable Future   01

1. Capitalism: The Ghost in the Machine   13

2. Capitalism: The Ghost Walks   43

3. What's Wrong with Money?   71

4. Pathways out of Capitalism: The Gift Economy   95

5. Pathways out of Capitalism: Democratic Socialism   123

6. Pathways out of Capitalism: Radical Reformism   149

7. Transitions to the Gift Economy   173

8. The Zapatistas: A State that is not a State   201

9. Anarchism, the State, and the Gift Economy   233

10. Prefiguring the Gift Economy: First Bite   261

11. Prefiguring the Gift Economy: Second Bite   281

12. Conclusions   303

Appendix A – Capitalist Patriarchy   319

Appendix B – The Gift Economy and the Anthropologists   327

Acknowledgements   341

Introduction

This book is based on the slogan often chanted at climate rallies. *System Change, not Climate Change.* A somewhat optimistic slogan, given that climate change is already happening and locked in, up to a point. At the same time, the basic meaning of this message is still valid. To have any kind of liveable future we need system change. Capitalism is a system that creates environmental problems through its basic economic structures. While we may begin to tackle the climate disaster through reforms within capitalism, these reforms are likely to fall short. We need something a lot more drastic.

Do you ever get the feeling that the population of the world is standing around like a deer caught in the headlights? Waiting for the end of the world. I mean most people know that the path we are on is catastrophic. But with some glorious exceptions, they are not doing that much about it. For the most part people in the rich countries are voting for mainstream parties and those in the global South are putting up with long established dictatorships, or oligarchic democracies.

When I was living in Newcastle in Australia, I started doing interviews and focus groups with local people. Newcastle is a large provincial industrial town. It is so mainstream in the Australian context that advertising companies try out their ads there. This was in the nineties when there still was a steel works in Newcastle. By 2003 I had worked with Jenny Gow to do a phone survey, to get some stats on how people were reading environmental issues. The results we got were astonishing. If you asked people what they thought was going to happen in the next fifty years, they would tell you that it would be disastrous. A catastrophic end to life as we know it. At this time, climate change was not so much on the radar as it is now. But the disasters they envisaged were things like an environmental crisis, an invasion by a foreign power, a nuclear war, a pandemic that would kill most of the population.[1]

This was pretty strange. I grew up in the fifties and sixties, with everyone believing that things could only get better as modern science created yet new wonders. Yet a decade or two of neoliberal insecurity and environmental alarm had wiped all that optimism away. Despite their pessimistic outlook, these interviewees were the same people who were voting for the two mainstream parties. The interviewees were not voting for these mainstream parties because they trusted them. They did not. Most believed governments were working hand in glove with corrupt business magnates. Politicians were only interested in their own advancement and business was only interested in profits. Nobody really cared about what happened to ordinary Australians.[2]

So why were they so passive in the face of impending doom? One thing was two track thinking. In one track, they expected business as usual to continue, an affluent modernity, in one of the lucky countries of the world. As political actors they operated in that world. Voting for the party that they thought might help them to get, or keep, a job. Spending their spare time in leisure rather than fruitless politics. But reflecting on things more deeply, their thinking took another track. The dark dreams in the middle of the night. Evil elites were running the world and driving us to catastrophe.[3]

The other reason for their fatalism was that they could not see any attractive alternative to the status quo. They were suspicious of environmentalists. They regarded environmentalists as extremists who might get the reins of government and destroy the economy and jobs. Regulating daily life to the point where it was not worth living. The nanny state. They would never vote for the Greens or get involved in environmentalist activism.[4]

This political scenario is not unique to Australia. Everyone knows that the current system is leading us to disaster. But they do not find any of the usual alternatives remotely appealing. Their anger finds expression in far-right gestures. Like Brexit, Trump, Bolsonaro,

Putin, Milei and the far-right wave in Europe. This response expresses paranoia and fear, rather than hope for new solutions. The demand is for freedom from the nanny state. Paradoxically, to be sought in yet another dictator. In a promise that the security and confidence of the past can be brought back. Make America Great *Again*.[5] In the South, that development can be put back on track.

Meanwhile, environmental disasters and signs of impending catastrophe just mount up. Bushfires and floods ravage urban neighbourhoods and pastoral idylls. Temperatures shoot up, bleaching coral reefs. The ice sheet shrinks. Wars in the Middle East and North Africa are fuelled by drought. The covid crisis drops on us like a ton of bricks. Plastics proliferate and take out ocean ecosystems. Nuclear plants melt down and destroy whole regions. Insect populations plummet, victims of pesticides and climate change. The IPCC tells us that we need to stop warming at 1.5 degrees but does not expect that to happen. Instead, they warn us of catastrophic runaway climate change.[6] For me the most chilling image is a map of heat zones on the globe in a period of paleo-climate history when parts per million of CO_2 got to where they are now. A world where you could not actually live anywhere south of London or north of Melbourne.[7] It is hard to believe that the human species is sleepwalking into a future where we destroy three quarters of our habitat. Knowing full well that we are doing that. It is equally difficult to fathom the moral incongruity of the situation. That this will come about as we switch on an electric kettle, drive to work, or turn on the ducted heating.

On the ground not a great deal is happening. It would be a mistake to say that governments are doing *nothing*. Governments in some rich countries are setting strong deadlines for phasing out fossil fuels. For example, the UK commitment in 2025 to cut emissions by 81% by 2035 to aim at net zero by 2050.[8] The EU has announced a ban on new internal combustion vehicles being sold. To start in 2035. With an exception for vehicles using biofuels. However, the ban will not affect existing vehicles, which will continue to run on fossil fuels.[9] To an extent, these are just promises. Right here right now only a small fraction of GDP is in fact going into this promised transition. For example, in the United States in 2023, GDP grew by 2.5%. Of that total growth, 6% was the growth in green energy. Meaning that out of the total GDP of the USA, only 0.15 per cent was being spent on the energy transition. China, usually seen as way ahead of the pack was spending 0.26 per cent of its GDP on the transition in 2023. In the EU, GDP growth was very sluggish at 0.52 per cent in 2023. Of their total GDP, only 0.16 per cent was being spent on the energy transition.[10] As Greta Thunberg and XR have been pointing out, there is *no emergency response*. Nothing proportional to the crisis we face. The Chinese government sees a golden opportunity selling electric vehicles and solar panels. While still building coal fired power stations.[11] Car companies in the rich countries are shocked by their earlier promises and wind back their deadlines for ending the sale of petrol and diesel cars.[12] Nothing can be done which does not maintain current lifestyles in the global North—and development in the global South.

Added to this is the impossibility of the transition that mainstream parties are promising. One hundred per cent renewables and every device and vehicle powered up with sustainable energy sources. It is totally unlikely that we will ever get the minerals we need for even one generation of that option. Michaux is a geologist, with special interest in minerals and mining. His report to the Geological Survey of Finland outlines the problems with optimistic scenarios based on replacing fossil fuels with renewables. 'Global reserves are not large enough to supply enough metals to build the renewable non-fossil fuels industrial system or satisfy long term demand in the current system'[13]. To transition to a renewable economy, we must create new machinery using minerals sourced via mining. There is no option to recycle minerals from machinery that we do not yet have. Yet there are insufficient global reserves of minerals such as lithium, nickel and cobalt, even copper. For example, with copper, a metal central to the electrification project:

> In 2019, global consumption of copper metal was 24.5 million
> tonnes and global copper reserves were reported at 870 million

tonnes (USGS mineral statistics). Using a straight and crude calculation, this means that current reserves represent 35.5 years of supply at 2019 mining and recycling rates. Copper demand is projected to increase to approximately 100 million tonnes per annum by the year 2100.[14]

A paper authored by Michaux and others includes a table that compares the mineral requirements for a fleet of EVs to match current internal combustion engines—with the known reserves of these minerals. Known reserves are between half and a quarter the size of requirements for zinc, lithium and graphite. Similar results apply if we compare known reserves of minerals to requirements for wind turbines and solar panels.[15] In another paper, Michaux is sceptical about the prospects for recycling. We have yet to construct the first generation of this machinery – so we will need mining to get those minerals in the first place. For future generations of this technology, the efficacy of recycling depends on the mineral in question. He does not expect much change from current rates of recycling – between one and fifty per cent.[16]

So, we have just *promises* to act and a commitment to implement an *unworkable* transition.

All this just gives people even more reasons for apocalyptic nightmares. Yet still the people of the world do nothing drastic. This book will look at this conundrum from the point of view of alternatives to the capitalist system. The situation we are in now is an effect of the basic economic structures of the global capitalist economy. The problem with proposed solutions for environmental problems is always this—that they might damage that capitalist economy. The long and the short of it. Businesses must make profit their priority. Workers must make having a job their priority. In the one track that is business as usual, every environmental proposal must run this gauntlet. Most of the time, the things that are drastic enough to deal with our problems do not get past this checkpoint. Reducing the consumer economy. Spending so much on energy transition that the rest of the economy goes into a tailspin. Redundancies for people working in the fossil fuel industries. Ending mass air travel. Localising agriculture. Banning long life plastics and toxic pesticides.

A typical example in Australia was the 2019 election in which Bill Shorten was the Labor (ALP) leader. An Indian magnate, Adani, wanted to open a huge coal mine in Queensland. Urban electorates that voted for the Greens opposed the mine. We do not need to export yet more fossil fuels to an overheated world. The Labor party was fearful of losing even more seats in these inner urban electorates. They hedged their position. They did not fully endorse the Adani mine. They left it open that they might shut it down – for environmental reasons. A convoy of environmentalists arrived in Queensland to pressure the Labor party. Wanting it to take a more definite environmentalist position and *stop* the Adani mine. That just stoked resentment from the Queensland electorate. These urban middle class environmentalists from the South are trying to take *our* jobs. The ALP was wiped out at the election. The seats they lost were all in working-class electorates. Even the CFMEU mining and construction union deserted the Labor party. Working class people across Australia voted in solidarity with a mere handful of workers—those who might *just possibly* have got a job in the Adani mine.[17] That was in 2019. Now in 2025 the Labor party still has no policy to phase out coal exports. The only energy policies that can be countenanced are:

- Policies that provide jobs – moving to renewables in Australia.
- Policies that do not increase the price of electricity.
- Policies that save the jobs of everyone working in fossil fuels.
- Policies that do not increase taxes.

Such constraints make an emergency response impossible.

Up to a point, people are aware that the system prevents us from blocking impending environmental disasters. Many people blame business for environmental problems. Others argue that environmentalists in government might wreck the economy.[18] Versions of the same insight.

This book will argue that a key problem is that the alternatives for system change that are most widely understood are both unpalatable and unworkable. This is the basic reason that they are not gaining large scale mass support. Because of this impasse, people do not bother to oppose capitalism or to demand action on the crises that face us. They know that current elites will do nothing. So why bother to make demands? They cannot imagine an alternative system that could work any better. So why bother to overthrow these elites and change the system? There are two models for system change that are dominant on the left. Neither of them is gaining much traction with the public.

1. The democratic socialist model. An economy with central planning and nationalisation of most production.

2. The steady state economy model pioneered by Herman Daly. A market economy where government regulation pulls growth back, leading to a final steady state.

An alternative that is less understood is the one this book is promoting. I am calling it here the 'grassroots gift economy', or simply the 'gift economy'. A version of anarchism, based in an economy without money or anything similar. 'Anarcho-communism', as originally proposed by Kropotkin. This has always looked like a utopian dream. Here I want to show how we could make it work, even in a high-tech complex economy.

The listing of these alternatives reveals another problem for those who want to promote system change. Disunity on *what* system we might change to. While the environmentalist left is united in seeing the capitalist system as the problem, there is no unity on what might replace capitalism. For the public at large, it looks like we do not know what we are doing. When the Occupy movement took off, it became obvious that participants were far from united on a preferable alternative to capitalism. One response was to argue that the alternative represented by Occupy was the system of decision making developed by Occupy itself. Anarchist principles of organisation—even when people had wildly differing opinions on system change.[19] I am sceptical. Participatory democracy is only a small part of an answer to the questions that people outside the left are asking. How do you propose to replace capitalism? How can we be sure that your ideas will really work?

What could bring about a more unified left? Effective coalition politics is part of it. At the same time, I would like to see the gift economy alternative gaining support from people who are now apolitical. Those who are discontented with capitalism and concerned about the environmental crisis. But cannot envisage an attractive alternative. I am hoping that those people will be inspired by the gift economy. Unifying the left around that option. This book hopes to recruit activists to the gift economy perspective. To sketch out the arguments we need to promote that alternative.

Let me now explain how this book has been put together. Spoiler alert. If you would rather be surprised, go now to the chapters and dive in!

I begin this book looking at how capitalism works as a system. Capitalism is a social invention, based on imagined and largely unconscious ideas. The capitalist social machine divides the population into classes. The ruling class maintains its power by exploiting people's work. A machine but also a game. As a social game it has a history— an effect of the actions of social groups. I consider four basic phases of capitalist history, from the seventeenth century to the present day. Why is the capitalist social machine coming unstuck now? What are the prospects for the future?

You may want to skip these two first chapters and just get straight into the topic of system change. Start with chapter three if you are feeling like that. Think of these first two chapters as a resource you might pick up later. On the other hand, if you want to start off by finding out how the systems we have are working now, go ahead and read these first two chapters.

The next section of the book, starting with chapter three, explains the problems with money and lays out the basic plans for a gift economy. Most people think of money as a useful tool—to facilitate exchange. A necessity to make a complex economy work. I challenge these ideas.

Money and the market go hand in hand. The market gives money priority. Social justice and environmental sanity take second place. The market and money depend on alienated labour. For a system that works for people and the planet we need to get rid of money.

The gift economy is one of three key proposals for system change and the one that this book promotes. The gift economy functions without money. Instead, collectives make agreements to supply goods and services to particular people and groups. Some working groups supply their own communities. Others are units in a production chain, linking up to assemble and distribute what they produce. How could a system like this ensure fair distribution, good environmental outcomes, and security for all?

There are two other models for post-capitalist systems that are much more influential than the gift economy. In the democratic socialist model, the state takes ownership of most of the means of production—on behalf of the people. A democratic government plans the economy to avoid environmental damage and ensure social justice. In my view, problems inherent in a monetary economy would still plague this proposal in practice.

The most popular alternative for system-change in the environmentalist movement is the steady state economy. Versions of this model feature in a great diversity of environmentalist writing. Because of this diversity I call this proposal 'radical reformism.' Radical in so far as it implies an end to capitalism. Reformist in so far as it intends to reform the market economy rather than replace it. Intensive government regulation and intervention winds back economic growth to zero. In the rich countries, degrowth is also necessary. Much of the economy remains in private hands. The market operates within government guidelines. Yet key proposals of this pathway are likely to undermine and even destroy a market economy—the whole foundation of this model. So, this is not a coherent alternative. If we tried it out, we would end up with something else.

A third part of this book, starting with chapter seven, looks at how we might get from where we are now to a gift economy. Also, at some of the prefiguring interventions that are being put in place around the world. I begin with a description of the Zapatista insurgency. The region of Mexico controlled by the Zapatistas is what I will call an 'autonomous zone'. How do the Zapatistas implement community control of economics and politics? This has been the most thorough attempt to set up a gift economy in recent history. It is also a hybrid of the gift economy and capitalism—with some of the problems that go with that. The 'state' cannot exist in a gift economy. Yet the Zapatistas show us how we might square this circle, with a governing federation that is not a 'state'.

For the transition to the gift economy there are a range of possible options. A popular revolution supported by armed force. An act of parliament following a landslide election victory. A multiplicity of 'prefiguring' grassroots initiatives links together and begins to operate without money, as the capitalist economy crumbles.

Following my account of the Zapatistas, I consider the question of whether a 'state' could be part of a gift economy. Anarchist authors reject the state. I consider this and look at several approaches. Anarchism is defined in relation to 'the state'. Anarchists oppose the state. I examine ideas about the state coming from Marx and Weber, founders of sociology. Marx and Engels see the revolution as a seizure of state power by the proletariat. Anarchists are critical of this model of transition, proposing a stateless post-capitalism. There is a gap between market and non-market anarchist writings. This difference is very relevant to intentions to abandon the state. If we had a revolution to a non-monetary gift economy, would a state be useful? I explain the argument that a state would be impossible in such a society. What version of territorial organisation might be possible? Would any such organisation be necessary?

I show how each of these options for a transition implies a period of prefiguring within the current economy. Of two kinds. In one, we try to carve off a piece of social space and run it like the post-capitalist society we are hoping for in the future. What I will call 'autonomous zones'. Another is what I call 'hybrids of the gift economy and capitalism'. These embody some aspects of the gift economy that prefigure a post capitalist system. This is combined with aspects of a current market-dominated economy. We can look at the market and gift economy aspects of these hybrids. I look at the tensions in trying to operate a gift economy ethics in a market economy context. Hybrids are a worthwhile strategy, but they are never without problems.

This is very much a *manual* for system change, system change made simple. I have written to avoid jargon and confusing verbiage. I have made a determined effort to answer all the tricky questions, rather than relying on vague slogans—that do not cut any ice with a sceptical public. Surely now is the time to end class society before it kills off the human species. To make a transition to a liveable future. To do that we need a system that can work, avoiding the destruction of the natural world through its basic make up. Rather than through an attempt to implement regulations that everyone hates.

Endnotes

[1] John [Jenny] Gow and Terry Leahy, 'Apocalypse Probably; Agency and Environmental Risk in the Hunter Region', *Journal of Sociology*, Vol. 41(2) 2005, pp. 1 – 25.

[2] Ibid.

[3] Terry Leahy, Vanessa Bowden, and Steven Threadgold, 'Stumbling Towards collapse: Coming to terms with the climate crisis', *Environmental Politics*, Vol. 19 2010, pp. 851-868.

[4] Leahy, Terry, 'Ecofeminism in Theory and Practice: Women's Responses to Environmental Issues', *Journal of Interdisciplinary Gender Studies*, 7(1 & 2) 2003, pp. 106 - 125.

[5] Arlie Hochschild, *Strangers in Their Own Land: Anger and Mourning on the American Right*, The New Press, New York, 2016.

[6] IPCC, *AR6 Synthesis Report: Climate Change 2023*, https://www.ipcc. ch/report/sixth-assessment-report-cycle/, viewed on 19 February 2025, Nick O'Malley, 'New studies suggest a key Paris warming target has been breached', *The Age*, 12 February, 2025.

[7] James Hansen, *Storms of My Grandchildren: The Truth About the Coming Climate Catastrophe and Our Last Chance to Save Humanity*, Bloomsbury Press, 2009.

[8] World Resources Institute, 'STATEMENT: UK Releases Ambitious 2035 NDC, Putting Country on Path to Net Zero', https://www.wri.org/news/, 30 January 2025, viewed on 19 February 2025.

[9] Sam Meredith, 'Sweden's Volvo Cars scraps plan to sell only electric vehicles by 2030', *Sustainable Future*, CNBC. 2024, https://www.cnbc.com/2024/09/04/; Greencell, 'Ban on Petrol and Diesel Cars – What Will Change in 2035?', 2024 https://greencell.global/en/gcnews/other/, viewed on 20 February, 2025.

[10] Laura Cozzi, Timur Gül, Thomas Spencer, Peter Levi, 'Clean Energy is Boosting Economic Growth', International Energy Agency, 18 April 2024, https://www.iea.org/commentaries/, viewed on 19 February, 2025.

[11] Nick O'Malley, 'With Trump declaring war on climate action, is this the last straw?', *The Age*, 18 February, 2025.

[12] Joshua Posaner, 'Germany rejects Commission's proposal for ending car engine impasse', *Politico*, 23 March 2023.

[13] Simon P. Michaux, *The Mining of Minerals and the Limits to Growth*, Report number: 16/2021, Geological Survey of Finland, Helskinki, 2021, p. 2.

[14] Ibid, p. 9.

[15] Simon P. Michaux, Tere Vadén, J.M. Korhonen and Jussi T. Eronen, *Assessment of the scope of tasks to completely phase out fossil fuels in Finland*, Report 18/2022, Geological Survey of Finland, Helskinki, 2021, p.81.

[16] Simon P. Michaux, ibid, p. 81, 2021.

[17] Anika Gaujer, Marian Sawer, Marian Simms, *Morrison's Miracle: The 2019 Australian Federal Election*, ANU Press, Canberra, 2020.

[18] Leahy, Bowden, Threadgold, op cit 2011.

[19] David Graeber, 'The New Anarchists', *New Left Review*, 13, Jan-Feb, 2002; Marisa Holmes, *Occupying Wall Street: This is Just Practice*, Palgrave Macmillan, Singapore, 2023.

Chapter 1
Capitalism: The Ghost in the Machine

A phrase you'll often hear is 'system change, not climate change'. This book explores that idea. How could we change the system? The capitalist system, the patriarchal system, the racist system. Systems that are destroying the planet. How did these systems come about? What connects them? So, this chapter and the next concentrate on capitalism as a key system of modern societies. But I will also consider the connections between capitalism and other social systems. .

Capitalism

I have called this chapter 'capitalism, the ghost in the machine'. Why am I talking about ghosts? Let me start off by saying what's wrong with conspiracy theories. Conspiracy theories have the idea that there's this shadowy elite that's up there pulling strings. If you look at capitalism in that way, it is obvious that the capitalist class is that evil elite. People like Rupert Murdoch, Jeff Bezos, Elon Musk and the like. The One Percent that the occupy movement talks about.

But what this populist analysis fails to grasp is the coherence of capitalism as a social machine. A social machine operates through the *combined* actions of the whole population. Including people that are not part of that elite class. People in general are caught up in this social machine and participate in its construction.

I like to use the phrase 'the ghost in the machine' to get to grips with how a social machine can operate without being *controlled* by a conspiracy at the top. Gilbert Ryle, a philosopher talking about mind-body problems, coined this phrase to talk about a theory he wanted to challenge.[1] But I want to use it more positively as a way of thinking about the nature of societies. My thinking on this owes much to Castoriadis, a Greek/French leftist and psychoanalytic theorist. He argues that societies are animated by a set of imaginary and largely unconscious ideas.[2] Almost everyone in any society takes these ideas for granted. We can think of this 'ghost' as the basic rules of the game that found a social machine. Operating like a game of chess or football, with various positions and rules. These constitute the background assumptions through which the game, as you see it on the TV, is played out.

Clearly this is not the first analysis to think of 'modes of production' as essentially 'games.'[3] With the 'social imaginary' that Castoriadis speaks about being conceived as a set of instructions for a game. For example, in *Beyond Money*, Anitra Nelson constantly refers to capitalism as a game and spells out the implications of that for the way social actors operate.[4], 'This is where capitalism is a game and, like all games, it involves skill, knowledge, experience and luck.'[5] Much of her analysis of the implications of capitalism as a game is replicated here in the accounts of my introductory chapters. Another example of game analysis in the social sciences is Bourdieu's framing of social action as moves in a social game.[6]

You can look at this 'game' analysis in terms of a variety of theories. Using the language of Foucault, we might refer to the ghost as a hegemonic discourse.[7] Or in a Marxist framing, we might think of the ghost as a dominant ideology.[8] The way Castoriadis frames it, this ghost is a set of largely unconscious assumptions about reality. These assumptions are in fact *imagined* and created over time by human actors. His example is the idea that you can *buy* someone's capacity to work. As Marx says, a foundational premise of capitalism. Castoriadis says that idea is no less imaginary than thinking that your ancestor is an owl.[9]

Social structures are relatively permanent features of social life. Repeated acts and events. The repetition and sameness of these events indicates that some governing social force is causing them to happen again and again. That governing force is the social adoption of a particular social game. Note here that while culture is all about what should happen and beliefs about what is happening, a structure is something that is just happening. These structural events are events that are taking place in the social world. Even in cases where people are deluded in their beliefs about them.

Like any game, social games imply structures. For example, in AFL that the two teams are opposing each other across the field, with one team trying to move the ball to the left and the other trying to move it to the right. This is a repeated pattern. It constitutes a social structure that is like a 'machine' in operation. So, in League matches there are five tackles allowed and the team with the ball tries to move up the field, passing the ball between their players. A structure. What you see in the League example is repeated drives by each team moving up the field and being tackled by the opposing team members. Just like in a clock what you see is one gear repeatedly moving another in a structured pattern. Society under the influence of a social game is exactly like that. A machine-like structure that comes out of the operation of the game in practice.

In all games, structures have force, they are backed by various kinds of incentives that bind players to implement those structures. In a case where players radically defy these structural requirements, the game is over, you are playing a different social game. For example, if in an AFL match, one team started to help the other team by consistently moving the ball in the same direction as the opposing team and consistently scoring 'own goals', we would have to say that we were not playing AFL anymore. That game would have been abandoned. Similarly, if we had a capitalist market economy and all the players stopped buying cheap and selling dear, we would be ending the market social game. For example, everyone might be giving stuff away for no money at all. The market economy would have ceased to dominate society as a social game.

Social games imply machine social structures that put particular groups of people into *roles* or *positions* in the social machine. In AFL, ruck, back etc. In capitalism, owner of property, capitalist, middle class person, unemployed. Each of these positions is rewarded and sanctioned by society to persuade or enforce participation in the game role. For example, a CEO is paid a huge salary that allows a vast choice of access to the products of other people's work. These sanctions ultimately work on aspects of human nature. The desire for autonomy (to get what you want), for approval (prestige, status, good company, for self-esteem).

What we can also say is that in a social game (as distinct from a game that is merely play) these sanctions and rewards are usually backed up by coercive force. If you steal the Rolex of some rich person, you may end up incarcerated or even killed. The machine structures of the social regime are enforced like this.

Note that as in any game, the social game allows—and indeed requires and expects—players to invent moves that fit within the game rules. This is the sense in which we are looking at a social *game* not just a social *structure*. Structures can remain the same even though moves in the game are different. The bishop in chess always moves diagonally, but *when* a player moves their bishop and *where* is an invention, a choice. The same applies to social games. Every social game has a history, an effect of the choices of players over time, working within the frameworks of the game. Or indeed sometimes working to go *outside* that game framework and undo it. Like the 1968 Paris uprising that attempted to *overthrow* capitalism.

The ghostly construction of capitalism

Looking at capitalism like this, capitalism is an invention of the human species, another kind of class society. Capitalism follows the model of earlier versions of class society, also invented and governed by a set of ghostly assumptions. Not that different to ancient Egypt or the Incas in many important respects. In Marxist language, capitalism is a 'mode of production'. A way people relate to each other around the production of material items. But behind this is a set of imaginary ideas, a largely unconscious agreement to play the social game in a particular way. To allocate social positions and capacities in relation to the rules of that game. Thereby creating a social machine—predictable and expected social actions and relationships. There are always a variety of causal influences on this process. The history of a social game is 'over determined' as Foucault shows.

Capitalism takes place in two distinct movements. The first stage of 'mercantilist' capitalism begins with the trading empires set up by Europe in the early period of imperial expansion. The political system in Europe at the time was dominated by absolute monarchs, a landed aristocracy and the church. Key events are Portugal opening a sea route to Asia, displacing the earlier Silk Road connection. Along with Columbus' 'discovery' of the Americas at the end of the fifteenth century. A second stage of capitalism involved the intensification of commodity production within Europe, with industrialisation of that production by the nineteenth century. An earlier stage of this process established factories that assembled hand powered machines under one roof. A later stage powered these machines with steam. Associated with this second stage, the various 'bourgeois' revolutions undermined the political power of the landed aristocracy.[11]

In human history taken as a whole we are looking at a mere five centuries. Yet many people think capitalism will never go away, which seems to me very unlikely. I am sure it will, eventually! So let us begin to look at this ghost more closely and describe the key animating ideas of capitalism. The following account is a way of interpreting some of Marx's analysis.[12]

The first aspect of the ghostly construction of capitalism is that things that produce useful material items are owned privately. What Marx calls the private ownership of 'the means of production'. And can be sold on the market. So, this is quite different from other class societies. For example, in Feudal Europe, the lord of the manor could not *sell* the manor, his land and residence. He had to pass it on to his heir, usually the eldest son. In turn, he had received it from his father and so on. Ultimately, it was the king who owned the manor and all land in his kingdom. The king *lent* the manor to the lord, who swore allegiance to the king. So, in Feudal Europe these complicated understandings about land imply that the means of production are not available on the market.[13] This is different in capitalist society.

The basic means of production can be sold on the market. If you're the owner of a factory, a farm, a bank, a power grid or whatever—ultimately, you can always sell it.

To maintain the value of your means of production, you must put that means of production into play. You can't just sock it away under the bed, just leave it in a bank. The value of any item of the means of production changes. You must put it out there and make it work. Say you have a factory. If you just leave it and do nothing with it, it is not realizing its potential value. It is not making money by producing things for sale. As well, the equipment you have starts to date. The original value of your factory declines. The minute you start making things and selling those things on the market, then your factory has value. In capitalism, the value of means of production is their potential to make money. To demonstrate this potential and maintain value, you must continue to *make* money.

The second aspect of the ghostly construction is that there's a distinction between employers and employees. Employers own the means of production. They pay people to work and produce value, making objects or services, which the owners can then sell on. Employees do not own the means of production. They cannot live by using means of production to produce the things they need. Instead, they must sell their labour capacity to an employer. So they can use their pay to buy what they need.

I have identified two basic social positions in the capitalist social game – employers and employees. People who are *not* employed and do not own the means of production occupy a third social position. They are scraping by at the edge of survival. These people are *potential* employees. If they could get a job, they would. Marxists refer to them as the 'reserve army of labour'. In today's world, these people are much more likely to be living in the global South. There are a billion people who are going hungry and another billion who are suffering from food deficiency diseases, wasting, anaemia, and the like. Because their income is insufficient to purchase a good diet.[14] Colonial governments took their 'means of production' and these are still in the hands of a rich elite, connected to global capitalism. Intense competition for work in those countries means that capitalists can pay the lowest possible wage to the people they *do* employ.[15]

A third aspect of the ghostly construction of the capitalist social machine is that labour is sold on the market. As 'free' labour. The employee owns their capacity to work and can sell it like any other commodity. They can *choose* their employer. This is completely different to other kinds of class society where the labour capacity of the subordinate class is not theirs to dispose of. In feudal society, each landlord has control over 'their' peasants. That landlord has the right to command their labour, to produce a tribute. In a slave society like Ancient Greece, the slave owner commands the work of the slave. Owning the slave *and* their labour power.

Nevertheless, as Marx says, while employees in capitalism may be free to choose their employer, they are *slaves* to the capitalist class, taken as a whole.[16] To live, you must sell your labour power—so you can buy what you need on the market. In selling your labour power, you lose the right to decide what to do with that capacity while you are at work. Your employer commands your labour. The contract to sell labour is regarded as giving the employer a moral right to obedience. Just like if you buy an orange, you have a moral right to eat it.

A fourth key feature of this ghostly construction is the way the social machine extracts a surplus from employees. In other words, a surplus over and above the value of what they are paid for their work. People get a wage, but the wage is not the full monetary value of what they produce. So, they might produce $300 worth of extra value to the capitalist firm, but they're only getting paid a hundred dollars of that value.

In other class societies, the extraction of a surplus is more transparent. The slave works on the master's fields and is only given a small portion of what they grow for their own use. Or the peasant in feudal society who works on their own field for four days a week and works on the lord's field for two days a week. Arrangements like that make the extraction of a surplus product obvious. For example, bags of wheat carried up to the lord's house. In capitalism, this extraction of surplus is concealed. The labour contract appears to involve two equal players who agree on a price for a labour service, a price determined by the market. But this apparent equality obscures the reality of class exploitation—the monopoly of the ownership of the means of production, the unequal deal of the wage contract, distribution by market processes.

This extraction of surplus is part of what produces the inequality that characterises capitalism. As the capitalist extracts surplus value from their workers, they can use that surplus to grow their means of production. The monopoly game in action. Let us look at some figures. The richest one percent of the global population owns fifty percent of global wealth. The richest ten percent of the population accounts for 85% of household wealth.[17] The average wealth of each adult in the top one per cent is more than 300 times the average wealth of someone in the bottom ninety per cent.[18] So, wealth is very unequally distributed. These figures include wealth in private personal possessions—such as houses and cars. The degree of inequality is even more extreme if we just look at disparities in the ownership of the wealth used to *produce* goods and services. The extreme skew of these figures backs up the Marxist account – the ruling class *owns* the means of production in capitalism just as surely as in other class societies.

These figures also suggest the existence of an important global middle class. One per cent own fifty percent of the global wealth and ten per cent own 85% of the global wealth. Meaning that the middle class of nine percent must own 35% of global wealth.

The fifth ghostly feature of capitalism is the process by which relevant players gain access to the various requirements of the game. For example, private ownership of the means of production. Where do these means of production come from? How do they enter the capitalist game and fall into the hands of capitalists? Likewise with free labour? Where do these people come from? This aspect of capitalism takes place off scene, outside of the game itself, as the condition that allows the game to take place. It is not in itself governed by the four ghostly rules described above.

As Marx uses the term, 'primitive accumulation' is the process by which the capitalist class first comes to own the means of production—which it then puts into circulation as capital.[19] A recent translation refers to this as 'original accumulation'. In the British case, the enclosure movement broke the tie between peasant agriculturalists and their land. In feudal Britain, lords owned estates that included peasant plots and common land used by villagers. The development of capitalism saw these peasants removed from their land. The lords appropriated the common land. This is what Marx is calling 'primitive' or 'original' accumulation. Meaning a *first* accumulation of means of production. In the next stage of this process the lords became capitalist farmers, growing agricultural commodities for sale and hiring labour. This enclosure of common land also provided capitalists with the labour they needed to run industrial businesses. The peasants lost their land to enclosures. Without a source of subsistence, they were thrown onto the streets as 'vagabonds.' Available for employment. Forcibly 'freed' from their connection to land.[20]

Marx also used the term 'primitive accumulation' to refer to the acquisition of means of production in colonized countries. Governments and firms from Europe took land by force. These thefts of the means of production enabled the growth of capitalist wealth in the global North. The land that was seized as colonies produced commodities such as cotton, spices, silk, sugar, wheat, timber, gold, silver. Later, minerals, oil, rubber, and more agricultural products. The wealth and 'modernity' of capitalist Europe and the settler colonies depended on these acquisitions. Samir Amin prefers the term 'dispossession' to the usual Marxist term 'primitive accumulation'. This is because accumulation through dispossession 'is a permanent feature in the history of capitalism'.[21] Historical capitalism, he argues, is imperialist by nature. It depends on these acquisitions. I will consider this in the next chapter. I like the term 'primitive accumulation' because it denotes a chronological relationship. Primitive accumulation must happen *first*, before the capitalist social machine can operate. This happens many times over the course of capitalist history. Putting yet new means of production into the hands of capitalists and yet new people into its employ.

Capitalism as a game

In many ways, the description of capitalism I have been giving follows Marx's writings on this topic, for example in *Wage Labour and Capital* or in the *Manifesto* or *Capital* itself. Usually, we treat the features of capitalism I have been talking about as a 'social structure', an analogy with the built environment of bricks and mortar. That is fair enough to an extent. This description represents a set of repeated practices that create a social machine. But we can also look at this as Nelson and Castoriadis suggest[22]. Many elements of this description refer to things that are completely imaginary. For example, it is a fiction that someone can *own* a piece of real estate or a factory or even a pop-up toaster. That this can happen is an idea that some people dreamed up. What makes it real is the way people orient their social conduct and their relationships with material things to this imagined 'ownership'. Similarly with concepts like selling and buying. The idea that we can buy something and by that change our practical relationship to that thing. Not to mention a whole set of moral claims going with that. Money itself, the most magical idea of all. That these figures, coins, pieces of paper have value and we can exchange them for the products of people's work. This capitalist social game is no less an imaginary invention than a football match such as an AFL (Australian Football League) game. These white sticks of wood represent 'goal posts.' The aim of this group of 'players' here is to kick this yellow leather oval between these posts, so 'scoring' a 'goal'. As with capitalism, this social game makes perfectly good sense. Because everyone is making the same imaginary assumptions and conducting themselves accordingly.

Other social machines linked to capitalism

Capitalism, throughout its history, exists alongside and in combination with other social machines. These social machines are articulated with capitalism. Capitalism, as it *actually operates*, depends on these links. It also intersects with these social machines to create 'racist capitalism', 'capitalist patriarchy' and so on.

Non-capitalist production relationships

In the previous discussion, I have characterised the exploitation of the subordinate class in capitalism as an exploitation of 'free labour'. A trajectory between feudal societies with *serf labour* and capitalism. A break between the *slave* societies of the ancient world and the free labour of modern capitalism. But this is very misleading when applied to the colonial period. I will discuss this in more detail in the next chapter. But clearly capitalism as a global system at that time included the colonized countries—where most of the population were working as slaves.[23] At the same time what they produced was integrated into the global capitalist market. Not just this, but countries that were part of the heartland of early capitalism were dependent on slave labour, an integral part of their market enterprises. These non-capitalist elements of empire still have an impact. The slavery of the colonial period has by no means totally vanished.[24] More commonly, a system of 'feudal dependency' or 'debt peonage' traps smallholder farmers in debt. They are tied to their landlord, owing them an unpayable amount of debt. Paying their landlord rents and servicing their debts, they scrape by in the most severe poverty. These situations are common in South Asia and the Americas.[25] This is not 'capitalism' as I have explained it in the first section of this chapter. Because the farm workers are not free wage labourers. They're chained down to a particular place. They are not the 'free labour' characteristic of the ghostly construction of capitalism. On the other hand, the things that they produce enter the global market as commodities, contributing to capitalist production in the global North. Cotton, sugar, rubber, tea, palm oil.

Unpaid subsistence work in the global South also articulates with capitalism without being 'capitalist' labour. Let us look at how things are in the east and southern countries of Africa colonized by the British—such as South Africa, Malawi, Zambia, Uganda, Zimbabwe, Namibia. During the colonial period lots of the best land went to white farmers. Even to the present day, white farmers still own much of this land. Other areas were reserved for the black population—the 'native reserves.' In this arrangement, women and children are staying home on their household farm in the native reserve, growing food for the family. Unemployed or retired men are sometimes helping with this family work. This work is *subsistence* agriculture. They're not selling that food. They're just eating it. In the meantime, the father is going to the city to get a job, working on a large commercial farm, or getting a job in a mine. They are earning a wage, some of which is being brought back to the family.[26]

The family depends on their rural subsistence production. The wage of the male 'breadwinner' is not enough to make ends meet. So, as with debt peonage, the capitalist system is linked up to some *other* social machine. The system of community title customary ownership and the subsistence production going with that. From a purely economic perspective, there are clear parallels with unpaid domestic work. Where this division is strongly marked by gender, this subsistence work can even be seen as a kind of domestic work. As with that, the successful operation of the capitalist part of the economy cannot go on without this non-capitalist social machine. The owner of capital depends on cheap labour to make a profit. They need a next generation fed and cared for in the native reserve areas. They are not paying for the reproduction of this labour force.

Racism

And then there's racism. I am taking it that racism is a social machine—in its own right. It is articulated with capitalism in various ways. Yet, the invention and dominance of racist thinking was not just an 'ideology' created to serve capitalism. It came out of European history, culture and science, all to a degree independent of capitalism. There are certainly niches within capitalism where racism fits. The rules of the capitalist game drive competitive expansion. Capitalism as an economic system seeks resources and capitalists are driven to constantly expand markets and means of production. This pressure to expand markets has driven colonisation and the longer-term economic domination of previous colonies. The rules of the capitalist game imply stratification within the subordinate class. Also, the inevitability of an underclass of the underemployed. Keeping wages down. These aspects of the capitalist machine create the context for racism.

At the same time, racism is its own social machine. A key version of European racism is based on a belief in the intrinsic inferiority of the racialized other – and a false theory of genetic endowment.[27] More recently this overt genetic theory has been replaced by a façade of reinterpretation. This respectable version of racism attributes inferiority to cultural difference. Yet an informal reality identifies the racialized other as the ones who *look* different.[28] All class societies dominate social groups that are constituted as 'the other'. However, *this* version of ethnocentrism is a particular invention of European societies.

There are two other types of racist discourse relevant to European imperialism. The early imperialism of the mercantilist period (1500 to 1800) was informed by a racist version of Christianity. The colonized were followers of the devil. They could be killed and exploited without qualms. Alternatively, colonisation was a sacred mission, to bring the gospel and convert the heathens.[29] Later, racism based on genetic theory was joined to an evolutionary theory of human social development. A supposed law of social change. Successively more advanced stages of civilisation replace an original barbarism—culminating in capitalism. The highest stage. A strange bedfellow of genetic racism. Since it implies the common humanity of each stage of human social development.[30] Current social science regards this evolutionary theory as outdated. Social change is the effect of random cultural inventions and interactions. What comes after is built on what came before. But it is not necessarily better. The claim that European imperialist capitalism is a 'better' social order than other societies is a myth. At the present time, facing climate extinction, it rings very hollow.

What has happened is that racist discourse has articulated with capitalism. Historically, racism justified the appropriation of colonial land in settler colonialism. For example, in Australia, the fiction of *terra nullius*. That Indigenous people did not really *own* their land.[31] Or in the United States, the racist idea that the Native Americans had not *improved* the land.[32] Likewise, racism justified colonial rule in countries where a white minority controlled a subordinate local population. The destiny of the white race. The 'white man's burden'. The 'barbarism' of the lesser races. The myth of the lazy native.[33] And so on. Following this colonial history, racism justifies the existence of a racialized underclass in many of the rich countries. It privileges the white working class. They come to see their domination by capital as self-chosen. They flatter themselves that their relative affluence is an outcome of their superior work ethic, intelligence, and moral probity—all qualities that are of great assistance to the capitalist class.[34] Like the Anglo taxi driver I met yesterday. He told me that all the 'ethnic' taxi drivers were cheating their customers. While he was a model of old school probity.

Historically and still today, the white working class acts globally as an intermediate class, providing the cannon fodder to maintain imperial control in the global South. They are ignorant of the unequal relationships that provide them with a standard of living premised on the exploitation of the global South.[35] This ignorance is fertilized with unexamined racist assumptions. The problems of the global South are because those countries are 'undeveloped', people there have too many children, or they are lazy and ignorant. So, racism provides an ideological backdrop. It allocates people for the role of an underclass within the global social machine.[36]

At the same time, racism is not *intrinsic* to the capitalist social machine. Racism has its own history. Within global capitalist society, racist regimes can be overthrown, and capitalism goes on happily.[37] People who are stigmatized as racially different in one century can be regarded as 'white' in another.[38] Some racialized groups are elevated while new targets for racism are invented. In one country a difference of appearance that would be racially marked elsewhere, is ignored. What all this speaks to is the partial independence of racism as a discourse articulated with capitalism.

A good example is the case of South Africa. Up until the end of apartheid in South Africa, a white minority governed South Africa, both politically and in the economy. The ANC was the party that led the anti-apartheid struggle and was victorious in 1994. The ANC policy in the period of struggle was a democratic socialist platform. Nationalize the leading industries. Redistribute land and wealth to solve the huge problems of poverty for the black underclass. In a fateful meeting in Davos, leaders of the capitalist world counselled Nelson Mandela against this. They threatened to withdraw international capital from the country and destroy the economy. The ANC became a convert to neoliberalism. In fact, entrepreneurial ideology came to dominate the thinking of the new middle class of black South Africans. White farmers retained most of the commercial farming land. Multinationals with white shareholders overseas dominated some economic sectors. While some token efforts were made to redistribute land to middle class black farmers, the terrible poverty of the rural villages—the large under class of under-employed blacks—remains.

Yet there has been industrialisation, and an export industry based in minerals and agricultural products. In most of the local economy the black middle class and small black-owned capitalist firms are in charge. The political system is dominated by a democratically elected black ANC government. The government departments are run by a black majority of civil servants. The humiliating stigma of cultural apartheid in daily life has mostly gone. Black entrepreneurs and civil servants have moved into white suburban enclaves. Popular TV shows represent an affluent black middle class.

Racism has ceased to be a central structural feature of the South African economy and daily life. On the other hand, South Africa is still part of the global South. The underemployed underclass still provides the leverage for an international exploitation of global South labour. The capitalist system and neoliberal economics receives the full support of the politically dominant ANC government.[39]

We could end racism tomorrow and still have capitalism—with its underclass and its postcolonial global inequality. While this may be possible in theory it may be unlikely to happen in practice. We could think of it as path dependency. Capitalism has done well out of racism. Racism has become entrenched, more so in certain countries and certain racialized relationships. It is hard to see it being undone in these contexts without a challenge to aspects of the ghostly capitalist machine. The smug work ethic of the advantaged, the underemployed underclass, the exploitation of the global South, the legitimacy of distribution and production decisions via the market.

Patriarchy

An aspect of modern patriarchy attached to capitalism is the machine of domestic labour, including the work of raising the next generation. This labour is largely the unpaid labour of women. The social machine of patriarchy allocates this work disproportionately to women, enabling men to participate more fully in the capitalist labour market. And consequently, to dominate women economically through their greater share of family income.[40] As with slavery and debt peonage this non-capitalist social machine is articulated *with* capitalism. The domestic work that women do is of course necessary for workers, both men and women, to enter the labour market. Selling their labour capacity as a commodity. Even in shopping, women do the work of turning consumer goods into things that are useful to the household. Thereby enabling the capitalist owner of the means of production to market goods and services to consumers.[41]

To an extent capitalism, as a purely economic system, could do without patriarchy and without these arrangements. Men and women could both be paid as wage workers, with no gendered differences in income. They could share the work of housework and childcare. The surplus value extracted by the capitalist class need be no different from what it is now—so long as men were paid less than they are today, and women were paid more. The gendered inequalities that are so ubiquitous do not come about because of the needs of capitalism as a system. But as an effect of the intersection of capitalism and patriarchy.[42]

If we look at the structure of the economy, the division between men's work, as part of 'the economy' and women's work as 'private' and domestic, did not apply in Feudal society. Most production, including agriculture, was organized by the household with complementary roles for men and women. For example, women making the cheese while the men are ploughing. At the same time, despite this complementarity in the economy, men dominated in families and in the broader political structures. Religion, the feudal political system, the use of armed force.[43] Men used the leverage they had in feudal patriarchy to institute capitalist patriarchy.

Eli Zaretsky, a new left author, starts with Marx and Weber. He points out that capitalism separates paid work outside the home from unpaid domestic work. The capitalist class did this because they wanted control over the paid work. The ownership of the means of production became privatized. The way you would make money out of the means of production was by producing more stuff and marketing and selling it. Making a profit through that and extracting surplus value. To facilitate this, in the first stage of industrialisation, cottage weavers were brought together in big factories.

The work that was left over in the home suddenly became separated from 'production'. In fact, all this domestic work is also productive. But the work that was paid and directly benefited the capitalist owner was the work outside the home. This paid work ended up being called 'productive' work—as opposed to unpaid domestic labour.[44]

Despite this, the transition to wage labour posed a challenge to the patriarchal relationships of the feudal period. In the feudal household the patriarch exercised direct and sometimes violent authority over his wife and children. As Batya Weinbaum and Heidi Hartmann point out, the post-feudal economy of wage labour meant that it was perfectly possible for young women, and adult children, to slip away from this authority. To go and live on a wage paid out by a capitalist boss.[45]

As these authors document, in England, the leading industrial country, this option was closed off through several strategic interventions. There was a cross-class alliance of upper-class philanthropists—alarmed at the 'moral' effects of factory work—and working-class male unionists—demanding exclusive access to higher paid positions. The factory acts restricted the hours women could work and excluded children from factory work—forcing women to return home to look after them. Along with this, men made demands to define their work as 'skilled' and to be paid at a higher rate than women. Together these strategies consolidated the link between women and domesticity. While ensuring that men achieved economic power through market employment.

These changes were also early steps in the developing moral economy of capitalist patriarchy. The role of the moral mother is to institute an early moral discipline.[46] To embody Victorian and puritanical moral ideals in her own conduct and to socialize children in those values. Values that make the capitalist machine possible. Most fundamentally the work ethic, but also the allied puritan values—sobriety, punctuality, honesty, respect for property rights, sexual propriety. This moral economy became the justification for the down grading of women's participation in the labour market. The stay-at-home mother became the acme of feminine virtue. As the working class gained income, working class women in rich countries left the labour market. Women who had to work could be paid a pittance because paid work was never a woman's true calling. The effect of this myth was to paint the home as a refuge of innocence from the dangerous public world. Implying that adult men had to be tough to survive this realm of nastiness and competition. A realm of good cops (husbands) and bad cops (the public sphere).[47]

Women are dependent on men economically. In the whole life course, they get only half the income of men of their own class.[48] So, husbands perform the role of the good cop, bringing home the income and protecting their families through that. Meanwhile men in general, men as a political and economic sex-class are the bad cops. Unless you're attached to a husband don't expect any help from us. Society will not come to your assistance. All those men will hang on to their control of income rather than see women get a fair share. There's no way to bring up a child comfortably without the support of a husband.

These dynamics still operate, after decades of feminist activism. These structures of income and control over money are part of the furniture of capitalist society. They are rarely seen clearly for what they mean to the gender regime.[49] (For a more extended discussion see Appendix A).

Psychological connections between patriarchy and capitalism

An equally important aspect of the articulation of capitalism and patriarchy is cultural and psychological. My argument, following second wave radical feminists (and most anthropological writing) is this. Patriarchy is not an invention of capitalism. More than this, it is not an invention of class society. It has also been typical in stateless classless societies, normally referred to as 'egalitarian' because *men* were equal to other *men*. Like radical feminists, I believe that this inequality has been rooted in women's role in reproduction. In social conflicts with men, women have been disadvantaged by wet nursing, birthing, pregnancy, and emotional ties to their children. Men have constituted themselves as a gender class and have been able to take power. While class society has not *invented* patriarchy, it has depended on it.[50]

1. An experience of family life in which the father and mother are radically unequal players. Creating an expectation that social life will embody these patterns. The desire to *be* led, as well as the desire to dominate.[51]

2. The relative absence of adult men within the lives of young boys leads adult men to become anxious, competitive, and insecure adults. They seek to gain advantage to establish their masculinity.[52]

These two factors linked to patriarchy have provided the psychological preconditions for all class societies. Necessary but not sufficient causes of class society. A refusal of empathy, a toxic masculinity, sustains every power dynamic. The ruling class distances itself from the subordinate classes and from foreign enemies. The army keeps a lid on the subordinate classes. They celebrate toxic masculinity as they go about the work of the ruling class. Putting down revolts, expanding the empire, and fighting off rival states. The ruling class are the 'fathers' of the society. One owes obedience, as to a patriarchal father. The ruling classes implement their power through hierarchical chains of command. Every petty commander acts as the supposedly benevolent ruler of the next link in the chain.

Queer sexualities and gender diversity

Clearly, capitalism, for a host of reasons, has treated homosexuality as a condition that disqualifies men as patriarchs. Connell talks of homosexuality as a 'subordinated' masculinity—a masculinity that is not hegemonic.[53] The patriarchal 'dividend' is only partly accessible to gay men. The (sparse) rewards of emphasized femininity are likewise denied to lesbians. These peculiarities of capitalism as a class society relate to its foundation in the culture of the puritan movement. A generalized attack on non-reproductive sex as 'unproductive'. Hence sinful. A division of labour between domestic work and public employment that does not fit gay men or lesbians. As Foucault explains, all this gets linked up to a medicalized 'scientific' discourse in which the sin of 'sodomy' gets re-cast as a discourse of natural conditions—a person's 'sexuality'.[54] In this discourse, homosexuality is an 'inversion' meaning that this subordinated masculinity is treated as 'effeminate' and stigmatized accordingly. As far as women are concerned, capitalist regimes of sexuality treat lesbian identities as a challenge to patriarchal power. No male authority, based in the family, runs the lives of lesbians. Butler synthesizes these issues, pointing out that the 'scientific' perspective is that sex (male or female) implies gender (masculine or feminine) that in turn implies sexual cathexis. Men are attracted to women and vice versa. This dominant discourse casts deviants as unnatural.[55]

This is a 'western' medicalized view of gender alternatives. It is not a pan universal of class societies. It is contradicted in gender regimes of the global South today that routinely use a different set of gender categories. Politically, there is a good case for linking alternative gender cathexis and gender identity to feminism. Along with trans and non-binary identities. All these interfere with the *naturalisation* of sex, gender and cathexis that Butler writes about. A naturalisation that has women as a key target for control and intervention. But the stretch to see these queer identities as necessarily 'anti-capitalist' is a leftism without nuance.

The capitalist machine in practice

What I've now outlined are the ghostly features, the rules of the game of capitalism and its links to other systems of domination. Now, I'm going to look at various effects of these rules as they operate in practice.

Market competition

Goods and the means of production can be sold on the market. They are privately owned. The way to make money and to become rich is by putting out goods for sale on the market. In fact, the only way to maintain the current value of your means of production is to use it to produce goods and services and market them. That means that different firms are in competition. They must sell what they produce, and they aim to get a bigger share of the money that consumers have available. Some degree of monopoly ownership changes this to an extent. Firms may collude on pricing. Large corporate monopolies invest in very expensive infrastructure. They cannot afford for this to become obsolete. They introduce new products that make use of the infrastructure they already have. They invest in patents to protect their market share. They ensure sales through manipulating the market, taking over rival firms. They attempt to avoid disruptive interventions from smaller players. On the other hand, there is always the possibility of money going to another branch of industry. For example, people may spend less at the supermarket and more on video games. The consequence is that money floats around, unpredictably to a large degree.

Accordingly, firms are in competition and must succeed in making a profit to be viable. You never know whether what you produce is going to do as well as you might hope. There is always the danger that sales could be lack lustre, that your loans will be hard to pay back, that your investors will desert you, that you may end up losing everything. It never makes any sense to aim for anything less than the highest possible profit.

One of the ways that capitalists do that is by adopting new technologies to reduce labour requirements. Paying less for labour. Doing that, they can put their goods on to the market at a lower price, increasing sales and market share. Getting more profits through that. Usually, by using more energy and raw materials for the same number of working hours in production. Alternatively, they can bring in new technology to produce a new and attractive product, also increasing market share. A new line in bread, a new kind of toothbrush. A totally new product, like the mobile phone. Private ownership of the means of production drives competition. In turn this drives the constant innovation that is such a feature of capitalist societies. By comparison the class societies of the past were technologically stagnant, despite some brilliant achievements.

Environmental damage

A related effect of this competitive pressure is economic growth. If every firm is competing to sell more and to produce more with less costs, the end result is growth. This growth creates an environmental impact. The economy makes more stuff, uses more resources, and produces more waste. At a rate of three per cent in annual growth there is a doubling of the economy every twenty-three years. So, by 69 years the economy is eight times as big.[56]

Environmental impact also comes out of this competitive context more directly. Capitalists *externalize* environmental costs to maximize profits—in a situation of competition. In other words, the impact is 'external' to the accounting of costs and losses on their balance sheets. If it's cheaper to produce things in a way that's environmentally damaging, the capitalist will do that—despite the environmental impact. They are forced by competition to run their production in the cheapest way possible. If they do not choose the cheapest method, another firm can undercut them and take their market. So, this environmental damage is built into the structure of capitalism. It does not come out of simple greed. It can happen even if all parties are aware of the damage they are doing.[57]

Historically, capitalism has seen a change from an economy based on an agricultural surplus (in the seventeenth and eighteenth century) to one where the surplus put into play consists of raw materials accumulated over geological time. Fossil fuels, metals, phosphorus, even sand and limestone. This historical development comes out of the competitive economic structure of capitalism—as firms found new ways of making money. The environmental consequences have been enormous, not to say disastrous.[58]

Technological complexity

I want to look at one more element of the machine in practice. How technological complexity in capitalism requires the active participation of the workforce. An insight from Paul Cardan's great book of the sixties, *Modern Capitalism and Revolution*.[59] To participate is to be involved, to do things on your own initiative, to think about the way things are working, making little adjustments when necessary. In this respect, capitalism is quite different to class societies of the past. In those earlier societies the work of the subordinate class was much more straightforward. Technologies of production hardly ever changed. Tradition laid down what you needed to do as a subordinate. It was easy for a supervisor to be on top of the whole process.

In capitalism, it's not like that. Constant technological change means that working people must be on the ball and participate. They are highly educated, and also familiar with the practical knowledge necessary to run their part of the productive machine. Jennifer Pont was researching a heart health project in the mining towns of the Hunter region. She interviewed workers at the aluminium plant. Time and motion experts had recently been appointed to speed up production. Her interviewees scoffed at their presumption, calling these professionals the 'theory wankers'. One of the aluminium pot lines, they explained, was out of date. They had to tinker with it constantly to make it work. They were the only ones who could understand its tricky requirements.[60]

So, capitalism requires participation if it is to work with complex technology. The consent of working people becomes a hidden necessity. This power is manifested in formal or informal pressure on the ruling elites. Representative democracy or informal political action can have an impact on the way the machine operates in practice. A recent telling example is the pressure ordinary Chinese people put on their government to wind back the elimination strategy for Covid—that had been an obsession of the ruling elites up until late 2022.[61] Ruling elites can always suppress discontent, so long as it is confined to a small faction. But the long-term cost is a loss of efficiency. The participation necessary to maintain a high-tech economy has been compromised.

Conclusions

This chapter has examined the construction of capitalism as an invented social machine. It is both that social machine, and also a ghostly presence based on shared imaginings. Capitalism in practice has depended on several partially independent social machines. Whether these are necessary for its functioning is always a tricky question. But we can certainly trace how capitalism has relied on them in practice. The basic ideas underlying capitalism have produced typical consequences in the way the machine works. The next chapter will show how capitalism has changed as the outcome of historical intervention. Capitalism as a game.

Endnotes

[1] Gilbert Ryle, *The Concept of Mind*, Must Have Books, Edinburgh 2023 (1949).

[2] Cornelius Castoriadis, *The Imaginary Institution of Society*, trans. Kathleen Blamey, Polity, London, 1987.

[3] My first use of this idea is in the joint paper, Terry Leahy, Vanessa Bowden, and Steven Threadgold, 'Stumbling Towards collapse:

Coming to terms with the climate crisis', *Environmental Politics*, Vol. 19 2010, pp. 851-868.

[4] Anitra, Nelson, *Beyond Money: A Post-Capitalist Strategy*, Pluto Press, London, 2022.

[5] Anitra, Nelson, *Beyond Money: A Post-Capitalist Strategy*, Pluto Press, London, 2022, p. 28, pp 125-126.

[6] Pierre Bourdieu, *Practical reason: On the theory of action*. Stanford, CA: Stanford University Press. 1998.

[7] Chris Weedon 1987, *Feminist Practice and Poststructuralist Theory*, Blackwell, Oxford.

[8] Karl Marx and Friedrich Engels, 'The German Ideology, Part One', C.J. Arthur (ed), International Publishers, New York, 1973.

[9] Castoriadis, *op.cit.* p. 157.

[10] Marx and Engels, *The German Ideology*.

[11] Samir Amin, *Global History: A View from the South*, Pambazuka Press, Capetown, 2011; Eduardo Galeano and Isabel Allende *Open Veins of Latin America: Five Centuries of the Pillage of a Continent*. Monthly Review Press, New York, 1997; David Van Reybrouck, *Revolusi: Indonesia and the Birth of the Modern World*, Penguin, UK, 2024; Erik Hobswbawm, *Industry and Empire: The Birth of the Industrial Revolution*, The New Press, New York, 1999.

[12] Karl Marx, 'Wage Labour and Capital', in *Marx and Engels: Selected Works, Vol One*, Progress Publishers, Moscow, pp. 172-174, 1969; Karl Marx and Friedrich Engels, The Communist Manifesto, Penguin, Harmondsworth 1967; Karl Marx, Capital, Volume 1, Progress Publishers, Moscow 1969 (1886).

[13] Marc Bloch, *Feudal Society, Vols 1 & 2*, Routledge, London 1989; D. Ross Gandy, *Marx and History: From primitive society to the communist future*, University of Texas Press, Austin 1979.

[14] Terry Leahy, *Food Security for Rural Africa: Feeding the farmers first*, Routledge, London 2019; UNICEF *Levels and Trends in Child Nutrition* 2017, Washington; International Food Policy Research Institute, *Global Nutrition Report*, Washington 2016.

[15] Michel Chossudovsky, *The Globalization of Poverty and the New World Order*, Global Research, Pincourt, Quebec 2003; Galeano *op. cit.*

[16] Marx, 'Wage Labour and Capital'.

[17] OXFAM, 'An economy for the 1%: how privilege and power in the economy drive extreme inequality and how this can be stopped', viewed on 14 March 2016, www.oxfam.org; UNU-Wider, 'Pioneering study shows richest two percent own half world wealth', in *United Nations University, World Institute for Development Economics Research*, viewed on 26 February 26, 2006, www.wider. unu.edu

[18] OXFAM.

[19] Marx and Engels, *The German Ideology*; Marx, *Capital Vols 1 and 3*.

[20] Michael Walzer, *Revolution of the Saints, A Study in the Origins of Radical Politics*, Scribner, New York, 1968.

[21] Samir Amin, *Global History: A View from the South*, Pambazuka Press, Capetown, 2011, p.166.

[22] Castoriadis, *The Imaginary Invention*; Nelson, *Beyond Money*.

[23] Amin *Global History*; Galeano *Open Veins*; Van Reybrouck *Revolusi*.

[24] Zach Hope and Kate Geraghty, 'Caught in a $60b scam, these workers tried to flee but the soldiers were waiting', *The Age*, 26 May, 2025.

[25] Galeano *Open Veins*.

[26] Terry Leahy, *Food Security for Rural Africa*.

[27] David Roediger, *The Wages of Whiteness: Race and the Making of the American Working Class*. Verso, London. 2022; Noel Ignatiev, *How the Irish Became White*. Routledge, London, 2008; Syed Hussein Alatas, *The Myth of the Lazy Native*, Frank Cass, London, 1977; Stuart Hall, *The Fateful Triangle: Race, ethnicity, nation*, Harvard University Press, 2017.

[28] Margot Ford, *In Your Face: A Case Study in Post-Multicultural Australia*. Charles Darwin University Press, Darwin, 2009.

[29] Sylvia Federici, *Caliban and the Witch: Women, the Body and Primitive Accumulation*. Autonomedia, New York, 2004.

[30] Herbert Spencer, *The Principles of Sociology*, Appleton & Co. New York, 1898.

[31] Aileen Moreton-Robinson, *The White Possessive: Property, Power, and Indigenous Sovereignty*. University of Minnesota Press, Minneapolis. 2015.

[32] Dee Brown, *Bury My Heart at Wounded Knee*, Holt, Rinehart & Winston, New York, 1970.

[33] Alatas, *The Myth of the Lazy Native*.

[34] Arlie Hochschild, *Strangers in Their Own Land, Anger and Mourning on the American Right*, The New Press, New York, 2016; Richard Sennett and Jonathan Cobb, *The Hidden Injuries of Class*, Vintage, New York 1978; Löic Wacquant, *Urban Outcasts: A Study of Advanced Marginality*. Polity, London, 2013; Stuart Hall, Chas Chrichter, Tony Jefferson, John Clarke, Brian Roberts, *Policing the Crisis: Mugging, the State and Law and Order*, Red Globe Press, London, 2013 (1978).

[35] Ulrich Brand & Marcus Wissen, *The Imperial Mode of Living: Everyday Life and the Ecological Crisis of Capitalism*. Verso, London, 2021.

[36] Terry Leahy 'The Australian Public, Developing Countries and the Environment', http://gifteconomy.au/permaculture/the-australian-public-developing-countries-and-the-environment/, viewed on 24 February 2025.

[37] Leahy, *Food Security for Rural Africa* 2019.

[38] Ignatiev, *How the Irish*.

[39] Terry Leahy, *Permaculture Strategy for the South African Villages*, Palmwoods Press, Queensland, 2009; Leahy, *Food Security for Rural Africa*, 2019.

[40] Michael Bittman and Jocelyn Pixley, *The Double Life of the Family: Myth, hope and experience*, Allen and Unwin, Sydney, 1997; Christine Delphy and Diane Leonard, *Familiar exploitation: a new analysis of marriage in contemporary Western societies*, Polity Press, Cambridge MA, 1992.

[41] Eli Zaretsky, *Capitalism, the Family and Personal Life*, Harper Collins, New York, 1986; Zillah Eisenstein (ed) *Capitalist Patriarchy and the Case for Socialist Feminism*. Monthly Review Press, New York, 1978; Sylvia Federici, *Caliban and the Witch: Women, the Body and Primitive Accumulation*. Autonomedia, New York, 2004; Cinzia Arruzza, Nancy Fraser and Tithi Bhattacharya, *Feminism for the 99%: A Manifesto*, Verso, London 2019.

42 Zillah Eisenstein, *Capitalist Patriarchy*, Batya Weinbaum, *The Curious Courtship of Women's Liberation and Socialism*, South End Press, Boston, 1978.

43 Bloch, Marc *Feudal Society, Vols 1 & 2*, Routledge, London 1989.

44 Zaretsky, *Capitalism, the Family*.

45 Heidi Hartmann, 'Capitalism, Patriarchy and Job Segregation by Sex', in *Capitalist Patriarchy and the Case for Socialist Feminism*, (ed) Z. Eisenstein, Monthly Review Press, New York, pp. 206-247, 1979; Batya Weinbaum, *The Curious Courtship*.

46 Ann Summers, *Damned Whores and God's Police*, UNSW Press, Sydney, 2016; Ruth H Bloch, 'American feminine ideals in transition: the rise of the moral mother, 1785-1815', *Feminist Studies* 4 (2) pp.101-126, 1978; Phillipe Aries, *Centuries of Childhood*, Pimlico, London, 1996.

47 Ellen Willis, 'Feminism, Moralism and Pornography', *New York Law School Review*, 38 (1), 1993.

48 Hugh Davies, and Heather Joshi, 'Gender and Income Inequality in the UK 1968-1990: the feminization of earnings or poverty?', *Journal of the Royal Statistical Society*, 161(1): 33-61, 1998.

49 Delphy and Leonard, *op. cit.*

50 Firestone, Shulamith, *The Dialectic of Sex*. Paladin, New York, 1972; Atkinson, Ti-Grace *Amazon Odyssey*. Link, New York, 1974; Michelle.Z. Rosaldo & Louise Lamphere (eds), *Woman, Culture and Society*, Stanford, Stanford University Press, 1974; Ernestine Friedl, *Women and Men: An Anthropological View*, Holt, Rinehart and Winston, New York, 1975.

51 Shulamith Firestone, *The Dialectic of Sex*.

52 Nancy Chodorow, 'Family Structure and Feminine Personality', in Michelle.Z. Rosaldo & Louise Lamphere (eds), *Woman, Culture and Society*, Stanford, Stanford University Press, pp. 43-66, 1974.

53 R W Connell, *Gender and Power*, Polity Press, Cambridge, 1987,

54 Michel Foucault, *The History of Sexuality Part 1*, Penguin Classics, 1976.

55 Judith Butler, *Gender Trouble*, Routledge, New York, 1990.

[56] Ted Trainer, *Renewable Energy Cannot Sustain A Consumer Society*, Springer, Dordrecht, 2007; Joel Kovel *The Enemy Of Nature: The End Of Capitalism Or The End Of The World?* Zed, London, 2007; Kohei Saito, *Slow Down: How degrowth communism can save the earth*, W & N, London, 2024.

[57] Andrew McLaughlin, *Regarding nature: Industrialism and deep ecology*. New York: State of NY Press, 1993; Robin Hahnel, *Green Economics: Confronting the ecological crisis*, Routledge, London, 2011.

[58] Eric Pineault, *The Social Ecology of Capital*, Pluto, London, 2023.

[59] Paul Cardan, *Modern Capitalism and Revolution*. Solidarity, London, 1974.

[60] Jennifer June Pont, *Heart Health Promotion in a Respectable Community: An Inside View of the Culture of the Coalfields of Northern New South Wales*, PhD Thesis, University of Newcastle, Australia, 1997.

[61] Nancy Qian, 'The Long Tail of China's Zero-Covid Policy', *The Strategist*, Australian Strategic Policy Institute, 21st Nov, 2023.

Chapter 2
Capitalism: The Ghost Walks

In the last chapter, we looked at the basic dynamics of how capitalism works. This chapter looks at how that worked out in practice. While capitalism is a social machine, it is also an ongoing outcome of interventions and practices. Like a game, as indicated in the previous chapter. I will introduce this by looking at globalising capitalism as a basic context. Given that background, capitalism from the mid nineteenth century developed through three episodes, as does any drama.

Globalising capitalism

As I have explained in the first chapter, the accumulation of wealth in capitalism is partly the effect of capitalist economic structures. But obviously, much of this wealth is also premised on the colonisation and political control of the global South. Before looking at how that all worked out, I will give some history to this imperialism.

I like Samir Amin's complex account.[1] In the pre-capitalist period before 1500, the basic mode of production for class societies in Europe and Asia was what Amin calls 'tributary'. Power was centralised under the control of imperial monarchs, taking tribute from the subordinate classes. A religious ideology justified this appropriation. As an example of this tributary system, a king might be backed up by a land-owning aristocratic class. The peasants on that land could provide tribute to their local aristocrat. For example, bags of wheat. In turn, their aristocrat would provide tribute to the king. For example, a platoon of soldiers armed to do the king's bidding.

Linked and somewhat similar regimes were what we usually

call 'civilisations'. For example, Ancient Egypt, the successive Mediterranean empires, China, India and so on. Europe as such, especially in the North and West, was peripheral. These civilisations mostly remained in their own regions. Nevertheless, trading relationships were significant. As far as Europe was concerned, the main trading route was the Silk Road.[2] This route gave a strategic importance to the Middle East as a mediating link. In all these tributary societies, a small merchant class operated with private property, monetary exchange and wage labour. A 'proto-capitalist' element, as Amin calls them. This merchant economy was 'cloistered in a world dominated by tributary relationships.'[3] The ruling family and the state-based aristocracy owned the basic means of production—the land. They controlled armed force, keeping the proto-capitalist sector within defined limits.[4]

Europe was the first of these civilisations to break out of the tributary mode of production. As a peripheral region of the world economy, the state was not powerful. A feudal fragmentation of power allowed merchant dominated cities to establish some independence. In the late feudal period, Europe saw a strengthening of proto-capitalist elements—private property supported by legal sanctions, commodity exchange of agricultural products, free wage labour in agriculture and craft production.[5]

This capitalist development was mercantile rather than industrial. The capitalists were merchants who made money siphoning a profit out of trading relationships. Not industrialists making money by directly producing goods for sale – as happened later. Amir sees the period of 1500 to 1800 as a transition to fully developed capitalism. With countries in Europe passing a torch as the capitalist system matured—from an early mercantile base to industrial production. As capitalist elements became more dominant, an alliance formed between new absolutist monarchies and the growing capitalist class. Two important initiatives strengthened their hand. The Portuguese developed the sea route to Asia. Ending the key role of the Middle East in world trade. Columbus opened the Americas to European conquest. 'From then on the Europeans knew they could conquer the world and went on to do so'.[6] The conquest of the Americas gave European capitalism leverage to enhance its domination. The wealth of American mines allowed Europe to offer products at lower prices and take over the global market. The result was to block proto-capitalist developments in other global centres, subordinating the global South to European imperialism. Amin argues that the military superiority of Europe was an effect of capitalism—in comparison to the tributary mode of production. As a more effective system for extracting surplus product. Competition between capitalist firms allowed a technological leap forward that European states leveraged as armed force.

European imperialism in the period since 1500 cannot be understood outside its capitalist context. Without this, the wealth generated through the conquest of the Americas might have just accumulated in vaults or financed large churches. In so far as this wealth contributed to *capitalist* enterprise this was an *effect* of the growing ascendancy of the capitalist mode of production. The drive to accumulate capital comes out of a competitive economic structure. The first moment is access to capital through primitive accumulation. An expansion of labour and resources that allows an expansion of markets and profits. Making for success in market competition. A process that, taken as a whole, equates to the European imperial project. The slavery and peonage of the New World was integrated into more directly capitalist enterprise in the core countries.[7] These colonial acquisitions enabled the beneficiaries to maximize their wealth in competition with other capitalists. The East India company, responsible for much of the conquest of India, is a good example. An earlier example is that of the Spanish conquistadors—obsessed with acquiring gold and silver in the Americas. They would loot gold and silver artefacts and establish mines serviced by slaves. This loot could be easily transported and taken back to Spain. In Spain it could be used to buy land and businesses. In other words, turned into capital. As Galeano points out, elites in Spain and Portugal bought manufactured goods from the centres of early capitalism in other countries of Europe. Huge debts to these European manufacturers were paid in silver and gold from the colonies of the Americas.

Fostering the early development of European industrialism.[8]

On the other hand, this exploitation was carried out by means which were rarely part of the 'capitalist' game in the narrow sense. For example, theft backed by armed force is not a business measure. Genocide to clear land for capitalist agriculture and remove whole populations. Landscapes depopulated through the impact of introduced pests and diseases.[9] Slavery, not wage labour. The export of slaves to the global North. But then again, consistent with the dynamics of capitalism, these exploiters were gaining surplus product from their slaves so that they could sell commodities on the market. These commodities were put into further circulation in other capitalist businesses. For example, cotton grown on land taken from Native Americans, worked by slaves from Africa, harvested and sold on global markets, turned into cloth in capitalist factories in Lancashire and sold again to a market of wage labourers.

Capitalism as a three-part drama

The discussion so far gives us a glimpse of the world prior to the development of mature 'industrial' capitalism in the mid-nineteenth century. I am going to look at capitalism since then as a drama in three parts, or episodes. The first is what I will call the 'first world bargain', a bargain with important consequences in the global South.

The first world bargain

The first world bargain began to be achieved in rich core countries of capitalism in the second half of the nineteenth century. Marx writes about the struggle for the ten-hour day in England.[10] Unions became legal entities. Men secured universal suffrage (the right to vote) first—and women by the early twentieth century. Working class pressure produced similar outcomes in the other rich countries. The broad outline of this bargain lasted till the mid-seventies.

The heart of the first world bargain is the political accommodation between capitalists and the working people in the core countries of global capitalism. Cardan's explanation makes sense.[11] Starting in the

1840s in Europe and the United States, political agitation threatened revolution and made demands to ameliorate capitalism. Pressure was applied through unions, working class parties, strikes, and riots.[12] The Factory Acts, and suffrage were early victories. Increasing technological power was an effect of the competitive economic structure of capitalism. This allowed the capitalist class to respond to pressure with wage rises and improvements in conditions. These increased wages also expanded the market, and with that, the profits of businesses selling to working people. The outcome was a gradual increase in the material well-being of the working class. Piketty's research suggests that wage increases in this early period did not eat into the *relative* wealth of the capitalist class. At the same time, the *absolute* standard of living of workers improved.[13]

The 1917 revolution in Russia was a warning and raised the stakes leading to more compromises. Likewise, the Nazi regime. While some capitalists saw the Nazis as an answer to the threat of leftist revolution, others were not enthusiasts. The fascist version of industrial society was not compatible with aspects of capitalism as a system— the free movement of wage labour, the rights of private property, the allocation of economic power by market forces. Large sections of the global capitalist class saw the Nazis as a threat and were willing to accommodate some reforms to forestall them.

These developments throughout the nineteenth and early twentieth century made capitalists amenable to compromise with the working class in the global North. That is why I call it a bargain. For the most part, the working class (the masses of ordinary people) gave up the goal of revolution. In Australia and the UK this was signalled, decades after the event, by Labor parties dropping their demand to 'socialise' the means of production. Ordinary people accepted alienated labour in return for increasing affluence. They put up with the extraction of surplus value, so long as their pay continued to rise.

This is how the bargain worked. The competition between firms ensured increasing technological power and productivity. It became possible to promise the working-class increasing affluence, measured by consumer goods and leisure options. Without eating into capitalist profits. An increasing supply of material goods for the same number of hours of work decade by decade. To make this bargain work, the competitive pressure on each capitalist—to drive down wages—had to be matched by coordinated working-class industrial power. To collaborate to put pressure on the capitalist class. Unions spanned different firms. Left parties introduced country wide legislation. Unions pushed this. The left parties pushed this. Gradually the wages and living standards of affluent workers in the rich countries increased. This process started in the 1850s and 1860s and continued right up to the mid-1970s. And even more recently as sections of what had been the global South joined this party. The technological complexity of capitalist production made these demands difficult to resist. If workers went on strike, it was hard to replace them.[14]

In the 1950s, this gradual increase in affluence grew to include the 'social wage'. The *proportion* of wealth and income held by the ruling class dropped significantly[15]. The social wage included unemployment benefits, free education, public health, public housing, transport services. The government owned more and more of the economy. These developments took place in all the countries of the global North.

Pineault considers the environmental impacts of these developments. Industrial capitalism meant that capitalists were making use of resources laid down over geological time. Accumulated in a useful form by processes taking millennia. Like coal, the fossilized bodies of plants, storing carbon. A key moment in this industrial development was the use of steam engines powered by coal. Their first use was to pump water out of coal mines, opening more coal seams for exploitation. Geological reserves of surplus used to expand the available surplus. This process continues to the present, expanding the use of geological reserves to expand production and markets. Pineault also notes the vast acceleration in the growth of the use of these resources from the 1950s. Politically, the capitalist class allowed wages to grow to accommodate the working class of the rich countries— following the second world war. The prestige gained by the Soviet Union had emboldened the working class and put capitalists on the back foot. They responded with an increased provision of wages—and with that consumer goods. The materials necessary to produce these consumer goods were resources laid down in geological time.[16]

The global South in the first world bargain

I will now explain the way the first world bargain affected the global South. The 'bargain', such as it is, never applied to the global South. Mostly, representative democracy has been patchy. Authoritarian governments have suppressed political agitation. Originally these were the colonial governments. Liberation struggles ensured local rule from the end of the second world war. Despite attempts to steer a new course, most ex-colonies replaced slave exploitation with wage labour exploitation. Periods of democratic government alternated with dictatorships run by ruling elites.[17] For example, the Sukarno and Suharto regimes in Indonesia, Marcos in the Philippines. Leftist revolutions did not lead to popular control. In some cases, they just installed a new ruling clique. In others, the revolution was reversed with a return to the old status quo.

This situation maintained the low cost of labour in the global South. Authoritarian governments suppressed working class agitation. It was hard to organize unions, go on strike and bargain for higher wages. It was difficult to get a social democratic government in power to enact welfare measures. It was virtually impossible to tax the rich. Competition between the countries of the global South meant they were forced to produce goods at the lowest possible prices. Their production was oriented to mining and agriculture—with industrial production being confined to the rich countries. Local elites in the South were bought off by global North money and adapted their economies to the needs of the global North. Revolts were suppressed by armed force.[18]

These countries now are parts of a global capitalist machine. There are local capitalists and a local middle class, tied in as junior partners in global capital. There is a mass of wage labourers on very low incomes. There is a large 'reserve army of labour'. People who have been deprived of their means of production and will take a job if they can get one. So, the global South is a functioning part of a global capitalist system. The *location* of the world's most extreme poverty in these countries comes out of the *history* of European imperialism. Giving advantage to the populations of the countries that began the process of European capitalist imperialism.

The low rate of employment in the global South reflects the fact that there is only a limited number of consumers in the rich countries who can buy what these countries produce. For example, in South Africa at the present time, there is a thirty per cent unemployment rate. For those between 15 and 24 the rate is 60 per cent. The 'expanded rate of unemployment', including those not registered as looking for work, is 44 per cent.[19] Unemployment like this drives down the price of labour—as people scramble for any job.[20]

This global inequality implies a mediated exploitation of third world workers by affluent first world workers. In 2006, I spent time in South Africa. Ordinary people in South Africa were getting AUS $40 a week. Much of this work was making things later bought by ordinary people in the rich countries. Like cars, macadamia nuts, platinum, citrus, tomatoes. How much were ordinary people in the rich countries getting paid? In Australia at that time, a typical wage for standard unskilled work was between $800 and a thousand dollars a week. The worker in Australia could buy *many* hours of labour, embodied in a product coming from South Africa, for the price of *one* hour of their own labour. A recent analysis by Hickel, Lemos and Barbour finds that 'in 2021, the economies of the global North net-appropriated 826 billion hours of embodied labour from the global South, across all skill levels and sectors.' Meaning that this embodied labour doubles the amount of labour available for consumption in the global North.[21]

I call this a 'mediated exploitation'. Mediated through market processes that are out of the hands of ordinary people in both countries. Largely, an exploitation that ordinary people in the rich countries fail to understand.[22] Despite this mediation, there is no doubt that everyday workers in the rich countries *are* exploiting people in the global South. A crucial part of the first world bargain. Ulrich Brand and Marcus Wissen recently coined the term, 'imperial mode of living', for this inequity. Earlier approaches use the terms 'dependency theory' and 'world systems theory' to consider relations between the rich countries and the global South. In the last few decades 'postcolonial theory' and theories of ecologically unequal exchange address similar issues.[23]

Rich country workers end up like the intermediate class of previous class societies. The soldiers in the Roman empire, the skilled craft workers of ancient Egypt. Such people live better than the great mass of the subordinate class and protect the ruling class. In this role in capitalism, the ordinary people of the rich countries are pressed into service to invade, colonize, and put down rebellions. A legion of folk songs from the nineteenth century shows this imperial mission was heartily endorsed. Take a look at the song 'Brave Wolfe'—sung by the Watersons in the folk revival. It stood in the oral tradition for more than 150 years, a testament to its popularity. It was collected in 1907 in Dorset and later in Hartford in England, as well as versions being found in North America. It commemorates the British victory over the French at the Heights of Abraham in 1759. The victory secured Canada for the British, appropriating the lands of the native Americans.

The very first broadside we gave to them
We wounded a hundred and fifty men
Well done me lads General Wolfe did say
Brave lads of honour, brave lads of honour
Old England she shall win the day

The very next broadside they gave to us
They wounded our general in his right breast
And from his breast precious blood did flow
Like any fountain, like any fountain
And all his men were filled with woe

Here's a hundred guineas all in bright gold
Take it, part it for my love's quite cold
And use your men as you did before
Your soldiers own, your soldiers own
And they will fight for ever more [24]

In the postcolonial period, local armies took on insurgencies with military aid from the global North. In Indonesia from 1965 to 1966, up to half a million leftists and *supposed* leftists were killed by the army and right-wing vigilantes.[25] With the cooperation of the CIA. In a few cases, the United States sent its own forces to prevent developments inimical to global capitalism. While the rhetoric was all about democracy, the interests of the global ruling class were always a key factor. Where to intervene to save democracy and where to make allies with right wing dictators. In Korea, Vietnam, Iraq, Afghanistan, to mention a few of the direct interventions. Indirect interventions assisted right wing coups. The overthrow of the Allende government in Chile, of Lumumba in the Congo. Economic embargoes against enemies of capital. For example, Cuba, Venezuela, Iran.[26]

Gilly gives us a detailed list of cases where external interventions have attempted, and often succeeded, in crushing revolutions.

> Examples would include Mexico (1910), Russia (1917), China (1949), Bolivia (1952), Korea (1953), Vietnam (1954), Algeria (1954), Guatemala (1954), Egypt (1956), Hungary (1956), Cuba (1959), Angola (1961), Guinea-Bissau (1963), Mozambique (1964), Czechoslovakia (1968), Chile (1970), Iran (1979), Nicaragua (1979), El Salvador (1980), and Grenada (1983).[27]

While what I have written so far is a good broad brushstrokes picture of the global South, I do not want to imply unrelieved misery and victimisation. The liberation struggles were effective in bringing about real changes. Patchy democracy, and even the more enlightened dictatorships, improved people's lives. Programs of public health, family planning, education. In some countries, aspects of the welfare state—South Africa, Brazil, Indonesia, China. Capitalism requires participation even in the global South and governments must negotiate that. If you spend time in these countries, you cannot help but notice that ordinary people aspire to 'development' and make considerable sacrifices to assist their children to become educated and get good jobs. In Indonesia recently I was driving with Jean Couteau who has lived in Bali for decades. Surrounding us in the busy traffic were motor bikes owned by many ordinary Indonesians. It was school pickup, and children wearing school uniform were riding pillion on many of the bikes. I was talking to Jean about the book, *The Imperial Mode of Living*[28] and he pointed to the people around us. These people, he said, compare their lives to those of their grandparents. An upward trajectory of affluence and modernity, not a nightmare of exploitation from the global North. While Bali is one of the more favoured parts of the global South, this sense of improvement is present in much of the global South. We can broaden this picture out to look at statistics for Indonesia—as an example of a global South country that has done relatively well. The 'human development index' measures life expectancy, health and education, as well as income. Between 1990, when these statistics were first collected and 2024, Indonesia climbed from 0.525 to 0.750, a marked improvement. At the same time, the Gini coefficient, a measure of inequality, is higher more recently (39 in 2017) than it was 27 years before (32 in 1990).[29] In other words, the improvement in living standards for the masses— represented by the human development index—has in fact gone together with increasing inequality.[30]

Capitalism, the second episode

The second episode is *globalization*. Several things happened, which ended up with globalization—the most significant development of this second episode. The term often used for this change is 'neo-liberalism'. For me, this is a smoke screen. Neo-liberalism is what the capitalist class could achieve *after* globalization had changed the balance of power.

Looking back at the seventies, we can see why the capitalist class was worried. Agitation and effective political action were eating away at the power of the capitalist class in the global North. Through the social wage, through full employment, job security and affluence. All of these strengthened the hand of the working class in the rich countries. There was an escalation of demands. To control production at each local site, for ever higher wages, for an increasing share of public ownership and public control, for increasing regulation.

The hippy generation attacked the work ethic and puritanical morality. Resistance to the (American) Vietnam war and to conscription galvanized young people. Women's liberation exposed the boring disaster of women's unpaid work. Feminists attacked hierarchical power in the family, comparing patriarchy to capitalism. The 1968 uprising in France allied students and workers with demands for workers' control of production. In the United States, riots by the black underclass destroyed whole suburbs. The rioters came from a class that was also the workforce in the US car industry. Left terrorist groups proposed an end to capitalism. The Baader-Meinhof group in Germany planted bombs. In Italy, left radicals ran a campaign of knee-capping—shooting capitalist magnates in the knee. Sabotage as resistance to capitalist work became widespread. For example, causing a stoppage of the production line to get an afternoon off. Strikes that were not authorized by unions, wildcat strikes. While all these were dramatic and disturbing, a quiet revolution, the advance of the welfare state, also plagued the capitalist class—an increasing share of the economy was being run by the government.[31]

All this was combined with revolutionary movements in the global South. The Vietnam war, pitting communists from North Vietnam against a pro-capitalist government in the South. Marxist insurgencies in Nepal, India and the Philippines. The revolutionary upheavals in Cuba, Guatemala, Nicaragua and Chile. Left-wing insurgencies in Algeria, Angola, Tanzania, Mozambique, South Africa and Zimbabwe. Leftist groups hoped for a world-wide revolution against capitalism.[32]

Globalization and the global South

Globalization was the dynamic that allowed the capitalist class to deal with the threats in the global North. This was not a conspiracy, a conscious decision to impose globalization as a strategy. It was more of a discovery, driven by the profit motive. Production was more profitable if wages were lower. Wages were lower in the global South. A simple move of manufacturing to the poor countries would undermine the power of the working class in the rich countries. You could put a factory in Indonesia or Taiwan or South Africa—knowing that in the last thirty years the government had educated the local workforce. Why leave your factory in Liverpool? Where the workers are so much trouble. Why not go to South Africa where wages are low? Where the police fire live bullets into crowds of striking unionists. So, this was no conspiracy, but became a trend as firms copied other firms. The effect was an exodus of manufacturing jobs from the rich countries. For example, in the UK 40 per cent of the workforce were in manufacturing jobs between the 1840s and the 1960s. Now there are only 8 per cent in manufacturing.

Globalisation was not just a response from global North companies. As well, some post-colonial countries developed a flourishing capitalist class. These new capitalists started out with joint ventures and moved on from that. They took advantage of the low wages in their home countries and undercut global North companies. Exporting to the affluent working class of the rich countries. China and the East Asian tiger economies pioneered this.

You could wonder why the capitalist class had never thought of this strategy before. In fact, several conditions for globalisation had only just been realized. The anti-colonial revolutions in the third world provided the conditions for education. The subordinate class became citizens, and education the pathway to development. For example, in Indonesia, Sukarno and Suharto established compulsory and free public education. In South Africa, majority rule extended educational opportunities to blacks. Creating a whole new cohort of the class system, the black middle class. Around the world, in even the poorest families, parents prized education as the route to social mobility. This educated population was a first condition for the extension of industrial production to the global South.

Ankie Hoogvelt mentions two others. The first is containerization. It was now possible to ship things around the world in standardized containers. These created the option of joining different parts of production in widely dispersed sites. You could make the gearbox in one country and the starter engine in another and assemble it all somewhere else. The second condition is digital communication. You could coordinate operations across several different countries at once. Large global firms also outsourced parts of their production to small contractors. Competition between contractors ensured the lowest cost. While one section of the global working class might achieve some power locally, you could always move production somewhere else. Where conditions were more favourable. An example is the history of the printing industry in Australia. As the printing industry left Australia, the first move was to Hong Kong. As wages there went up, the industry re-located to Taiwan. Then to the Philippines. Now India.

The consequences of globalization in the rich countries

These are the things that enabled globalization. What were the effects in the rich countries?

More inequality

Stagnation of wages for the ordinary masses of working people in the rich countries and a corresponding rise in the wealth of the top end. The bottom twenty per cent of the population have experienced a decline in incomes. Meanwhile incomes and wealth at the top end have been going up.

Piketty traces some of these developments. Let us look at how this worked out in the leading capitalist country of this period, the United States—for the top *ten per cent*. Between 1910 and 1940, the top 10 per cent were getting 43% of national income. From 1945 to 1980, with higher taxes, the top ten per cent was only getting 33%. By 1980 to 2000, after twenty years of globalisation, their share of national income jumped to 50%. Most this growth was in the top one per cent. For Europe the share of the top ten per cent in the national income started out at 47 per cent in 1910 and dropped steadily to 32 per cent by 1950. It had gone down to 28 per cent by 1980. But between 1980 and 2010 it climbed again to 35 per cent.[36]

There was a similar pattern for the top ten per cent in national wealth. For example, in Britain the top ten per cent held 90 per cent of national wealth in 1910. This fell steadily to 65 per cent by 1970, stayed flat at this level to 1990 and then started to climb, getting to 70 per cent by 2010.[37]

Let's look at the share of national income going to capital (as dividends, rent etc.) and the share going to labour (as wages). For example, in Britain, the share going to capital stayed at between 30 and 40 per cent between 1770 and 1910. It then fell with the depression and rose again to 30 per cent by 1940. Between 1940 and 1970, the height of the welfare state, it stayed at close to 20 per cent (meaning 80 per cent was going to labour). Between 1970 and 2010 the share going to capital climbed again reaching 28 per cent.[38]

Governments cut back but also expand

The second consequence was a change in the way governments operated in the economy—neoliberalism. Neoliberal propaganda traded on the resistance to taxes that came with a stagnation in real wages and job insecurity. The rhetoric of spending cuts was not always matched by the reality.

There was a fall in public ownership of the economy, relative to the share owned by private capital. Piketty surveys eight rich countries. In 1970 the worth of public capital as a percentage of annual national income was between nought and 100 per cent. By 2010 it had dropped to between minus 70 per cent and plus 70 per cent. Meanwhile the worth of private capital started out in 1970 as between 200 and 350 per cent of national income—and climbed to between 400 and 700 per cent.[39]

Along with this fall in public ownership, there was a winding back of some government services. To take Australia as a typical example. While public health insurance remained, the government paid less out of a typical doctor's fee—with patients paying the gap. Work pressure on medical staff in hospitals intensified. Services were more often inadequate. More parents chose private schools and were paying more. In universities, class sizes doubled. Student loans replaced free tertiary education. The government funded technical education sector

(TAFE) was decimated, and fees were increased. Public transport was privatized. Likewise, the banking sector and energy. Public housing provision was pretty well discontinued. The real value of unemployment payments decreased. The endless box ticking required to access benefits increased.

Despite all this contraction, there was in fact an *increase* in some government spending. Take the UK as an example. Between 1949 at the beginning of the welfare state period and 1982 at its close, government spending as a share of GDP climbed from 37 per cent to 56 per cent. Then, in harmony with the rhetoric of neoliberalism, government spending fell to 39 per cent by 2000. However, it then climbed again, reaching 48 per cent in 2011. The percentage of GDP going to social expenditure was 10 per cent in 1960, 15 per cent in 1980 and 23 per cent in 2010. Public social spending includes such things as health, family services, disability payments, housing, unemployment benefits, age pensions. There were similar patterns of change in the other rich countries. In 1960 public spending in the USA was 30 per cent of GDP, 36 per cent in 1980 and 43 per cent by 2011. In Australia, while overall government spending declined from 44 per cent of GDP in 1980 to 37 per cent by 2011, the proportion of *social* spending continued to go up, from 12 per cent of GDP in 1985 to 18 per cent in 2016.[40]

These patterns reflect a shift in government spending. More money is being spent on social welfare. Less is available for key public services. The effect of globalization is to shift power to the rich. What the rich have done is to undermine the conditions of employment. So instead of getting a regular full-time job, more people are employed in casual or part time jobs. When one of these ends, they must make do till they find another one. The effect is an increase in registered unemployment and undeclared periods of underemployment. There is also increasing pressure on the system from this economic insecurity. Appearing as mental and physical illness, drug use, crime and other social damage. All of which increases the number of people drawing on government provision[41]. In the welfare state period, unemployment in Australia was typically close to two per cent. That is hard to believe now, when unemployment is considered low at six per cent and averages out at 7 per cent. In real terms, it is much higher than this. Government statistics now count anyone as employed who has some hours of work.

These conditions have been worse in other rich countries. For example, in 1985 in Spain, the unemployment rate was 17 per cent. However, another 28 per cent were not bothering to register as unemployed. In 2020, European countries had rates of 'labour underutilization' between 19 per cent (France) and 26 per cent (Spain and Italy). These hidden unemployed are not looking for work, because they don't expect to get a job, or working less hours than they need.[42]

Governments spend money mopping up the consequences of this shift in the labour market—and there is less available for other government services.

The cost of basic necessities goes up

Real conditions have been undermined by the galloping costs of essentials. While it looks as though wages have *stagnated*, this is misleading. Within that wage packet, the cost of consumer goods has declined. While the cost of essential goods and services has gone up. Electronics, white goods, cars and like items have become cheaper relative to income. These goods are now manufactured in the global South where wages are low. But the cost of essential goods has gone through the roof. For example, in Australia between 2005 and 2020, spending on education increased by 89 per cent, spending on health by 84 per cent and spending on housing by 64 per cent. Meanwhile the prices for many everyday consumer items, now coming from the global South, declined.[43]

During the welfare state era, owning a house in Australia was affordable for a sizeable majority. This is no longer the case. Between 1960 and 2006 real house prices increased at an average of 2.7 per cent per annum while household incomes were only going up at 1.9 per cent. In 1966, 73 per cent of households in Australia owned or were buying a home. By 2023 that had fallen to 63 per cent.[44] The average property now costs nine times an ordinary income. Three times what it was in 2000.[45] This graph from the Australian Bureau of Statistics says it all.[46]

Ratio of home prices to wages and incomes

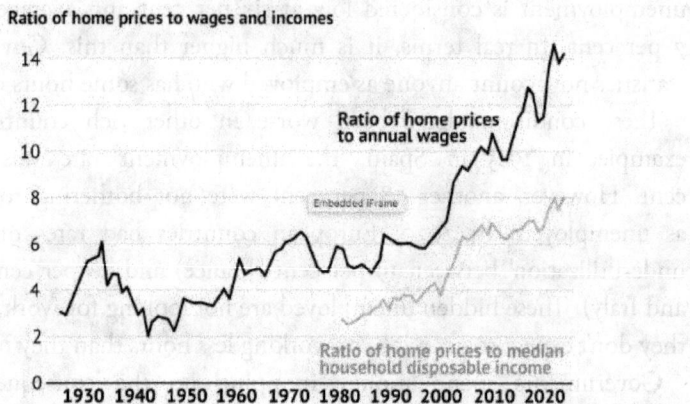

Ratio of home prices to annual wages

Ratio of home prices to median household disposable income

1930 1940 1950 1960 1970 1980 1990 2000 2010 2020

Source: ABS, Cotality, AMP

Various neoliberal measures have produced this consequence. The decline in public housing construction – removing competing low prices from the housing market. Tax breaks for investors renting out their real estate. The opening of the housing market to the upper echelons of other countries. Investment in rental housing as superannuation. Low interest rates.

Conditions like this are ubiquitous in the global North. Living standards for average workers in the global North have *deteriorated*. Despite income figures that imply stagnation.

Capitalism, the third episode

The third episode is a cliff-hanger. We don't know what might happen.

There is no doubt that the first world bargain is finished. The first world bargain was increasing affluence. Productivity increases because of technological inventions. Caused in turn by competition. The cooperation of the ordinary people of the global North with the capitalist class. The social compact. What's killing that off?

First is globalization, as explained. The capitalist class does not have to accommodate popular pressure in the rich countries. They no longer need industrial labour from the rich countries.

Secondly, the environmental crisis. There is no way to maintain the affluence of ordinary people in the rich countries and deal with the climate disaster and other kinds of environmental problem—like the plastics crisis, the energy crisis, and the global water crisis, to mention typical issues. Solving any of these problems costs money that cannot fund everyday consumer goods and government services. *Not* solving any of these problems also costs money. In Australia the recent bush fires and floods—the impact of climate change—showed the second side of this dilemma. These catastrophes destroyed many homes. Insurance companies will not pay the owners to rebuild in the same locations. They cannot sell their properties for anything like what they were worth before these disasters. A catch 22 of capitalism. Government assistance is a joke.

It may also be that we are past the peak of invention, that we are beginning to run out of technologies that can produce things more cheaply with less labour and fewer materials.[47]

Of course, globalization has produced some small gains for the global middle-class and some parts of the working class. Like workers in South Africa with jobs in car factories. These workers are surely doing better than they would starving in a rural village. Yet what gets ignored in paeans of praise for globalisation is this. There are still more than a billion people without adequate food and another billion suffering from severe food insecurity. For example, in Africa and South Asia between 25 and 50 per cent of children under five years old are stunted from malnutrition.[48] The cause is poor food supply exacerbated by gastric infections. A consequence of inadequate sanitation. Capitalism, despite its glitzy achievements, is hardly an epitome of efficiency. In meeting human needs, it's a complete schemozzle.

An impasse for reformists

The third episode of capitalism implies the insufficiency of reformist options. Reforming and regulating capitalism to make these problems go away. Starting in the nineteenth century and accelerating in the 1950s, working class pressure reformed capitalism. Improving people's lives substantially in the rich countries and even in the global South. The vote, the welfare state, better wages and conditions, shorter working hours, some regulation of environmental impacts. These strategies worked—that is not an illusion.[49] But extending these reformist options is no longer viable for the rich countries. Even less likely for the global South.

If you tried now to enact a strong program of reform—for example like those proposed by Jeremy Corbyn or Bernie Sanders—big business would move their operations to countries that are maintaining a 'favourable' economic strategy.

Globalization is a trap for reformists. An 'own goal' for the left where social democratic parties implemented it. The only way to make strong reformist proposals work would be to cut your country off from the rest of the world. To start producing for local consumption. Running your own show without the constant threat of 'offshoring'. But if you do that, what happens next? The price of consumer goods goes through the roof. Re-planting the manufacturing industry is expensive enough. Then there is the cost of the environmentalist retrofit we need. Not to mention the high cost of labour with local manufacturing. If a reformist government attempted all this, they could expect to lose the next election—as it became clear what was involved. The continuation of alienated labour and the privileged lifestyles of the rich—combined with hikes in taxes and the price of everything.

As explained above, the environmental crisis is also a barrier to reformist options. The basic compensation for alienated work in rich countries has always been an increasing supply of consumer goods and leisure options.[50] You cannot reconcile this with measures to deal with the environmental crisis. Not dealing with it entails the same problems—declining affluence for ordinary consumers. Capitalism by its very nature creates pressures to grow the economy and cut corners to externalize environmental damage. Reform adequate to deal with these problems kills economic growth, destroys jobs, and implies a vast bureaucratic oversight—itself a huge cost. More on these issues in the following chapters.

Promises of reform made along these lines are either disingenuous or naïve. No leftist mainstream party is going to restore tariffs and end globalisation. Or institute environmentalist policies adequate to the science. If they do attempt this policy in good faith, they will be voted out. For the most part, when politicians on the right promise to restore local manufacturing, it is a straight lie. They are also aware of the likely electoral consequences. Trump is a special case here. He imagines the symbolic power of patriotic gestures will be amplified by an economic context that *reduces* living conditions. More deflection. More scapegoating. Allowing an oligarchic demolition of representative democracy.

It seems to me that now there are two drastic alternatives, we can either have a re-feudalisation of class society, or we can have de-growth and revolution.

Re-feudalisation

What does a re-feudalisation of class society look like? Like more of the same. The tendencies already present in globalisation are intensified. Markets target the rich. Most production is oriented to the top ten per cent. The bottom 90 per cent are gradually losing out. Malnutrition would become common in the rich countries, just like in the global South.

To stay on top in this situation, the capitalist class would have to abandon representative democracy and get populist support for authoritarian solutions. Authoritarian governments are already typical in the global South. In the rich countries the ordinary population has been raised on a diet of increasing affluence as compensation for wage labour. As the pressures in play remove this entitlement, the ordinary people of the rich countries are furious. Sections of the capitalist class will call on authoritarian solutions to cap this discontent. The Trump regime is an early adopter. The conversion of Elon Musk to Qanon and the far right is telling. Along with Vice President Vance's endorsement of far-right parties for Europe. Putin's Russia is a model.[51]

While this is the political scenario, the economic scenario is 'corporatism'. A mafioso version of a monetary economy—but not really capitalism. Certain companies are allies of the ruling cliques and get favoured treatment. The government dismantles companies owned by disloyal capitalists. The competitive market vanishes. There are monopolies authorized by the state. As in mercantilist Europe. In the long term, without a competitive global market economy, technological innovation and increases in productivity disappear. Not just in one country but in the whole world.

This is not a good setting for effective action on climate and other environmental catastrophes. Of course, technological stagnation and corrupt cronyism reduce the chances of coming up with workable environmental solutions. But the political issues are just as relevant. The ruling elites would have to watch their backs before anything else. They would be plagued by the threat of rebellion from below and by coups from disaffected elites. So environmental action would become window dressing, stage props for doing nothing. Worse even than the current scenario. Collapse within a hundred years or less.

This scenario is misunderstood if it is conceived as a continuation of capitalism, an *adaptation* of the capitalist economy. It maintains the power of certain sections of the capitalist class. But the social machine, the mode of production, is not capitalism.

Degrowth and revolution

The other alternative is de-growth and revolution. That is the one I'm looking forward to. The population of the world goes, 'You know what? This is not working. We need to do something completely different.' And in the rich countries people are willing to accept a cut in their consumer affluence. In the global South they accept that the American dream will never happen.

Affluence, measured in material goods, is no longer an option. Renewable energy technologies are insufficient to provide a rich world energy diet for the whole globe. There are not enough minerals to make the batteries. Not enough mountain valleys for pumped hydro power storage.[52] To preserve global biodiversity, we must cut back our impact in agriculture, timber, energy, land clearing, toxic waste. Recycling and removing toxins, the 'circular economy', implies more hours of work and less production.

But what is the payback, the compensation for these losses in consumer goods? A successful and sensible alternative to capitalism could promise quite a lot. Firstly, security in your basic material needs. Your housing would be secure, your food would be sufficient. You would not expect any sudden changes in your conditions. Control of everyday life. In a gift economy, people doing the work would decide what they wanted to produce—in consultation with their communities. They would have complete control over how their work was organised. Their work would not be commanded by any boss. They would be doing things that they themselves thought to be useful. Everyday material security, along with creative and social pleasures, would compensate for the loss of consumer goods.

This combination of de-growth and revolution could in fact get support. People are much more aware of the necessity for degrowth than you might imagine. They just cannot see how it can happen without Mad Max or Hunger Games coming along for the ride. But of course, the current mainstream strategy of doing nothing does not *prevent* nasty feudalism. The prospect of collapse becomes more real every decade. Hanging on to the dreams of the past looks more and more delusional.

The de-growth and revolution option fits with grassroots strategies in much of the global South. It has become obvious that insertion into the global agricultural economy is no solution for the rural poor. Moving to the big city and getting a global factory job works for a minority. But most are not finding 'development' a brilliant solution. Meanwhile we know that a simple permaculture agroecology strategy can make huge improvements in nutrition and health. With only minimal use of industrial products like mosquito nets, cement, wire, and poly-pipe tubing. So long as people have control over their own land. None of this is rocket science. These experiments are being tried in a patchwork of projects in the global South.[53] On a larger scale by revolutionary movements—such as the Zapatistas and the Rojava Kurds.[54]

These provide a living model of how well de-growth can work. The ordinary people of the rich countries could end up seeing *this* as the way forward. A revolution in the rich countries would localize production. Complementing this, revolutions in the global South could block the drain of wealth to the North. System change to a gift economy could undermine the racist lifeboat mentality so common in the North now. 'We are the little red hen, we do the work, while you come begging for our help.' These paranoid views reflect the very real insecurity plaguing ordinary people in the rich North.[55] With that insecurity gone, these globally privileged classes might develop a more generous practice. Global production today is excessive, and consumption is confined to elites. There is more than enough for us all to live a simple sufficiency. While also looking after our planet.

So, this is the basic history of the social machine that is capitalism. The following chapters will look at alternative pathways out of capitalism. Starting with a chapter on what's wrong with money!

Endnotes

[1] Samir Amin, *Global History: A View from the South*, Pambazuka Press, Capetown 2019.
[2] Peter Frankopan, *The Silk Roads: A new history of the world*, Bloomsbury, London, 2015.
[3] Amin, *Global History*, p.18.
[4] Karl Polanyi, *The Great Transformation*, Penguin, Harmondsworth, 2024.
[5] Amin, *Global History*.
[6] ibid., p.30; David Van Reybrouck, *Revolusi: Indonesia and the Birth of the Modern World*, Penguin, UK, 2024.
[7] Chris Hesketh, 'Debating modes of production in Latin America'. *Progress in Political Economy*, 12 September 2023; Eduardo Galeano and Isabel Allende *Open Veins of Latin America: Five Centuries of the Pillage of a Continent*. Monthly Review Press, New York, 1997; Andre Gunder Frank, *Dependent Accumulation*. Monthly Review Press, New York, 1979; Immanuel Wallerstein, *The Capitalist World Economy*. Cambridge University Press, 1979.
[8] Galeano, *Open Veins*, Alf Hornborg, *Global Magic: Technologies of Appropriation from Ancient Rome to Wall Street*, Palgrave Macmillan, London 2016.

[9] Alfred J Crosby, *Ecological Imperialism: The Biological Expansion of Europe, 900-1900*, Cambridge University Press, 1986.

[10] Karl Marx, *Capital, Volume 1*, Progress Publishers, Moscow 1969 (1886).

[11] Paul Cardan, *Modern Capitalism and Revolution*. Solidarity, London, 1974.

[12] Edward P. Thompson, *The Making of the English Working Class*, Vintage, New York, 1966.

[13] Thomas Piketty, *Capital in the Twenty-First Century*, Harvard University Press, Cambridge, MA, 2014.

[14] Wolfgang Streeck, *Buying Time: The Delayed Crisis of Democratic Capitalism*. 2nd ed., Verso, London, 2017.

[15] Piketty, *Capital*.

[16] Eric Pineault, *A Social Ecology of Capital*. Pluto Press, London, 2023.

[17] David Van Reybrouck, *Revolusi*; Galeano, *Open Veins*, Leahy, *Food Security*.

[18] Galeano, *Open Veins*.

[19] Statista, 'Unemployment rate in South Africa from Q1 2019 to Q3 2022, by age group', in *Statista*, viewed on 27 December 2023, https://www.statista.com/statistics/1129482/unemployment-rate-by-age-group-in-south-africa/; Business Tech, 'The provinces in south africa where more people are unemployed than working', in *Business Tech 2022*. viewed on 27 December, 2023, https://businesstech.co.za/news/business/650185/the-south-african-provinces-that-have-more-people-unemployed-than-working.

[20] Narotsky, Susana, *New Directions in Economic Anthropology*, Pluto, London, 1997.

[21] Jason Hickel, Morena Hanbury Lemos and Felix Barbour, 2024, "Unequal exchange of labour in the world Economy," *Nature Communications*, 15: 6298.

[22] Leahy, Terry 'The Australian Public, Developing Countries and the Environment', http://gifteconomy.au/permaculture/the-australian-public-developing-countries-and-the-environment/, viewed on 24 February 2025.

[23] Ulrich Brand, & Marcus Wissen, *The Imperial Mode of Living: Everyday Life and the Ecological Crisis of Capitalism*. Verso, London, 2021; Frank, *Dependent Accumulation*; Wallerstein *The Capitalist World*; Julian Go, *Postcolonial Thought and Social Theory*, Oxford University Press, 2016, Hornborg, *Global Magic*.

[24] *Henry's Songbook*, http://mysongbook.de/msb/songs/b/bravewol.html, viewed on 5th March 2025; Bob Copper, *A Song for Every Season*, Paladin, St Albans, 1975.

[25] Van Reybrouck, *Revolusi*.

[26] Noam Chomsky, *Turning the Tide: U.S. Intervention in Central America and the Struggle for Peace*, Paperback, Haymarket Books, New York, 2015; Vincent Bevins, *The Jakarta Method: Washington's Anti-communist Crusade and the Mass Murder Program that Shaped Our World*, Public Affairs, New York, 2021; Noam Chomsky, *Towards a New Cold War*. Pantheon Books. New York, 1982.

[27] Adolfo Gilly, *Paths of Revolution*. Verso, London, 2022, pp. 207-208.

[28] Brand and Wissen, *The Imperial Mode*.

[29] Yenny Tjoe, *Two Decades of Economic Growth*, https://blogs.griffith.edu.au/asiainsights/two-decades-of-economic-growth-benefited-only-the-richest-20-how-severe-is-inequality-in-indonesia/, Griffiths Asia Institute, 2018, viewed on 6 March, 2025.

[30] Pam Nilan, *Decolonizing Social Science Research in Southeast Asia*, Palgrave, Singapore, 2025.

[31] Luc Boltanski and Eve Chiapello, *The New Spirit of Capitalism*. Verso, London, 2007; Piketty, Capital.

[32] Horowitz, David, *Imperialism and Revolution*. Allen Lane, London. 1969; Chomsky, Noam, *Towards a New Cold War*. Pantheon Books. New York, 1982.

[33] The Economist, 'Britain's manufacturing sector is changing beyond all recognition', in *The Economist*, 5 May 2016, viewed on 27 December 2023, https://www.economist.com/britain/2016/11/05/britains-manufacturing-sector-is-changing-beyond-all-recognition?; Hans-Peter Martin, and Harald Schumann, *The Global Trap: Globalization and the Assault on Prosperity and Democracy*, Zed Books, London, 1997.

[34] Ankie Hoogvelt, *Globalization and the Postcolonial World: The New Political Economy of Development*. Palgrave, Basingstoke, U.K.

[35] Hoogvelt, *Globalization*.

[36] Piketty, op.cit., pp. 291, 324.

[37] Piketty, op.cit., p. 344.

[38] Piketty, op.cit., p. 200.

[39] Piketty, op.cit., p. 184.

[40] Our World in Data, 'Public Social Spending 1880–2011 as share of national GDP', in *Our World in Data*. 2023, viewed on 29 December 29, 2023, https://ourworldindata.org/government-spending

[41] ibid.

[42] ILOSTAT, 'Statistics on unemployment and labour underutilization', in *ILOSTAT*. 2023, viewed on 29 December 2023, https://ilostat. ilo.org/topics/unemployment-and-labour-underutilization; Olivier Blanchard, Charles Bean and Wolfgang Munchau, 'European unemployment: the evolution of facts and ideas'. *Economic Policy*, vol. 21 (45) 2006, pp.7-59.

[43] Michael Janda, 2021, "Inflation Analysis Shows Costs of Necessities Rising Fast As Many 'Wants' Become Cheaper," *ABC News*, May 26, 2021.

[44] Shane Oliver 2023, "Australian homeownership peaked in 1966, How do we make property more affordable?", *Livewire*, May 23, https://www.livewiremarkets.com/wires/australian-home-ownership-peaked-in-1966-how-do-we-make-property-more-affordable, viewed January 28, 2023. Judith Yates, 2008, "Australia's Housing Affordability Crisis," *The Australian Economic Review* 41 (2): 200-214. Yuhno, Cho, May Li, Shuyun and Lawrence Uren 2021, "Understanding Housing Affordability in Australia," *Australian Economic Review* 54 (3): 375-386.

[45] Alan Kohler, *The Great Divide: Australia's Housing Mess and How to Fix It*, Quarterly Essay, QE92, Melbourne, 2023.

[46] Australian Bureau of Statistics, 'Ratio of Home Prices to Wages and Incomes.' https://www.abs.gov.au

[47] Wolfgang Streeck, How Will Capitalism End? Verso, London 2016.

[48] FAO 2022, *The State of Food Security and Nutrition in the World*, Rome, United Nations.

[49] Wolfgang, Streeck, *Buying Time: The Delayed Crisis of Democratic Capitalism*. 2nd ed., Verso, London, 2017; Raewyn Connell, Ashenden, D. J., Kessler, S. & G.W. Dowsett, *Making the Difference: Schools, Families and Social Division*, George Allen & Unwin, Sydney, 1982.

[50] Cardan, *Modern Capitalism*.

[51] Catherine Belton, *Putin's People: How the KGB took back Russia and then took on the West*, William Collins, London, 2020.

[52] Ted Trainer 2022, "Can Australia Run on Renewable Energy: Unsettled Issues and Implications," *Biophysical Economics and Sustainability* 7 (10): 1-17.

[53] Terry Leahy, *Food Security for Rural Africa; Feeding the farmers first*, Routledge, London, 2019.

[54] Dylan Eldredge Fitzwater, *Autonomy Is in Our Hearts: Zapatista Autonomous Government through the Lens of the Tsotsil Language*, PM Press, Oakland CA., 2019; Ashish Kothari, Ariel Salleh, Arturo Escobar, Federico Demaria and Alberto Acosta (eds), *Pluriverse, A Post-Development Dictionary*, Tulika Books, New Delhi, 2019.

[55] Leahy, *The Australian Public*.

Chapter 3
What's Wrong with Money?

In the last two chapters, we looked at capitalism as a system. What are the ghostly features of capitalism? As I called them. How does capitalism operate like a game? The early history of capitalism and the three episodes of mature capitalism. Why capitalism has no future.

As you may well understand from those chapters, capitalism is totally founded on money. The means of production, like land and factories, are owned as capital. This means that they have a monetary value. To maintain that monetary value, capital must work. To make more money. Every firm is in competition with other firms. To even stay in the same place, they must try to make more money. So clearly money is central to the capitalist system.

This chapter explores money in more detail. To explain why money is a problem. Our efforts to bring about system change will run into endless difficulties if we try to maintain a monetary economy.

Most people, and most mainstream economists, think that money is primarily a means of exchange, that money makes exchange easy. So, I've got an apple that I don't want, and Robert has an orange that I do want. I sell the apple to Mary and use that money to buy the orange from Robert. The other thing people think is that money is necessary in a complex society. Handing things over to other people without money being used is okay in a simple pre-industrial society. But you cannot make an industrial society work without money and the market.[1] The market is the network of monetary exchanges between people. Most people believe the mainstream view of economists. The market is an efficient way of linking people's desires for consumer goods and the production of those goods. If people want more apples than farmers are selling on the market, the price of apples will go up. This is a price 'signal' to farmers to grow more apples. The result is that more people can satisfy their desire for apples, their preference. The market and money are just an information system that links preferences and production.[2]

A common belief is that every society has had markets. It is ridiculous to think we could do without them. Also, as the market is simply an information system, it is politically neutral. Whether you are on the left or the right, you can use the market to implement your preferences and manage the market to embody ethically sound policies.[3]

I will challenge a number of these ideas in this and subsequent chapters. Markets are not politically neutral. Capitalism absolutely depends upon money, and if you could get rid of money you would get rid of capitalism. The combination of money and the market is disastrous, for the environment, for social justice and for the wellbeing of the people doing the work. The market is the opposite of an efficient mechanism for adjusting production to people's preferences. Not every society has had money. Egalitarian stateless societies did not have any money at all.[4] This is no surprise when you understand how money does in fact function. The market is not actually necessary to make a complex society work.

The Origins of Money

This is a startling set of claims, and I will take it slowly. Let us start off by looking at the origins of money with early states. David Graeber talks about this in his book, *Debt. The first 5,000 years*.[5] The early states needed to pay their soldiers. They needed some way of giving soldiers access to goods and services, especially food. They began the cycle by minting money and paying their soldiers. Along with this they forced the peasant classes to pay tribute in money. To pay their taxes, the peasants needed to produce something for the market. They had to sell something to get the money to pay their taxes. The soldiers had money and needed to get food. They bought the food from the peasants, providing the cash that the peasants needed to pay their taxes.

The state pays their soldiers. The peasants grow food. The soldiers buy it. The peasants pay their taxes. A cycle.

Graeber cites sources from a variety of early states, in India, Iran and China to back up this analysis. Original sources and archaeology show that ruling elites were well aware of the connections between mines (for precious metals), soldiers, taxes and food. These sources concluded,

> The creation of markets of this sort was not just convenient for feeding soldiers, but useful in all sorts of ways, since it meant officials no longer had to requisition everything they needed directly from the populace, or figure out a way to produce it on royal estates or royal workshops.[6]

In *Beyond Money*, Anitra Nelson makes a similar analysis of the connection between money, the state and taxes. She draws on evidence from ancient Egypt, in the third millennium BC (3,000 to 2,000). There the development of money coincides with the change from an egalitarian tribal society to a class society. She also draws on research on Sumer, the first class society and first state, dating back to before 4,000 BC. She argues that money and the market can be found established in an early form as debt tokens in the seventh century in Sumer. The Greek cities originated money, as we now know it, in the fifth century BC. Again, in the context of a state-based class society.[7]

In this early history of money, the work that the peasants were doing to provide food for the market was 'alienated labour', as Marx calls it.[8] It was forced upon them. They had to grow food for the market to get cash to pay their taxes. If they failed to pay their taxes, they would be punished. A system of surplus extraction in which money played a key part. The state was freed from the necessity to source food to feed their army directly.

What this little story suggests is that the state, money, and alienated labour were connected at the point of origin of money. And I would argue that thereafter, they are always connected.

Money and Alienated Labour

What is money? I am going to explain what are called credit theories of money. And in this, I owe a lot to Anitra Nelson who has written much on this topic. Her recent book is *Beyond Money, A Post-Capitalist Strategy*.[9] In credit theories of money, having money is as though society owes you a debt. Society guarantees that you will be able to use your money to buy something on the market. When you have made this purchase, society will have paid off the debt. The point of money is that you will be able to buy things. Then what is your money? It is a claim on the social product. It is a promise from society that you will be able to access a certain amount of the social product.

> When you have money in a market society, you have a generic credit from society as a whole.[10]

As Nelson points out, the assumption that you make when using the money is that the market will continue to produce goods and services that you can use your money to buy. In other words, the whole of society is committed to maintaining the capitalist economy to realize the value of money as credit.[11]

Having money is like having a record of a promise from society at large, that you will be able to buy something. When you buy something, society will pay back the debt that the money represents. This has certain implications. Money and alienated labour are linked. In capitalism, the ability of your money to buy things depends on the fact that other people have been forced by economic necessity to sell their working hours, making things that can be sold on the market. You would not be able to buy *anything* unless other people had to do work and get paid for that work and put things on the market. So, the fact that your money is useful to *you* is because *other* people's labour is forced labour. Just like in the story of the origins of money, where farmers were forced to produce food for the market, because they needed to get money to pay their taxes.[12]

How people have been forced into alienated work varies from case to case. In the most general account, the subordinates of any class society have been deprived of their means of production. They cannot use the society's means of production to make the things they need to maintain their lives. To access their livelihoods, they must work as instructed by a ruling class. Let's look at tributary societies where monetary exchange is just a small part of the total economy. The most basic structure is the extraction of a surplus of food grown by peasants—and going to a class of landlords. An unpaid labour. This is alienated labour. The subordinate class (peasants, slaves) do not have any choice but to provide this tribute. A part of the surplus they produce enters the realm of monetary exchange. The landlords mint money and use it to pay soldiers, craft workers or merchants—for goods and services. These middle classes use their money to buy food. They are like the peasants in one respect. They do not control the means of production of food. Their labour is *also* alienated. They must do the things that the landlord class *wants* to get money and through that food. Like making weapons, putting down a rebellion, building a castle, trading a silk cloth. Two kinds of alienated labour, that of the peasants and that of the middle classes. With money mediating this arrangement.

But, as I am sure you may have heard, market constraint is no problem. People are doing things that produce goods and services which people are prepared to buy! In other words, they must be doing *some* sort of useful work as they are forced to enter the market.

So let us look at the implications of this alienation. This market work is not necessarily the work that people would prefer to be doing. They must choose the work that will get them an income, regardless of their preferences. It could be work that is monumentally boring, useless as far as they are concerned, or controlled by a tyrannical boss.[13] The whole point is to produce something that can be sold to make money on the market. For example, you might be growing strawberries when you might rather be working in aged care.

In the most usual case, someone else owns the means of production with which you are working. The fact that the capitalist class owns the means of production is what forces you to get a job, to earn money by putting goods for sale on the market. The owner of the means of production for your job controls your work. So, a primary factor in alienated labour is the absence of control over the process of labour. While you are at work you must do what you are told. At best you are consulted and given discretion when the boss thinks it is in their interest.

Another aspect of this market alienation relates to distribution. The recipient is not necessarily the person you would have chosen to receive your production. As in the example of the previous paragraphs, you might be growing strawberries. You know that they will be bought by the people whose high income makes such a luxury an option. You might prefer that they go to people in the outer suburbs. But you would not be able to make that distribution decision. If your intended buyers had no money to buy strawberries, there would be no point in growing strawberries for them. So, distribution is also something that the market decides.

How is this alienated labour a problem? Well, no one should be expected to live their life doing what the market demands. It is a sort of slavery to have to work to fit with the dictates of the market—a social machine working beyond your control. In fact, beyond the control of any person or group of people. It is like being a slave to an automaton, a cyber person. Even worse when you are also directly controlled by an employer while you are at work. This is just the beginning of the problems with markets and money.

The hidden foot of money

I'm going to now turn to the topic of whether money is politically neutral. To talk about the ways in which money has predictable political effects. I'm going to call this the *hidden* foot of money. Adam Smith talks about the hidden hand of the market. Well, this is the hidden foot of money. Money is 'naturalized' in the sense that we don't really think about it a lot—we treat it as though it was a natural phenomenon. There are assumptions about money that we make without even realizing we are doing that. But in fact, they are central to how money works.

And the main one is that the market and money depend upon a hegemonic discourse. A way of thinking that is dominant in society. Namely this. When you are using money, you will buy cheap and sell dear. That practice is what a market and money imply and also *depend* upon. You will try to get the 'best value' by buying the cheapest. If you are selling you will try to get the most money you can. Durggh. Where your labour is alienated—you are being forced to work to get money—it makes absolute sense to try and get the most out of your money. Every bit of your money has cost you. For example, you go to the supermarket and see a whole shelf of things lined up and you look at them. And you think, well, these are all basically the same, but this one's lots cheaper and you buy it. In almost every case. As Nelson puts it,

> Consumers tend to purchase the cheaper options among commodities with similar values.[14]

The owners of business, just like anyone selling something, attempt to achieve the highest price – selling dear. And are punished economically if they do not. As Nelson notes,

> If a capitalist departs from the basic principle of cutting costs and selling as much as they can at as high a price level as consumers can bear, they heighten their risks of losing money (capital) and going bankrupt.[15]

It seems sensible to behave like this because everybody else is doing this. And this is in fact what makes prices predictable and makes markets work. The hidden hand of the market that Adam Smith talks about absolutely depends upon this. That is why I call it the hidden foot. This is the socially dominant discourse. A way of behaving. How most of the time, most people use their money, and think about money. But you are actually *free*, in any particular instance, to do the opposite of this and buy the dearest product on the shelf. You do not realize that there is a social compulsion to behave according to the hidden foot. Because at any particular moment, you can do the opposite and make a totally stupid decision. It never occurs to you that money as a *system* requires you to keep buying the cheapest. That the whole system *only works* because you are most likely to buy the cheapest product when you are buying—and to aim at the highest price when you are selling.

The political consequences

This discourse and the use of money in this way has a huge effect. The effect is to prioritize monetary efficiency. What costs less in any purchasing or production decision. As a seller you want to produce things that are going to cost you less and get the highest possible prices. What that means is that *other* values, use values for humans and values for other species take second place. For example, for the workforce. In many cases, managers find it cheaper to organize production so that their workers are doing work which is mind numbingly boring. Because that's more efficient from a monetary point of view. But of course, from the point of view of the people doing the work it's a disaster. Likewise, it may be sensible from a monetary point of view to have your workers doing a 12-hour day. This is the situation today in much of the global South. Twelve hours a day, six days a week. Of the most boring work possible. Is that a way to live your life?

To take an environmental example. Production and distribution depend on energy. The more production and distribution, the more money is being made. Fossil fuels have been cheaper than renewables. They probably still are, if you fully account for storage costs with renewables.[16] That is why the capitalist class is hanging onto fossil fuels as the main energy source. It is not just the cost per kilowatt hour. It is also the cost of transition. They are making better money using the fossil fuel infrastructure that is already in place. Rather than spending a lot of money to move to renewables.[17] Whether through taxes to fund a transition or through purchase to pay directly for renewable energy. The monetary system operates like this in every case. For example, old growth forest. You can make more money cutting down an old growth forest and sawing it up for timber. Starting a new plantation on farming land and waiting for the forest to mature is the expensive option.[18]

The same implications of the market create social injustice. A factory making leather seats for Mercedes cars. For the two per cent of the global population who can afford to buy them. That makes more market sense than making bicycles for people living in African villages.

It's not that capitalism hates the environment and wants to keep the poor in their place. But people in the market system will make decisions to buy cheap and sell dear all the way along the line. Because that's how the market operates.

Money and inequality

Money creates inequality. Monetary transactions are always competitive because both parties are trying to get the best deal. And one party can only get a better deal when the other party gets a worse deal. For example, a firm gets a higher price for their widget and the consumer must pay more, getting a monetary loss. Who can get the best deal is always an issue. The effect in the long-term is to create winners and losers from any equal starting point. Some people gradually accumulate money and by using more money, they're able to accumulate even more and so it goes. This is how the 'Monopoly' board game plays out. Let us dream up a fictional example to see how this works. We can assume two players who are getting different amounts of weekly income. Maurice gets $500 a week and spends all of it on necessities. Peter gets $1000 a week and usually has $500 left over at the end of the week. So, Peter is getting twice the income in the first week. In the second week, Peter decides to invest his spare $500 in something that he knows will earn another $500 in the week. So, on the Friday of the second week, Maurice is getting his $500 income and Peter is getting his usual $1000 plus another $1000. $500 of this is carried over from the previous week, so we could say that Peter's new income at the end of the second week is $1500. Three times what Maurice is getting. The ratio of inequality in weekly income has gone from 2 to 1 up to 3 to 1.

Accidental factors put some people in an advantageous position in the market, and they come to the top. Their good luck allows them to use their advantage to amass greater and greater wealth. As Piketty points out, this can only be countered, *to some extent*, by the strongest political pressures and regulatory policies.[19] There is a presumption that legally acquired advantage in the market is ethically acceptable and even meritocratic. After all, we are all in the same market business of buying cheap and selling dear. The wealth of the elite is just another example of the same processes that operate in our own lives. And are regarded as perfectly acceptable in that context. We end up with a system where one per cent of the global population owns as much wealth as the bottom fifty per cent. Where a third of the population of the world are not getting enough to eat.[20]

Let us look at how this played out in the relationship between the Germans and the Greeks. This drama has been considered by Yanis Varoufakis, a minister in the Syriza leftist government in Greece. And by Wolfgang Streeck, a German sociologist.[21] Their conclusions are very similar.

Germany produces industrial goods, which are high cost and high value. Most Greeks could not afford to buy them. So, what did the German banks do? They offered the Greeks cheap loans to buy these goods. You can see how this move was a great benefit to German industry. They could expand their market, make more money and pay more workers in Germany. Then at the end of the day, the Greeks had a huge debt crisis. The leftist government in Greece went to the EU, controlled by the German banks. They asked for more time and lower repayments for their loans. This was refused. Instead, the EU demanded that the Greek government cut back its spending. With the consequence that social services in Greece were cut so much that many Greeks went hungry.

How was this episode understood in Germany and the rest of the EU? The Greeks were lazy. They were not working hard enough to pay off their debts. Spendthrift. They were taking out loans that they could not afford to pay back. They were stupid, thinking they could receive government services without paying for them in taxes.

But in fact, the Germans were just *lucky* that they got these industries up and running decades before. They had cornered the market before the Greeks could get into the same game. It was German banks and industry that saw a profit in lending money to the Greeks—and did super well out of that decision. This unequal situation, and the unforgiveable suffering of the Greeks, is justified by claims that treat the market as an *ethical* institution. As though it's all about real values, about who has earned their advantages through their hard work.

The inequality that comes out of the market means that those with more money have more influence on decisions about production and distribution than those with less. Praises for the market treat markets as a kind of democracy. Instead of voting, you put your money where your mouth is. Doing that, your preference is translated into decisions about production and distribution. But in the market these votes are *not* equal. The weight of your 'vote' totally depends on the amount of money you can put into it. That is why it makes more sense to produce leather upholstery for a Mercedes than a bike for an African villager.[22]

Money and capitalism

As I explained in the last chapter, capitalism is the only society where the means of production—like farms, factories, and banks—can be privately owned and sold on the market as commodities. The second thing that is unique to capitalism is that the subordinate class offers their labour power on the market as a commodity. Compared to other class societies, capitalism is the class society that is most strongly organized around money and markets. The class structure of capitalism depends upon the way the market operates. The capitalists are those who have the most money and use their money to grow their capital. The working class and the middle-class are those who have to offer their services, skills and labour power on the market—to make money to live.

The effect of competitive private ownership in capitalism is to create various problems. If you are the owner of the means of production in capitalism, you must make the most possible profit. The market is very insecure. You can take out a loan and use it to put a whole lot of stuff into production and then put it on the market—only to find some competitor has a new technology and they are selling their products at a lower price. Or there is a downturn in the economy and your consumers cannot afford your product. Suddenly all the money that you spent on your production is worth nothing. To avoid going under when something like this happens, you must make the most possible profit that you can. To create a buffer, a hedge in case things go haywire. So, every firm is competing to make a bigger profit. How do they do this? They do this by cutting their staff and paying less for their workforce. They do this by getting in new machinery, that produces things at a cheaper price. They do this by expanding their markets and selling the same thing to more people. If every firm is doing this, the effect is growth. Everybody is behaving in this way, and you cannot stop them behaving this way. Because in a monetary market economy these strategies make sense. Managers of firms would be mad to do anything else. From a planetary point of view, we have come to the end of that game. It is not going to work anymore. We need to get away from capitalism, and we need to invent a system that does not depend on money and the market.

Cooperatives and the solidarity economy

Getting to understand what is wrong with capitalism, a lot of people think, 'I know what we'll do. We'll run a market economy. That'll be fine. But instead of those evil capitalists controlling every firm, we're going to have a co-operative of workers controlling every firm'. Recently, this proposal is often referred to as the 'solidarity economy'.[23] One problem is that you would end up with just the same kind of evil consequences that you get with any kind of market economy. It's great that you don't have a boss. That relieves some problems, but far from all of them. Thinking through this shows us some of the issues intrinsic to markets. Let us imagine how a solidarity economy might work out. Almost all the means of production are owned by cooperatives and the rest is in the hands of governments or small family-owned businesses.

The first thing is you have still got alienated labour. What people must do in these cooperatives is to produce for the market. They are making use of the resources they have, to find a market niche that suits what they can do. So, their cooperative can get an income and they can get paid. As with capitalism today, they're producing for those who can afford to buy stuff. Those who can't afford to buy stuff miss out. What does all that mean? That they cannot decide to make things for people who cannot afford to buy them. They're constrained by the market to that extent. Their labour is alienated. They're not actually making creative decisions about how to contribute through their work. Instead, they are trying to find something that provides an income by making good market sense.

Their own labour conditions are also constrained by market competition. Your cooperative is competing with all other cooperatives for market share. Doing that, there's a limit to how much you can improve your labour conditions. For example, if you work a three-hour day, you are not going to be competitive with other cooperatives working longer hours. This is endless.

There are the same problems that you get with the capitalist economy where environmental and social justice issues are concerned. Cutting corners is necessary to stay in the game. To compete on profit, you must make profit your priority. As with any market economy, market competition drives growth. An environmental problem in its own right.

The Mondragon collectives provide an illustration of the problems cooperatives face. Mondragon in Spain is a place where a cluster of industrial cooperatives started up during the Franco regime. They produce industrial whitegoods, like washing machines, and fridges. And this went all very well. And their cooperative is certainly a great improvement on the organisation of most capitalist firms. But let's look at what happened during the globalization of the seventies and eighties. Suddenly these industrial cooperatives were no longer competitive. They were in competition with firms that had moved their manufacturing to low wage countries. The Mondragon collectives responded by outsourcing some of *their* industrial work to countries of the global South—where labour was cheaper. These workers were not *members* of the cooperative. They were working with the same pay and conditions as other workers *in their own countries*. You may see this as an unethical decision. Nevertheless, it was a decision that made good market sense.[24]

A solidarity economy would end up with inequality just like in capitalism. In the solidarity version of a market economy, cooperatives compete for market share. Some cooperatives win these competitions and others lose them. The result is that some cooperatives, some workers, some regions, some countries end up losing out vis a vis other firms, workers and countries. The ones that continue to win these market contests use their money to gain further advantages and yet more wealth. They become a part of a new solidarity de facto capitalist class. They can dictate terms to other cooperatives. The notion that you can create an egalitarian society through workers' cooperatives ignores the way the market works.

Michael Lebowitz is one of the key socialist advocates of the solidarity economy. He promoted the revolution in Venezuela as working towards that model. He also looked at the problems that took place when Yugoslavia attempted an economy based on workers' cooperatives. Workers' councils left decisions on marketing and production in the hands of managers and technical experts. With long working days, workers were too tired to manage their firms. Cooperatives competed on prices and quality. As you might well expect in any market economy! Some firms did well in the market. The firms that were not doing well were reluctant to lay off their workers. They went to the banks to get loans to pay workers who were in fact redundant. In defiance of market logic, the banks provided them with help. Why? Members of the regional government were also serving on these state banks. They preferred this solution to paying unemployment benefits. Also, firms that had been successful were entrenched on bank boards. They used the leverage of these loans to confirm their market advantage. In the end, workers doing the same jobs were being paid at wildly different rates, depending on what firm they were working for. There was a lot of resentment and hostility on both sides. Our taxes are being used to pay for these idle workers. We are being screwed by these lucky workers. Ethnic tensions escalated. Managers worried more about their political connections than about market efficiency.[25]

The last thing I want to mention is alienated labour and compensation. One of the features of capitalism that I've talked about in the second chapter is the first world bargain. Workers compensate themselves for their alienated labour—with increasing consumption. This has been possible with increasing productivity, producing more with less labour. The worker can buy more and more stuff. This leisure consumption compensates people for the absence of creative control in their workplace. A system of market-based cooperatives run by workers does not get around that problem. Labour is still alienated. The outcome is political pressures for growth. Workers' cooperatives hope to do better in the market and get more income. They end up supporting policies that might grow the economy. With predictable environmental impacts.

Ethics tames the market?

When you pose these kinds of questions to people who support the solidarity economy, their reply is always exactly the same. Where we have a solidarity economy and it is backed up by strong public support, workers restrain their competitive market behaviour. They do this because there is an ethic of cooperation and egalitarianism. An ethic of environmental care. For example, Lebowitz, writing optimistically about the revolution in Venezuela in 2006 quotes their Bolivarian constitution:

> The constitution envisages an alternative economic model, one marked by concepts of justice, equality, solidarity, democracy, and social responsibility. Guided by those ideas of the constitution, I suggest you can avoid many of the problems that plagued the Yugoslav model—particularly those that resulted from their focus on self-interest, rather than the interests of the working class as a whole.[26]

This answer assumes that the problem of capitalism is the greed of the capitalist class. We get rid of all these greedy capitalists. We have an ethical revolution, a cultural revolution. If we run everything through worker's cooperatives, we're not going to have problems. My reply is this. The problems with capitalism are not an effect of the personalities of capitalists. Instead, they come from the market economy and the way that money operates. The ghost and the machine.

One way of looking at this is to say you cannot have a market economy and run it ethically. But now I want to look at this in reverse. If you start to behave ethically you will not be able to run a market economy. A thought experiment. In this thought experiment, the solidarity economy has become a reality. Ethical cooperatives own the means of production. The priority is ethics, not market success.

These workers are going to go, 'Okay, how can we run our cooperative ethically? We're not going to be dominated by the market. When an ethical decision is not a good market decision, we're going to make the ethical decision rather than the optimal market decision. None of the consequences of the market that you have been talking about will apply because we will be making these ethical decisions, not the market decisions.' So how would an economy like this work out in practice?

I am going to give an illustration that starts off with Firm A, a steel works in a rich European country. They have decided they're going to sell a batch of steel that they made last year to Firm B for $2,000. Meanwhile. Guess what? Firm C is prepared to buy their batch of steel for $10,000. So why is Firm A knocking back this fabulous profitable offer? They are giving a huge discount to Firm B. Firm B is a cooperative in an African village. They are going to use the steel to make windmills for their electric power and irrigation pumps. So, Firm A is making the right ethical decision. They don't care about the money. They have decided not to worry about the market imperatives. All power to their elbow, way to go! And are they worried? No, they are not a little bit worried. Why not? You would think they might be worried, only getting $2,000 for their batch of steel. However, they have a plan. They are going to use that $2,000 to buy a batch of guitar amps from Firm W. Normally the price of these guitar amps would be $10,000. But not in this case! The workers in Firm W are into heavy metal music. They know that workers in Firm A are also heavy metal fans. So, their cooperative has decided to express their aesthetic taste through a cheap offer to Firm A. The cooperative running Firm W believes that their ethical responsibility is to make sure that their workers get some leverage over distribution.

This is a somewhat fanciful example of how a society, based on market cooperatives, *which are also ethical cooperatives*, might work. What can you say about this? Well, imagine that every cooperative in the market behaved like this. Market prices would be completely unpredictable. Without Adam Smith's hidden foot (buy cheap and sell dear), the market and money could not actually work. At all. Nobody would know what it would cost to buy a guitar amp, what it would cost to buy a batch of steel. You would not have the faintest clue. The value of money would change from one deal to the next. The worst effects of the Soviet Union's central planning would look like a model of efficiency. In this situation, markets and money would have little influence over production and distribution. Adam Smith's hidden foot would be absent. Without it the hidden hand could never work. Instead, it would make sense for the cooperatives to make decisions through meetings and agreements. Firm A would send representatives to meet with Firm B and promise Firm B a certain amount of steel next year. They would send representatives to meet with Firm W to hear that they would be getting a batch of guitar amps next year. A solid promise. Money would not be relevant. In other words, the solidarity economy in practice could only operate as a *gift economy*. I will discuss that option in the next chapter.

JK Gibson-Graham, Eric Olin Wright, Michael Lebowitz and others have a vision of an ethically charged cooperative solidarity market economy.[27] I am arguing that this vision is in fact incoherent. It could not possibly work.

Bitcoin

Let's now look briefly at digital currencies like Bitcoin. Some anarchists are attracted by the idea of Bitcoin, and they are part of a whole digital currency wonk movement, sometimes referred to by the term P2P—peer to peer.[28] So let me make a few comments about that. The problems with markets that I have explained also operate with digital currencies. Bitcoins are only useful if other people are being forced to perform alienated labour and put what they produce on the market. Buying cheap and selling dear is the only way to make money work. Bitcoin must work like that and so must any digital currency. As I have explained, the discourse of using money by buying cheap and selling dear has a raft of problematic implications.

Far from Bitcoin being a form of money that has no connection to the state, it is entangled with the state in several ways. In a global society where states create money, the value of any money is quantifiable relative to state currencies. The default value of any unit of digital currency is always a quantity of a currency guaranteed by a state. We all know how much Bitcoin is worth in US dollars. It is inconceivable that it could be worth anything at all without us being able to quantify that value—relative to monies authorized by states. In turn, as we have seen, state-based currencies are an inevitable tool of state power in any society that has money and the market.

There is a second kind of state entanglement implied in Bitcoin. The assumption that people make when they transact deals in Bitcoin is at least this. That the state will protect the assets they purchase using Bitcoin. That the state will recognize their 'ownership' within the market system that the state validates and regulates. If you buy a house with Bitcoin, you will expect the seller to give you the title deeds. You will expect the state to recognize and protect that title. If a gang of squatters invades your house, you will expect the police and the courts to look after you. These bitcoin devotees want to have their cake and eat it. They want to engage in monetary deals with Bitcoin that evade the scrutiny of the state. To avoid taxation. To run a criminal business. To protect their wealth from their ex. But at the same time, they assume that the state will step in to protect their ownership of goods bought with Bitcoin.[29] This may be a tempting scam, but it is hardly a viable long-term strategy. If we want to get rid of the state, we must get rid of money.

A market without a state?

It is apt to talk about the view of some anarchists that we can have a market economy *without a state*. These anarchists are either.

1. 'Anarcho-capitalists', a branch of right-wing libertarianism.
or
2. Leftist anarchists, who want market-based workers' cooperatives, but see no need for the state.

These related positions are both untenable. As I have explained, the market and money imply a competitive economy. It is always tempting to make a better deal by cheating—theft, embezzlement, fraud, insider trading, Ponzi schemes, debt default, contracts that are not met, shoddy work. You name it. We hear about incidents like this every day. For a market to function, the state must act as a neutral arbitrator, at least to a certain extent. Making sure that the obligations implied by market transactions are met—and are not just empty promises.[30] If we were to abolish the state and wanted to keep money, these enforcement functions would have to be parcelled out to private companies. Companies of mercenaries funded to enforce contracts for the oligarchs who were paying them. The market would no longer function as a market. Success in this post-market environment would depend on localized armed enforcement. Not upon sales, consumer demand and commodity prices. Not unlike the situation of feudal societies. It would not be a market economy without a state—but a warlord economy without a state.

This may be regarded as an unfair critique of left anarchists who endorse a vision of this kind. Including people like the IWW, Murray Bookchin and Noam Chomsky.[31] Clearly these anarchists envision workers' cooperatives suspending market competition to achieve egalitarian and cooperative outcomes. As I have explained above, such a suspension implies the end of money as a *useful* tool—and with that the impossibility of *market-based* cooperatives.

What to do now we understand money

What are the implications of this critique of money? This critique does not imply that we must begin to do without money right here, right now. You might want to live a hair shirt existence up in the country using as little money as possible. And I like that as an experiment, pointing the way forward. However, most of us are not going to do that. The current operation of money is a social fact, and it makes sense to adapt to it.

What the middle class left needs to do right now is at least to use money wisely and be good at the market game. We look forward to a society without money. Nevertheless, money is now a means to access the social product. We must use it to finance our activism.

We need to support attempts to do without money. Strategies like those of ZAD (Zone a Defendre), which has taken over a whole district in France and largely operates without money. Other initiatives like the Zapatistas and the Rojava Kurdish resistance making some moves in this direction.[32] What I will call 'Autonomous Zones'.[33]

We need to back prefiguring strategies that operate the market in ways that defy market logic. To use the very limited amount of money that we have, to get the most political impact. In part, by breaking the rules of market discourse. Making gifts to people and the planet. Defying the discourse of buying cheap and selling dear. Even if we go into a supermarket and buy the organic tomatoes, we're doing that to an extent. Later chapters will consider more elaborate examples.

Finally, we need to promote a post-capitalism without money and the market. We don't want to engage in yet another failed revolution that tries to make use of the state and money. We do not want to settle for this failed solution. As though it was the only pragmatic option. Let's forget that pipe dream and go for a gift economy. The next chapter will explore that option.

Endnotes

[1] Andrew Sayer, *Radical Political Economy: Critique and reformulation*, Wiley Blackwell, Oxford, 1995.

[2] Anitra Nelson, *Beyond Money: A Post-Capitalist Strategy*, Pluto Press, London, 2022; Susana Narotsky, *New Directions in Economic Anthropology*, Pluto Press, London, 1997; John Jackson, Ron Mc Iver, Campbell McConnell, Stanley Brue, *Economics, 4th Edition*, McGraw Hill, New York, 1997.

[3] Sayer, *Radical Political Economy*; Herman E, Daly and Jonathan Cobb, *For the Common Good: Redirecting the economy toward community, the environment and a sustainable future*, Beacon Press, Boston, 1989.

[4] David Graeber, *Debt, The first 5,000 years*, Melville House, New York, 2011; Chris Gregory, *Gifts and Commodities*, Academic Press, London, 2015 (1982).

[5] Graeber, *Debt*.

[6] Graeber, *Debt*, p. 50.

[7] Nelson, *Beyond Money*, pp. 22, 156.

[8] Karl Marx, *Writings of the Young Marx on Philosophy and Society*, eds Loyd D. Easton, & Kurt H. Guddat, Doubleday, New York, 1967.

[9] Nelson, *Beyond Money*.

[10] Nelson, *Beyond Money*, p. 25.

[11] Nelson, *Beyond Money*, p. 25.

[12] Karl Marx, 'Wage Labour and Capital', in *Marx and Engels: Selected Works, Vol One*, Progress Publishers, Moscow, pp. 172-174, 1969.

[13] Studs Terkel, *Working: People Talk About What They Do All Day and How They Feel About What They Do*, The New Press, New York, 1997; Barbara Ehrenreich, *Nickel and Dimed: On (Not) Getting by in America*, Picador, New York, 2021; David Graeber, *Bullshit Jobs, Bullshit Jobs: A Theory*, Penguin, London, 2019.

[14] Nelson, *Beyond Money*, p. 28.

[15] Nelson, *Beyond Money*, p. 28.

[16] Ted Trainer, 'Can Australia run on renewable energy: unsettled issues and implications', *Biophysical Economics and Sustainability*, vol. 7(10), 2022, pp.1-17.

[17] Terry Leahy, 'Renewable energy: Are optimistic scenarios feasible?', *Green Agenda*, 21 June, 2024, https://greenagenda.org.au/2024/06/critique-of-the-path-to-a-sustainable-civilisation/

[18] Andrew McLaughlin, *Regarding Nature: Industrialism and Deep Ecology*, SUNY, New York, 1993; Nelson, *Beyond Money*.

[19] Thomas Piketty, *Capital in the Twenty-First Century*, Harvard University Press, Cambridge, MA, 2014.

[20] OXFAM, 'An economy for the 1%: how privilege and power in the economy drive extreme inequality and how this can be stopped', viewed on 14 March 2016, www.oxfam.org.

[21] Wolfgang Streeck, *How Will Capitalism End?* Verso, London 2016; Yanis Varoufakis, *And the Weak Suffer What They Must: Europe, Austerity and the Threat to Global Stability*. Vintage, New York, 2016.

[22] Nelson, *Beyond Money*.

[23] Michael A Lebowitz, *The Socialist Alternative: Real Human Development*, Monthly Review Press, New York, 2010.

[24] Lynne Weiss, 'The Mondragon cooperatives', *What I'm Seeing and Hearing*, 21 September, 2022, viewed on 6 July 2023, https://lynneweisswriter.com; Nick Romeo, 'How Mondragon became the world's largest co-op', *New Yorker*, 27 August 2022; Anjel Mari Errasti, Inaki Heras, Baleren Bakaikoa and Pilar Elgoibar, 'The internationalisation of cooperatives: the case of the Mondragon cooperative corporation', *Annals of Public and Cooperative Economics*, vol. 74:4, 2003, pp. 553-684.

[25] Michael A. Lebowitz, *Build It Now: Socialism for the Twenty-First Century*, Monthly Review Press, New York, 2006.

[26] ibid., p. 98.

[27] Lebowitz, *Build It Now*; Erik Olin Wright, *Envisioning Real Utopias*, Verso, New York, 2010; Julie Katharine Gibson-Graham, *A Postcapitalist Politics*. University of Minnesota Press: Minneapolis, 2006; Michael Albert, *No Bosses: A New Economy for a Better World*, Zero Books, Winchester, Hampshire, U.K., 2021; Yanis, Varoufakis, *Another Now: Dispatches from an Alternative Present*, The Bodley Head, London, 2020.

28 Michel Bauwens, Vasilis Kostakis and Alex Pazaitis, *Peer to Peer: The Commons Manifesto*, University of Westminster Press, 2019; Los Indianos, *The P2P Mode of Production: An Indiano Manifesto*, Grupo Cooperativo de Las Indias, 2015.

29 Rob Harris, 'The wealth is digital, the violence is analog': How the crypto rich got caught up in a new crime wave, *The Age*, Melbourne, 25th May, 2025.

30 Graeber, *Debt*.

31 Murray Bookchin, 'Market Economy or Moral Economy?' Keynote address to the New England Organic Farmers Association, July, https://sniadecki.wordpress.com/2019/09/21/bookchin-economy/, 1983; Noam Chomsky and Nathan Schneider, *On Anarchism*, Penguin, Harmondsworth, 2014.

32 Mauvaise Troupe Collective, *The Zad and NoTAV: Territorial Struggles and the Making of a New Political Intelligence*, London, Verso, 2018; Dylan Eldredge Fitzwater, *Autonomy Is in Our Hearts: Zapatista Autonomous Government through the Lens of the Tsotsil Language*, PM Press, Oakland CA., 2019; Anonymous, 'Revolution and cooperatives: thoughts about my time with the economic committee in Rojava cooperatives as a revolutionary strategy – facing capitalist modernity', 2020, viewed on 9 January 2023, https://internationalist commune.com.

33 Bey, Hakim, 'T.A.Z.: The Temporary Autonomous Zone, Ontological Anarchy, Poetic Terrorism', in The Anarchist Library, 1985, viewed on 24 April 2023, https://theanarchistlibrary. org/library/hakim-bey-t-a-z-the-temporaryautonomous-zone-ontological-anarchy-poetic-terrorism; Bey, Hakim, *Immediatism*, AK Press, Chico, California, 1994.

Chapter 4
Pathways out of Capitalism: The Gift Economy

The first of these chapters on pathways out of capitalism is on the gift economy. In the last chapter, I talked about the problems with a monetary system and markets. So, this chapter explains how we could have a society that doesn't use money. There is more than one name for this idea. Kropotkin's 'anarchist communism' is a close fit.[1] A term common in the European left is an 'economy of the commons.' This concept is *sometimes* used to refer to what I am talking about as the gift economy.[2] Anitra Nelson is a participant in the global degrowth movement. She has written about a system like this as 'Non-Market Socialism'.[3] Also as the 'Community Mode of Production' and an economy based on 'real values.' Social ownership of the means of production, but with no money and no state.[4] Lately, she is calling it 'The Community Mode of Provisioning.'[5] Other authors with a similar critique of money and a similar take on post-capitalism are Friederike Habermann, John Holloway and Jasper Bernes.[6] The term 'gift economy,' comes from the French 'Situationists'.[7] I like it because it sounds less academic, but it can be a bit misleading. If you think gifts are always gratuitous, unpredictable, and totally voluntary! In the gift economy I am talking about, those assumptions do not apply.

Origin of the term 'gift economy'

As you may know, the concept of the 'gift economy' comes from the anthropologist, Marcel Mauss.[8] He based his theories on research in pre-colonial societies of Northwest America, Melanesia and the

Pacific. Things were exchanged but the aim was not to get the best deal. Instead, it was to gain prestige through giving a bigger gift. In return for the one you received. These return gifts were presented in a ceremony with feasting. In some examples, donors did not expect a return gift. The first recipient was instead obliged to *pass on the gift* to a third party and they would pass it on to a fourth party. Leading to a whole cycle of gifts. In the long run the first donor would receive a return gift—at the end of the cycle.

The anthropological term, 'the gift economy' was taken up by the 'Situationists' in France in the 1960s. This was one of the political currents that contributed to the uprising in 1968. They painted Paris with slogans like 'Take Your Dreams for Reality' and 'Beneath the Pavement, the Beach'! Raoul Vaneigem's *Revolution of Everyday Life* explains their understanding of the 'gift economy.'[9] They re-purposed Mauss's concept. Much about their proposals differs from the anthropological accounts that initiated the concept.

My use of the term and other uses

To avoid confusion with a variety of uses of the term 'gift economy', I could call my version by another name. I am not going to take that route. I like the short version. The great benefit is to stress that in a gift economy, the ultimate prerogative of producers is to 'give' what they produce, to be responsible for the choice of recipient. There is no higher authority commanding their labour. Let me call this the 'grassroots gift economy'. Stressing that decisions about production and distribution are made at the grassroots. That these links of production and reception constitute a grassroots network of social connection.

So, how does *my* use differ from that of others who have used the term? The gifts Mauss describes function in a form of patriarchal status competition. Men compete to give more than their rivals. I am hoping for an economic system that does not operate in that way. There are other differences, and I have more to say about this topic in Appendix B—for those who are interested.

In the Situationist writings, gifts are portrayed as gratuitous and random. What holds this system together is the abundance possible with modern technology. A society of 'masters without slaves', as Raoul Vaneigem puts it.[10] Yet by now it is obvious we cannot produce gifts that waste scarce resources. As well, the recipients of gifts need to play a part in working out what gifts are suitable. Gifts that are not random and gratuitous. 'Compacts'—promises to produce and receive gifts—are worked out between voluntary work groups and the communities they serve.

In Genevieve Vaughan's use of the term, there is much that I share. The key difference is in the way she conceives gifts as purely altruistic. She relates this to her understanding of mothering.

> The logic of mothering requires that the nurturer give attention to the needs of the other person. The reward for this behavior is the well-being of the other.[11]

She opposes this to 'exchange', which is 'giving order to receive'.[12] The altruism she is talking about is certainly an aspect of the gift economy I am writing about. However, I will not deny the relevance of more self-interested motives. For a start, the reward of pleasure taken in an act of kindness. The rewards in appreciation and status you get from being the donor. The economic rewards coming out of a realistic expectation of reciprocity. The creative pleasure of producing something that changes the world. The enjoyment you get from being part of a joint project. Unlike Vaughan, I will use the term 'exchange' in the broadest possible sense. So 'exchange' takes place when someone transfers an object or service to someone else. Whether reciprocity is expected or not.

Marx's 'communism' as the gift economy

Marx's work has inspired much of what I am writing in this book. This chapter is no exception. In Marx's early writings, he proposes a utopian project based on a theory of human nature.[13] The contrast is between the dystopia of capitalist society and the future utopia of communism. Both are social orders that depend upon and work through aspects of human nature. The logic of this analysis is not too different from that of classical philosophers such as Aristotle or Hobbes. Also writing about a perfect social system, working with human nature to meet human needs.

The argument turns on Marx's division of human nature into two parts. What he calls our 'animal nature' are the drives for food, shelter and reproduction. What he calls our 'human nature' are our capacities for sociability, creative production and conscious action. Today, we would take issue with Marx's failure to understand *other* animals. We might make a different interpretation of this division in human nature. Still, there is much that is relevant.

In the capitalist dystopia, the means of production are owned by the capitalist class. To meet their *animal* needs, most people must work for a capitalist boss. They get a wage and use the money to satisfy their animal needs, buying food and shelter. However, the cost they pay for this submission is the denial of their *human* needs. Marx speaks of this as 'alienation'. We are alienated (cut off) from our capacities to take conscious action, to express ourselves creatively and to relate to other people socially. At work, we have little choice. The boss commands us. Decisions about work are not the result of our *own* conscious choice. Our capacity to create beautiful and useful things is suspended. We do what we are told. We are deprived of the material resources we need to express our creative capacity. Our own ideas about what to make are irrelevant. Our capacity to find pleasure in the well-being of other people is truncated. We are pitted into inevitable antagonism with the capitalist class. We have an ambivalent relationship with fellow workers—also competing for favours.

For Marx, this whole arrangement is unnecessarily complex, as well as damaging. He proposes communism as a system using human nature in a totally different way. The people own the means of production. In their work, they take conscious action to express their creative drives. Making beautiful and significant cultural objects. They express their sociable side by making *useful* things for other people and distributing them. Also, by joining with their communities to produce these gifts. Receiving these gifts, people satisfy their animal needs for food and shelter. In a passage from the early writings Marx maintains:

> In my production I would have objectified my individuality and its particularity, and in the course of the activity I would have enjoyed an individual life; viewing the object I would have experienced the individual joy of knowing my personality as an objective, sensuously perceptible and indubitable power. In your satisfaction and your use of my product I would have had the direct and conscious satisfaction that my work satisfied human need, that it objectified human nature, and that it created an object appropriate to the need of another human being. I would have been affirmed in your thought as well as in your love.[15]

In the following description of the gift economy, key parts of Marx's analysis are relevant to how a gift economy might work—and what could be good about it. Although Marx does not use the term 'gift economy', these writings are foundational.

Why the gift economy seems an unlikely improvement

The idea that there could be a society without money and without the state strikes most people as a joke. A typical reaction is to assume you are talking about a neo-feudalism, like Hobbit villages. That's not what I intend. The gift economy is meant to be technologically complex. At least to a degree. People will say, how could you organize that technological complexity without money—and without a state? People worry about whether conduct could be regulated without a monetary economy. How would you get people to work? How could you guarantee fairness? How would you prevent inequality— some people living in comfort while others were in poverty? What sanctions would prevent environmental vandalism? If everyone's free to do whatever they like, surely some people are going to cause environmental damage. What about patriarchy and racism? What about crime or warlord usurpers? Does a gift economy mean there is no army and no police force? How do you manage that? If this is meant to be a pathway out of capitalism it would have to be politically feasible. But the idea of having no money and no state produces vertigo. What do you really mean by that? That sounds ridiculous. So, I will have to reassure you on all these points. I'm going to start off with a basic map.

The basic operation of the gift economy

Well, first, there's no money. It's not a society based on barter where people exchange equivalent objects, one for another, trying to get the same value. Instead, it's based on agreements to supply and receive. That's why it's called a *gift* economy. Agreement to supply means you guarantee to supply, for example, 20 carrots to this household, within the next six months. And agreements to receive. The community that's about to receive knows this is going to happen. They say, 'Yes, we want this.' And 'Yeah, that'd be great, we expect it in November.' Anitra Nelson calls these agreements 'compacts.'[16]

Equivalence, as in fairness in distribution and reward for effort. You're giving things to other people. How can you be sure you're going to get something equal back? Because we are not using money and this is not a system of barter, you can't be totally sure. Equivalence and fairness are the long-term outcomes of this economic structure. While you are distributing what you make through compacts to supply, other people are supplying you. This goes around in multiple networks. The aim of all players is a fair share for everyone, and that people get what they need. The Indonesian concept of *gotong royong*. What anthropologists call 'generalized reciprocity'. [17]

The basic unit of the gift economy is a voluntary group, which produces goods or services. It can be anything from washing up to a bus service or a hospital. So voluntary groups produce and supply stuff. They may be working for their own community. Self-provision is a part of the gift economy. Like a community garden supplying vegetables to a local neighbourhood. Or there can be a compact to supply a group outside of the immediate community. If you're making things, you will need inputs from other collectives. For example, if you're a community garden growing cabbages, you will need fencing mesh to keep the goats out. You're depending upon another voluntary group to supply you with that. That ends up with a chain of production. From the very beginning, in mining or sourcing minerals from recycling. Through all the stages of production. Up to the final product, and then to its distribution. Each of these links works in the same way— production, supply, production, supply, production, supply, and so on in that chain. These chains of production form networks. There are the people making mesh fencing, and the people growing carrots. There's the community eating the carrots. Other people in the carrot eating community are making chairs for the community making the mesh fencing. What goes around comes around.

Most production in a gift economy is localized for environmental reasons. We have an impossible situation now, relying on fossil fuels to produce vast amounts of energy. We can't replace this amount of energy with renewables. It makes sense to localize production—to reduce the energy used in transport. Localizing food growing and sewerage treatment. Producing a lot with locally available resources. Energy supply, furniture, transport, housing. Where local production is not feasible, we will transport goods with renewable energy—electric trains, sailing ships, airships. Production chains move goods from one link in the chain to another—via transport powered with renewable energy.

How does work get distributed in the gift economy? Within each voluntary collective, there are tasks that nobody wants to do all the time. To share this around, the collective will roster these. You do it this week and I do it next week. Assuming nobody is incapable of skilled work. And everyone has a responsibility to do some mundane work. Capitalism has produced an education system that fails people at the bottom of the heap. We need to organize production so that everyone is doing some creative, highly skilled and interesting work.

The gift economy on the ground

What might the sustainable gift economy look like on the ground?

The following vision is based on my understanding of current technology. Showing what might be practicable. Much of this design follows the writings of Ted Trainer, an Australian advocate of 'the simpler way', as he calls it.[18]

Villages and small rural towns would be connected by a network of railways or by canals, sailing ships and airships. Train services would run on solar power or wind power. Avoiding the necessity for batteries if we were only running the trains when energy was available.

The use of rare earth metals has been seen as a problem for renewable technologies. With everyone on the planet using renewables, we will soon run out. Apparently, these minerals are only necessary to reduce the weight and bulk of our devices, from mobile phones to wind turbines. In a decentralized economy with low consumption, the weight and bulk of devices might not be a major problem. We could do without a lot of the rare earth minerals we might appear to need. Local transport would use bicycles, oxcart, donkey carts. Emergency vehicles, power tools and earth moving equipment would run on biodiesel or batteries. There would be small farmsteads, providing for themselves and distributing a surplus to the community. Or community housing with a community farm. Organic agriculture with an emphasis on tree crops. Localized irrigation using dams and contour bunds. Sewerage and water provision also local. In other words, permaculture.[19]

Local energy provision would use solar, wind power, local hydro, biofuels. Buildings would use electricity for lighting, digital entertainment, communication and computing. But space heating and cooling, cooking and hot water would not be powered by electricity. Passive solar design of houses would be part of the solution. Solar hot water panels and solar cooking. Wood burning stoves a final resort. Powered refrigeration would be uncommon. Cool cupboards and cellars would do for vegetable crops. With milk and meat from local farms as and when needed.

These local sites would also specialize in industrial production. For example, fencing mesh from one town. Wire for that from another town. Steel for that wire from another town. These chains would send goods by train to the next site. Some towns would specialize in high-tech services—like a hospital in one, a university in another. There would be a lot of recycling. There would be no planned obsolescence. Things would be made to be repaired and last for a very long time. Villages and towns would be connected by digital communication. Phones, the internet, TV, films, recorded music. Transport powered with renewable energy. These high technologies would be manufactured by chains of production, linking villages and towns. With each link producing a part of the product.

The debate about renewables

Faced by this vision, most middle-class leftists that I talk to say that it seems very austere. Comparing it unfavourably to the modernity of the rich countries today. As though this 'simpler way' vision is *choosing* a politically motivated austerity. What is more politically practicable, they say, is current affluence *with renewables*. Space heating, air con and refrigeration—all running on wind, solar and batteries. Planes, cars and trucks—running with batteries, hydrogen, ammonia or biofuel. Urbanism—with international travel for holidays.

We need to untangle the political and the technological issues. These middle-class leftists may well be right about the political problems of a 'simpler way' vision. But from a technological perspective, what I have described is the BEST we can possibly expect. There are two basic problems for the affluence with renewables scenario. *One* is that the minerals we would use are not inexhaustible. Even if only the affluent of the world (the top ten to twenty per cent) were to go for this solution we would quickly run out of essential minerals. Like lithium and nickel. Even copper.[20] The *second* basic problem is that with renewables we need lots of energy storage. Making energy a lot more expensive. For example, say we had 20 panels and a battery to provide all the power we would need on a day when the sun is shining. But we could need another 120 panels and 6 more batteries to store energy from that sunny day. For a following stretch of six cloudy days.[21] Presuming the batteries *could* store power for the whole six days! It becomes less economically damaging to *abandon* some rich world lifestyles—urbanism, cheap cars, air con, flights to Hawaii. Compared to devoting a huge chunk of the economy to propping these up with renewables.

How do questions of cost translate to a gift economy context? Prices are the way that a market economy deals with costs. In a gift economy, we must look at human needs and natural realities. How does the need for air con compare with the workload to provide it? Could we find minerals for that?

If you think this is austere, please come up with a better scenario. With a low energy budget. Something like 5 per cent of what we now get per capita (with fossil fuels) in the rich countries. On the current trajectory, the most likely outcome is a renewables revolution with the one per cent using electric cars, travelling overseas for holidays, and switching on the air con. While the rest of us are living a worse than feudal existence. I have pictured an alternative to that nightmare. It may be that in the gift economy, we will come up with sustainable technologies to provide air conditioning and quick trips to international destinations. I am not holding my breath. Let us get off this side track.

Organizing production and distribution without central planning

So how would you organize production and plan for production in a gift economy. How would you know how much steel mesh to produce? If you were the town producing the steel, how much steel would you need for that mesh? Where would it go?

The gift economy is not *that* different to a market economy. A market economy doesn't have central planning. People respond to market signals, producing for demand. The gift economy does not work through *market* demand. Demands in a gift economy are simply people's wants and needs, expressed in a variety of ways – via media, as discovered from social research, through direct requests. You get prestige and appreciation supplying these. It's strange that people worry that such a system cannot be efficient. When the market economy also operates through decentralized supply chains.

In a gift economy, compacts to supply will be motivated by self-interest when people are producing for their own community. Where other communities are concerned, one motive is the good will that comes from supplying a real need. Also, the excitement that comes from participation in a production chain providing for other communities. Directly, you're not getting any benefit. What you're producing is going to the next stage of the production chain. Nevertheless, you know that the whole production chain is making something useful for all these communities. You know the benefits of the gift economy depend on voluntary local action. You are proud to be contributing.

We can think of various ways to coordinate a production chain. One would be that each of the towns and villages in a bioregion would decide how many metres of fencing mesh they required. Then those figures would be passed on to the town making the mesh. Imagine a team of scouts from the town supplying the fencing mesh. Checking these figures. And then the factory producing the mesh would respond to each village. For instance, 'Well, by next November, we can make 56 metres of fencing mesh for your village. Is that okay?' And they come to an agreement (a compact) and you go from there. The factory making the fencing mesh would negotiate in the same way—with the people making the fencing wire. And so on, through the whole chain of production.

The gift economy and the environment

So why is the gift economy uniquely suited to look after the environment? These questions are crucial in relation to the issue of 'planning' in a gift economy. We would want to be reassured that the outcomes of production do not destroy the environment. 'Planning', such as there is in a gift economy, must effectively do that. The key point is that such production planning does not take place through any central organising point, however 'democratically' it may be organized. As explained, production decisions ultimately come from the various producer collectives, organising liaisons with each other and with the communities that they provide. The plan, looked at from an eagle's viewpoint, is merely the total outcome of all these partly independent and partly coordinated decisions. I can see why that vision of a complex technological society may seem surprising, but I do not find it unthinkable.

I have explained why a capitalist economy is a disaster as far as the environment goes. Here's what the gift economy does. There's no motive to produce for money and ignore the environmental consequences. Your own standard of living depends upon the gifts that come from other producers. You can produce as much as you like, but at the end of the day, that is not going to get you extra goods and services. The wire that you're making just passes onto the next community, which is making the mesh fencing. They're not paying you back for that wire. There's no motive to produce a vast amount of unnecessary stuff. The motive to produce things for other people is prestige, affection, long-term reciprocity. You will also make room for plenty of leisure time, for arts and slacking about. Enjoying what your work has made possible.

Prestige comes from a gift that looks after the environment. The local community where you are doing the work will not want you damaging *their* environment. You will not get any status producing wonderful things—at the expense of your local community. This extends further afield. So, if you're producing for another community—and what you are doing is harming the global environment—they're not going to like that. You are giving them a poisoned gift. That harms the environment in which *they* also live.

The reason why these things are such a problem *today* is that capitalist economies give managers so many motives to act unsustainably. Those motives are completely absent in a gift economy. The opposite motives become dominant. Everybody understands the prestige of getting it right. The pleasure of living in a good environment. That what we are doing now is going to kick on to our grandchildren's generation. These are all things that people think about. I was interviewing two Newcastle steelworkers. They told me about the terrible pollution of the Hunter River. How the steel works drained toxic waste into the river. And they said, 'Yeah, we know about this, but we don't say anything because we'll lose our jobs'. These steelworkers *were* concerned. They loved fishing and knew the toxic waste was not good for the fish. But they needed to keep their jobs.

In a gift economy, producers who were in any doubt would seek the advice of a science collective. Like, the helmeted honey eater of Victoria. Now on the extinct and endangered list. If you had a patch of bushland that could host the helmeted honey eater, a great project would be to introduce them and look after their habitat. Not knock it down for a new apartment. You would find out how to look after the helmeted honeyeater by asking bird watchers and biological scientists. There would be no need for state enforced regulation because there would be no motive to get it wrong.

In the gift economy, if you felt that there was a need for coercive enforcement to save the environment, you'd just do that. Let's look at a local village. You might appoint a group to go round making sure that people were handling the sewerage correctly. And these people would be unlikely to turn up fully armed and in uniform. They'd be more likely to appear in civvies as an advice team. 'This is a composting toilet. The problem here is you're not putting enough straw in your compost, and when you lift the lid, you can see how much it smells. Okay. That's because you're getting anaerobic composting. Let me explain that.' But at the same time, there's five local people who are not happy with what you're doing. You get to know that. And if necessary, they take over and say, 'Well, you're obviously not handling this. And this is a danger to the whole community. So, we'll roster someone on to come and help.' This logic could apply on any scale, from the village, to global.

People often wonder how we could coordinate a global response to climate change in a gift economy. One answer is you'd coordinate it through meetings of representatives. Who would take back ideas and information to their towns and villages. That would be part of it. The bottom line is that you would not have any motive for causing such an awful ungodly disaster. I am assuming that we could in the end prevent the earth from becoming uninhabitable. By ending the use of fossil fuels. By using biochar, tree planting and seaweed farming to draw down carbon.

Social justice and the gift economy

How could we ensure just distribution in a gift economy? How are we going to make sure people don't just get rich and look after their own interests? Without anything going to those who really need it. Most people assume that the only way to get just distribution is to coercively enforce redistribution—through a state apparatus. Let us look at a few issues.

The gift economy is predicated on an ethic of fairness. We're looking for a cultural change. I don't think that's impossible. A lot of people would like to see a move in that direction. But capitalism makes it difficult. The voluntary collectives and the community forums that run local affairs in a gift economy are run democratically. These collectives would look after all their members, while considering differences in people's needs. It is possible, even likely, that these collectives would consider the interests of their own communities, first. Theoretically that could lead to inequality. But people would produce more than enough. With a surplus they would face the question. Well, what do we want to do with this? Most likely, they would want to look after people with the most need. A community that already has plenty of fencing wire is not going to want more. Why would they want that? The community that needs fencing wire. If you provide it to them, they're very appreciative. Fairness and just distribution would come out of the desire to be appreciated. You want to produce gifts that will make a difference.

Distribution to equalize world living standards makes sense. People in the impoverished backwaters of the world economy would be a lot happier, more productive and contribute more—if they could sort out the life and death problems that now preoccupy them. In any case, global warming is a global problem. We need changes in systems of production and environmental restoration in every part of the world. In a gift economy a combination of useful assistance and an end to exploitation would enable this. The rich countries would stop exploiting the Global South through trade and the market. If rich countries produced things for the South, they would be gifts. All that they might expect would be long-term reciprocity. There would be no expectation of equivalence, and no way of measuring it. Trading relationships that end up with debt and impoverishment would go.

In the rich countries we would be looking after our own needs to a much greater extent. Let's look at Australia. The supermarket shelves are stocked with foods produced in the global South. Coffee, tea, chocolate. I could go on. The only reason these foods are not grown in Australia is the cost of labour here. There is nothing about our climate or soils that prevents us growing all these foods. The same applies to the industrial goods we now receive from China—toasters, laptops, and washing machines. The clothing from India.[23] Produced by people working twelve-hour days, with one day off for 'weekends' per month. In factories where workers are unable to escape a fire— because management locks the doors. In a gift economy we would be producing these goods in our own communities. With voluntary collectives making sure that work was fun and not a torment.

Racism, patriarchy, and the gift economy

Would a gift economy solve the problems of racism and patriarchy? As a purely *economic* format, the gift economy does not imply an end to racism or patriarchy. If we look at pre-colonial stateless societies, a lot were 'ethnocentric' and 'patriarchal.' For example, men would gain prestige by going on midnight raids to other villages. Coming back after taking heads. They'd refer to their own tribe as 'the people'—others were less than human.[24] These societies were gift economies. There was no money, there was no state. People came to agreements and decided what to produce. Gifts were the vehicle for economic exchange.[25]

So, the short message is that we need to work on racism and patriarchy independently. As well as working towards a gift economy.

We require a cultural shift. Along with anti-racist structures built into the new gift economy. The same thing with patriarchy. We need a cultural change and new gender arrangements. An independent women's movement. So that's the short message. A longer message would talk about why the gift economy makes it easier to dissolve racism and patriarchy.

Racism

Let us imagine there is a global revolution to implement a gift economy. In Alabama, the white majority want a white ethno-state. They want freedom and an end to elites. They end up convinced that a gift economy is the way to go. They implement their ethno-state and their non-monetary economy with that. Thankfully, people who are not happy with these developments leave peacefully and go where they are more welcome. In the rest of the United States, anti-racist gift economies dominate. How do they respond to these developments in Alabama? They close off their economic links. The production chains that make the former United States viable as a technologically complex society. No one wants to make deals with these racist idiots. They get no gifts from regions where the refugees from Alabama have any say. Their racism seems more and more quixotic. Their children desert them.

In other words, racism is an impediment to a flourishing global gift economy, and this becomes apparent. What we would also want from an anti-racist global economy is an end to the post-colonial structures considered in the first two chapters. A generous gift exchange between the global North and the South. The end of white racism in the global North.

Patriarchy

Where patriarchy is concerned, the economic format of the gift economy makes it a lot easier to solve some of the tricky problems. The gender order in capitalism is backed up by the division between unpaid domestic work and paid public work.[26] Domestic work by and large the responsibility of women. Paid work is where men gain economic advantage. In a gift economy, there's *no* paid work! This dichotomy vanishes. The unpaid side of the economy expands to fill the whole economic space. That makes it easy to roster housework. The understanding is that in any household, there's a certain amount of domestic work to be done. That will be shared equally by the members of the household, whether we are talking about a couple or a commune. Just like the boring jobs are rotated in any voluntary producer collective. Each work task takes time, requires skills, and will be rewarded with status and acknowledgement.

Patriarchy and class society

The gift economy is a pathway out of class society. Patriarchy has always provided the seeds for class society. If our gift economy does not get rid of patriarchy, class society will eventually renew its evil reign. The psychology of class society is based on the patriarchal structures of the family.

Patriarchal families instil the deep belief that somebody must always be the boss. All class societies model themselves on the patriarchal family.[27] The ruling class, king or state represent the father. The duty of the subordinate classes is to obey and love these figures. The chains of command that make up a class society depend on people taking up these two roles. Father and child. A point made by the leftist psychoanalytic literature from Reich to Firestone.[28]

Further than this, patriarchal families create the competitive masculinity that is essential to the functioning of any class society. Men anxious to prove they are *really* men. What has aptly been named 'toxic masculinity'. How patriarchy recruits biological men to hegemonic masculinity. This emotional pattern is not innate to men as biological creatures. In a brilliant survey of the anthropological literature, Chodorow explains this process—as a cross-cultural constant of patriarchal societies.[29] Toxic masculinity comes out of a family structure in which women are the main nurturing figures. Men are somewhat remote, avoid much of the work associated with childcare, and operate in the public sphere to gain power. Young boys have little intimate engagement with men. *Becoming* 'a man' is a puzzling challenge. One way to prove your manhood is to reject femininity. The women looking after you as a young child nurtured you. To be a man is to do the opposite. Cutting the apron strings. Cruelty as the proof of manhood. Another strategy is to challenge other men—to prove yourself a man. Sorting the men from the boys.

This detachment, this denial of empathy is an essential foundation for class societies. Where the suffering of the subordinate classes is concerned, the ruling class feel no qualms. The armies prove their manly prowess defending the state. Expanding the empire through conquest.

These two mechanisms are key aspects of the way class societies work. So, getting rid of patriarchy is a very good idea, if you want to *maintain* a gift economy. Putting this bluntly, if men do not want to be oppressed by ruling classes, they need to help women destroy patriarchy.

Crime, violence and the police

What about criminal gangs and warlord usurpers? People who steal things and take over. For many, the Mad Max, zombie apocalypse scenario is very plausible. After the collapse of capitalism warlords take control. People assume you need a benevolent state and a police force, to prevent this.[30] For reasons that I will explain in later chapters, a gift economy could not have a state. Not having a state, it could not have a police force. On the other hand, there is no doubt that violence could undo a gift economy—stepping in to override compacts and hand ownership over to thugs. So how would a gift economy deal with that?

First, the gift economy would end many of the motives people have for crime. Poverty is a huge motive for crime. There would be no poverty.

In capitalism, the sense of being a failure is ubiquitous. No achievement can reassure you that you have done enough. There is always someone who has done more.[31] A veneer of meritocracy. Crime can be an arena of control and achievement, a 'deviant career' as sociologists call it.[32] In a gift economy, control and achievement come from participation in production and distribution. The economy runs on gifts—implying every day that other people appreciate you.

In the world today, many criminal gangs depend on the drug

trade. This works because people medicate themselves to relieve the traumas of capitalism and patriarchy.[33] The state backs the sensible hard-working mainstream, the ideology of duty and the fiction of the meritocracy.[34] It tries to alleviate the worst effects of dysfunction through tough policing. Boosting the cost of drugs and forcing addicts into crime. In a gift economy we would expect these issues to be handled differently. Less trauma all round. Drug use as recreational or at most a health issue.

We can look at crime today as 'lateral violence'.[35] Capitalism is a violent society. The subordinate classes are exploited and dominated.[36] The state backs up these humiliations with force. People become angry and turn on the people who are easy to violate. People in their immediate vicinity. Through domestic violence or street fights. The capitalist class—and the economic structure itself—are difficult to target in 'vertical' violence. There is not much point if you believe things cannot be any better. These motives for lateral violence would be absent in a gift economy. An egalitarian society with the means of production controlled by voluntary collectives.

Competitive masculinity is one of the drivers of crime. Men try to prove their masculinity by defeating other men. If a war is not on the cards, crime is a good second option. Especially for those who are failing at work, wages, and domestic power.[37] Domestic violence is another expression of this toxic masculinity. At least you are not letting a woman tell you what to do! In a society where feminism had become successful, we would expect men to be doing an equal share of housework. Including childcare. We would expect women to be full participants in the public sphere. These changes would undo the psychological roots of toxic masculinity. Some of the criminal violence plaguing us would just evaporate.

In a gift economy, incidents of assault or property damage would mostly be handled through mediation, compensation, and treatment— rather than enforcement and policing.[38] Or direct intervention on the spot if that was a practical response. These strategies are being promoted today by the transformative justice movement. If we look at stateless societies of the past, that's exactly how they worked.[39]

So, we can summarize this by saying first, that there are less motives for engaging in violent attacks on other people in the gift economy. And secondly, mediations and compromises might solve some of these problems—without a police force.

Ultimately, however, the gift economy is like any other social formation. It assumes a willingness to use coercive violence to maintain that social order. The revolution itself is a key instance. It is an exercise of force by the great majority against the capitalist class. If we're looking at daily life situations in the gift economy, people would expect civilian intervention to defend community norms. For example, if you were witnessing domestic violence, you might intervene, with force if necessary. If it was safe to do so. For more extreme situations, we could have local enforcer clubs vetted and approved by their communities, with a rotation of these roles. For instance, if a little gang started forming up and going around intimidating people, then you'd form an enforcer club to control them. If a whole town in your bioregion decided to become an empire and take over the whole bioregion, you'd have to get together, setting up your militia groups, arming yourselves to control that.[40] I'm not anticipating a warlord insurgency as a daily occurrence. Something of that kind may never happen. Nevertheless, if it did happen, there would be a way to deal with that. I will return to these issues in other chapters. If a 'state' is impossible in the gift economy, what territorial organisation could work?

Child raising in the capitalist world and in the gift economy

There is another thing we might think about relevant to crime and violent assaults. The socialisation of children within capitalism could be designed to create insecurity and anxiety. Not about the obvious things like climate Armageddon and wars. But more personal issues that can be grafted on to any situation.

Let us consider a culture radically different to Western capitalist culture. The Anbarra of Northern Territory Australia. The anthropologist, Annette Hamilton, went to stay with this group.[41]

When she went there, aspects of their original Aboriginal culture had been retained despite the devastation of colonisation. In the camp, the infants were usually being held in arms, on laps, picked up or hugged. If there was any problem they were given the breast, for comfort if not for food. They rarely cried. Older children looked after the early toddlers as much as the mothers and their friends. If a younger child wanted a toy, the older child would give it over. In their play groups, they were kind to each other rather than competitive. Infants slept with their parents. Adults asked children to do things, but the child could say no. It was expected that they would want to help. There was no punishment for refusing an instruction.

The Anbarra child raising culture is not unique and seems to have been present in stateless societies the world over, persisting to today.[42] Hamilton's conclusion. This kind of child raising produces adults who expect other people will look after them. Their needs will be met. They do not need to hoard and hang on to things. This works with a gift economy based in generosity.

As she says, Western child raising has been quite different. Phillipe Aries documents these developments in Europe in the seventeenth and eighteenth century.[43] 'Spare the rod and spoil the child.' Just a few examples from more recent times. After birth in a hospital, mother and newborn were separated—so the mother could rest. At home, four-hour schedule feeding was recommended. The mother might shut the crying child in a cot—in a separate bedroom—trying to ignore the wails. Picking up and comforting a crying child is seen as 'reinforcing' bad behaviour. Controlled crying is a technique used to train an infant to sleep in their 'own cot' in their 'own bedroom'. Punishments are to be expected. From the mildness of the 'naughty corner' to beatings. As for breast feeding and toilet training, getting your child to finalize these stages early is a sign of your hard work and their amazing abilities. The dummy is a point of contention. Experts warn that the use of a dummy can deform the jaw, leading to expensive orthodontic work. The basic lesson for the child is learning to stifle your emotions.

The opposite behaviour is equally damaging. The child behaves in a very anti-social way. A tantrum and throwing things around. Being insufferably rude. The parent ineffectually asks them to stop. They give in to some crazy demand after refusing the first time. After an endless set of manipulations. They never express anger, never let the child know how they really feel. With the steely gaze and the tone of voice that says, 'You won't ignore me'. For the child this emotionally absent parenting is like living with a ghost robot. What the Supernanny was trying to address.

It is no surprise that adults in Western culture are very anxious. Crimes are committed because the perpetrators are insecure. They are not getting what they need. They lash out at people who have nothing to do with these feelings. We could expect punitive child raising to disappear in a gift economy. One where the adults were trying to look after each other and the rest of the planet. There is already a movement to change things for the better. Montessori education. Child centred pedagogy. I am expecting these changes to spread as we work on the grassroots initiatives for a new system.

How likely is this alternative?

So, I come to my last point in this chapter. Is a gift economy politically unlikely? Well, not necessarily. I could certainly agree that it seems unlikely this week. Most people are voting for a mainstream party. In Australia, the combination of preferential and compulsory voting means that minority voices *are* represented in voting preferences. There is only a small minority voting for a left alternative to capitalism. Between ten and fifteen per cent. Mostly for the Greens, with a miniscule handful of Socialist voters. You could argue from these voting figures that most people are happy with capitalism as it is now. People don't see any better options around the corner. Nevertheless, we are facing an impending collapse. The most recent report of the IPCC makes it quite clear that climate change is going to destroy our current civilisation—if nothing drastic is done. It is difficult for the ruling class to make the drastic u-turn we need. It seems unlikely that people will maintain their faith in the system as these disasters bite.

Let's look at the argument that most people don't want to move to anything drastically different from capitalism. With several colleagues, I have done a random sample survey of 300 people in the Hunter region, along with a set of face-to-face interviews.[44] Our findings are backed up by studies in a range of countries.[45] The term we came up with was 'two track thinking.' In *one track* people believe we are headed for collapse. Environmental crisis or some other catastrophe. We need to be doing something radically different. Government is working hand in glove with big business. Failing to deal with the problems. Up to twenty per cent believe we need system change to socialism or the gift economy. About fifty per cent think we need drastic government intervention. So, this is *one* of the two tracks. The *other track* forgets all this doom and gloom. It assumes business as usual will continue. In this track people worry about the jobs their children might get. They hope their kids will be able to afford a house. They expect them to fly off for a holiday after high school. To marry and have children. To own a car and an outboard for fishing. So that's the second track. Normal life and business as usual.

When people go out to vote, they are thinking within the second track. They worry about the market and their chances within the economy. The other track, the dark thoughts in the middle of the night, they forget about that. So, something as wacky and radical as a gift economy could happen at any time given the right circumstances. The point where people realize that the business-as-usual track is no longer relevant. That's not out of the question and it could happen quite soon. Most commentators on politics overestimate the stability of the market, the economy, and the political system. They don't take two track thinking into account. They just look at the one track reflected in voting behaviour.

So, as a global collapse becomes more and more real—and the ruling class fails to deal with it—people will look for alternatives. Even if the gift economy is massively unlikely, it is the best thing to be advocating. It is the only thing that would really give us a better life on this planet. To escape one of the other sticky ends that are more likely. Like ninety per cent of the world's population die. We end up with feudal lords who screw the peasants into the ground—accompanied by plagues, famines and stupid wars.

Other options

In the next two chapters I will consider the two main alternatives for system change coming from the environment movement and the left. One is the democratic socialist option. The other is what I will call 'radical reformism'. The founder of radical reformism is Herman Daly with his 'steady state economy' concept. A stronger government regulation of the market economy, ultimately achieving a steady state.

Endnotes

[1] Pëtr Kropotkin, *The Conquest of Bread*, theanarchistlibrary.org, 1892.

[2] Friederike Habermann, *Ecomony:UmCare zum Miteinander*, Ulrike Helmer-Verlag, Sukzbach, 2016.

[3] Anitra Nelson and Frans Timmerman (eds), *Life Without Money*, Pluto Press, London, 2011.

[4] Anitra, Nelson, *Beyond Money: A Post-Capitalist Strategy*, Pluto Press, London, 2022.

[5] Anitra Nelson, 'Metamorphoses to a Postcapitalist Community Mode of Provisioning,' in *Democratic Economic Planning for the Future: Directing Institutional, Social Metabolic and Technological Change* edited by Project Society After Money.

[6] Habermann, *Ecomony*;, John Holloway, *Hope in Hopeless Times*, Pluto Press. London, 2022; Jasper Bernes, *The Future of Revolution: Communist Prospects from the Paris Commune to the George Floyd Uprising*, Verso, London, 2025.

[7] Raoul, Vaneigem, *The Revolution of Everyday Life*, D. Nicholson-Smith (trans), Left Bank Books and Rebel Press, London, 1983.

[8] Marcel Mauss, *The Gift: Forms and functions of exchange in archaic societies*, Trans. Ian Cunnison, Routledge and Kegan Paul, London, 1970.

[9] Vaneigem, *The Revolution of Everyday Life*.

[10] Vaneigem, *Revolution of Everyday Life*.

[11] Genevieve Vaughan, *For-Giving: A feminist criticism of exchange*, Plain View Press, Austin, Texas, 1997, p. 20.

[12] Mauss. p. 16.

[13] Karl Marx, *Writings of the Young Marx on Philosophy and Society*, D.L. Easton and K.H. Guddat (eds), Doubleday, New York, 1967; see also Leahy, Terry *Humanist Realism for Sociologists*, Routledge, London, 2017.

[14] Karl, Marx, *Early Writings*, trans. T.B. Bottomore, C.A. Watts $ Co. London, 1963, p. 125.

[15] Marx, *Writings of the Young Marx*, p. 281.

[16] Nelson, *Beyond Money*, pp. 49-50.

[17] Chris Gregory, *Gifts and Commodities*, Academic Press, London, 2015 (1982).

[18] Ted Trainer, *The Transition to a Sustainable and Just World*, Envirobook, London, 2010.

[19] Bill Mollison, *Permaculture: A Designers' Manual*, Tyalgum, Australia: Tagari Publications, 1988, Rosemary Morrow, *Earth User's Guide to Permaculture*, Kenthurst, Australia: Kangaroo Press, 1993; Terry Leahy, *Food Security for Rural Africa: Feeding the farmers first*, Routledge, London 2019.

[20] Simon P. Michaux, *The Mining of Minerals and the Limits to Growth*, Report number: 16/2021, Geological Survey of Finland, Helskinki, 2021; Simon P. Michaux, Tere Vadén, J.M. Korhonen and Jussi T. Eronen, *Assessment of the scope of tasks to completely phase out fossil fuels in Finland*, Report 18/2022, Geological Survey of Finland, Helskinki, 2021.

[21] Ted Trainer, *Renewable Energy Cannot Sustain a Consumer Society*, Springer, Dordrecht, 2007; Ted Trainer, 'Can Australia run on renewable energy: Unsettled issues and implications', *Biophysical Economics and Sustainability*, vol. 7(10), 2022, pp. 1-11; Terry Leahy, 'A degrowth scenario: Can permaculture feed Melbourne', in *Food for Degrowth: Perspectives and Practices*, Anitra Nelson and Ferne Edwards (eds), Routledge, London, 2022, chapter 14; Terry Leahy, 'Renewable energy: Are optimistic scenarios feasible?', *Green Agenda*,

22nd June, 2024, https://greenagenda.org.au/2024/06/critique-of-the-path-to-a-sustainable-civilisation/

[22] See also Nelson's discussion of Yenomon for ideas on this. Nelson, *Beyond Money*, 46-58.

[23] Ulrich Brand & Marcus Wissen, *The Imperial Mode of Living: Everyday Life and the Ecological Crisis of Capitalism*. Verso, London, 2021; Julian Go, *Postcolonial Thought and Social Theory*. OUP, Oxford, 2016.

[24] Yolanda & Robert Francis Murphy, 2004, *Women of the Forest*, Columbia University Press, New York; Michael J. Johnson, *Ojibwa: People of the Forests and Plains*, Firefly Books, New York, 2016.

[25] Marshall Sahlins, *Stone Age Economics*, Tavistock, London 1974.

[26] Heidi Hartmann, 1979, 'Capitalism, Patriarchy and Job Segregation by Sex', in *Capitalist Patriarchy and the Case for Socialist Feminism*, (ed) Z. Eisenstein, Monthly Review Press, New York, pp. 206-247.

[27] Shulamith Firestone, 1972, *The Dialectic of Sex: the case for feminist revolution*, New York, Paladin.

[28] Wilhelm Reich, *The Mass Psychology of Fascism*. V.R. Carfagno (trans), Penguin, Harmondsworth, 1970. Firestone, *The Dialectic of Sex*.

[29] Nancy Chodorow, 'Family structure and feminine personality', in *Woman, Culture and Society*, Michelle Z. Rosaldo, & Louise Lamphere (eds), Stanford University Press: Stanford, CA., 1974, pp. 43–66.

[30] Steven Pinker, *The Blank Slate: The Modern Denial of Human Nature*, Penguin Books, London, 2002.

[31] Richard Sennett and Jonathon Cobb, *Hidden Injuries of Class*, Vintage, New York, 1973.

[32] Raewyn Connell, *Masculinities*, University of California Press, 2005; Pam Nilan, *Young People and the Far Right*, Routledge, London, 2021.

[33] Gabor Maté and Peter A. Levine, *In the Realm of Hungry Ghosts: Close Encounters with Addiction*, North Atlantic Books, 2010.

[34] Stuart Hall, Chas Chrichter, Tony Jefferson, John Clarke and Brian Roberts, *Policing the Crisis: Mugging, the State and Law and Order*, Red Globe Press, London, 2013 (1978).

[35] Geraldine Moane, *Gender and Colonialism: a psychological analysis of oppression and liberation* (Rev. ed.). Palgrave Macmillan, Basingstoke, 2011.

[36] Loic Wacquant, *Punishing the Poor: The neoliberal government of social insecurity*, Duke University Press, Durham NC, 2009.

[37] Connell, *Masculinities*, Nilan, *Young People and the Far Right*.

[38] Leah Lakshmi Piepzna-Samarasinha and Ejeris Dixon (Eds), *Beyond Survival: Strategies and stories from the transformative justice movement*, AK Press, California, 2020.

[39] E. E. Evans Pritchard, 'The Nuer of Southern Sudan', in Meyer Fortes and E. E. Evans-Pritchard. *African Political Systems*, Oxford University Press, 1940, pp. 272-296; Max Gluckman, *Politics, Law and Ritual in Tribal Society*, Basil Blackwell, Oxford, 1965; Ken Maddock, *The Australian Aborigines: A portrait of their society*, Penguin, Harmondsworth, 1974.

[40] Starhawk, *The Fifth Sacred Thing*, Bantam Dell, New York, 1994.

[41] Annette Hamilton, *Nature and Nurture: Aboriginal Child Rearing in North-Central Arnhem Land.* Canberra: Australian Institute of Aboriginal Studies, 1981.

[42] Jean Liedloff, *The Continuum Concept*, London: Duckworth, 1975.

[43] Phillipe Aries, *Centuries of Childhood*, Pimlico, London. 1996 [1960]

[44] Terry Leahy, Vanessa Bowden, and Stephen Threadgold, 'Stumbling towards collapse: Coming to terms with the climate crisis', *Environmental Politics*, vol. 19(6), 2010, pp.851–868; Gow, John & Terry Leahy, 'Apocalypse probably: agency and environmental risk in the Hunter region', *Journal of Sociology*, vol 41(2), June 2005.

[45] Arlie Russell, Hochschild, *Strangers in Their Own Land: Anger and Mourning on the American Right*, The New Press, New York, 2016; Norgaard, Kari M. *Living in Denial: Climate Change, Emotions and Everyday Life*, MIT Press, Cambridge, MA., 2011.

Chapter 5
Pathways out of capitalism:
Democratic Socialism

This is the second of three chapters on pathways out of capitalism. How can we replace capitalism with something more benevolent? I'm looking at the models that are the most popular. The gift economy, democratic socialism, and the steady state economy. Other options are usually variations on these themes. In the last chapter I wrote about the gift economy as my preferred model. What I'm looking at in this chapter is democratic socialism. The title for this chapter opens up a minefield of terminological confusion. The order of the the adjective and its noun is crucial. The difference between 'democratic socialism' and 'social democracy' has a meaning in contemporary political discussion that does not apply to the use of these terms before about 1930. In contemporary terminology this chapter is about democratic socialism and not about social democracy. In everyday usage now, the term 'social democrat' is most typically used when we are describing *people* as 'social democrats'. Like left members of the ALP and other Labor parties around the world.

This is just a beginning. An umbrella term 'democratic eco-socialist' more defines the topic of the chapter.

I am indebted for this introductory discussion to my friend Hans Baer, who identifies as a 'democratic socialist'. He claims that he and his co-author, Merrill Singer coined the term 'democratic eco-socialist' to explain their approach to reforming health systems in the textbook *Introducing Health Anthropology*, in 2007 (the first edition)[1]. At that time, they wanted to insist on the need for democracy in the light of the failures of the Soviet system. They had in mind two kinds of democratic mechanisms—representative democracy and participatory democracy. They were using the term 'socialist' to refer to public ownership of the means of production. The prefix 'eco' was intended to indicate the necessity for an ecological reorganisation of civilisation, something that some strands of Marxist 'democratic socialism' had not really embraced. Either by ignoring the issue, or by promoting an unrealistic promethean and productivist vision. Looking at the landscape of terminology as it exists today, Hans acknowledges that 'eco-socialists' as a broad church include authors whose version of 'public ownership' differs from that more usually associated with the phrase 'democratic socialist'. Namely two other strands. A non-monetary, commoning strand of eco-socialism (Nelson, Saito, Bernes).[2] A solidarity economy market cooperative strand (Lebowitz).

The term 'democratic socialist' is used in this chapter as follows. Taking over the means of production, nationalizing things, a planned economy, all that. Whereas the term 'social democrat' refers to the left wing of the Labor parties. A welfare state regulation of capitalism. In contrast to that reformist program, the key idea of 'democratic socialism' is to *end* capitalism. The state owns the means of production on behalf of the people. The commanding heights of the economy are nationalized—energy, transport, education, and health. Even mining and agriculture.

Different democratic socialists plan to set the boundary between the private economy and government ownership differently. But they all believe that the public should own the most basic parts of the economy. When they talk about the people 'taking ownership' of the means of production, they mean through a democratically controlled state. Also, through participatory control in workplaces and communities. The state nationalizes central parts of the economy. So, what are the other parts of the economy? This is a shifting boundary, depending on who you're talking to. The private parts of the economy could include small businesses, like the local shop or a local electrician. Or bigger enterprises such as market-based cooperatives, supported by the state. The monetary economy might be backed by some unpaid community work. Such as community gardens. The state would closely supervise privately owned businesses. Allowing overall control through representative democracy. Access to goods and services would be through a wage or a state pension. You could be working for a state company or a private business. Or you might get a state pension, such as an old age pension or supporting parents' benefit. Some government services would be free.

The term 'democratic socialism' is used to clearly distinguish this pathway for system change from Soviet style regimes which claimed to be socialist. What's 'democratic' about this new version? Well, representative democracy implies an elected government—with different parties promoting alternatives. Democratic socialists insist on freedom of speech and freedom of association. They also recommend workers' participation. Through local community and municipal democracy, through workers' councils managing government departments, as well as through worker-owned cooperatives.

This expanded representative democracy oversees a planned economy and regulates environmental outcomes. Parliament decides how to run the economy and plans it. The government allocates money to government departments to implement these plans. In doing this 'central planning', the elected government also plans for environmental outcomes. Because government departments are not working to make a profit, they are not tempted to cause environmental damage. Instead, they will follow democratically decided environmental regulations. Those who see democratic socialism as a way of getting past the environmental disasters of capitalism describe themselves as 'eco-socialists.' As explained above, there are a variety of positions described by that term. In this chapter I will only be talking about eco-socialists who are *also* 'democratic socialists', in the sense I am making of that phrase for this chapter.

Adolfo Gilly was imprisoned by the Mexican government in 1966 and in his appeal hearing he explained the aims of the Trotskyist 'Workers Revolutionary Party'.

Nationalization, without compensation, of imperialist enterprises and major national enterprises; transfer of all land to the peasantry, to be collectively cultivated; planning of the economy by, and at the service of, mass organizations; workers' control of production; pay increases and a sliding pay-scale; full employment; democratic rights; education in service of the people and its needs; a government of workers and peasants; and socialism.[3]

This is a succinct and clear statement of a democratic socialist program, couched with Mexico in mind, but relevant more generally.

Democratic Eco-Socialist Visions

Eco-socialist writers vary in the extent to which they articulate the detail of their post-capitalist vision. Let us look at Joel Kovel's *The Enemy of Nature* first. In a series of passages towards the end of the book, Kovel explains his model.

The first of these passages is an account of the structure of the eco-socialist party. The vanguard party of the revolution. It should be grounded in communities of resistance and production – in other words, activist pressure groups and workplace unions. These will 'supply the cadre of party activists' and 'the assembly that is its strategic and deliberative body'.[4] Delegates to this decision-making body and members of administrative task forces will be rotated and subject to recall. So, this is a representative structure—local bodies elect delegates to a central decision-making body.

Kovel affirms the 'right of an individual to freely appropriate the means of self-expression'. For example, an individual or family has a right to good housing. But 'the ownership as such of the housing and the land upon which it stands is collective and is granted by the collectivity.'[5] This collective is the democratically elected state body in charge of this process. In other words, what Kovel calls 'collective ownership' is ownership by an elected state body.

The role of the state in the revolution is emphasized in a passage that worries about the state becoming an 'alienating agency'—as in the Soviet Union. This must be considered 'since the gain of state power by the revolution is essential for redirecting society.'[6] The revolution will seize the executive power of the state to 'direct society'. Immediately after the revolution, an 'interim assembly of delegates from the revolutionary communities of resistance constitutes itself as an agency to handle the redistribution of social roles and assets, to make sure that all are provided for out of common stocks, and to exert such force as is necessary to reorganize society.'[7] These communities of resistance are being represented through the eco-socialist party. Accordingly, the party, acting through the assembly, is using armed force, when required, to determine distribution and reorganize society.

Each local area will be run by a town government elected by all inhabitants. 'The assembly will convene in widespread locations and send delegations to regional, state, national and international bodies.'[8] In other words, a system of nested territorial governance based on representative democracy, with voting units being 'communities of resistance'. The central assembly will monitor communities according to their ecological contribution and 'give a kind of weight to communities' proportional to their contribution.[9] Meaning that the central assembly will reward towns for ecological conduct and sanction the wrongdoers. These central bodies will provide society wide services such as 'rail systems, the allocation of resources, the reinvestment of the social product, and the harmonization of relations between regions.'[10] In other words, what earlier democratic socialists have called 'central planning'.

Cooperatives become the units of the new economy and existing cooperatives (communities of resistance) organize other workers into this network of productive communities. Many of these are envisaged as money making cooperatives putting goods for sale onto the market. Others must clearly be government departments. During the transition, 'incomes will be guaranteed.'[11] The state centrally controls incomes. State shops or market cooperatives provide goods and services to buy with those incomes. Ultimately money will be based on 'ecocentric value.'[12] A quantitative measure of value—working just like money in all essential respects. Childcare work and similar unpaid services will be transformed into 'productive communities.'[13] Meaning that workers in these services will be paid a wage, since no one will go without 'remuneration'.

Let us look now at another account of the eco-socialist vision that is essentially similar. In *Global Capitalism and Climate Change*, Hans Baer lays out the principles of 'democratic eco-socialism' as an economy oriented to meeting basic needs, a high degree of social equality, public ownership of the means of production, representative and participatory democracy and environmental sustainability.[14] Socialization of private wealth would be a first step. Governments would own much of the economy. Workers' cooperatives would own another major part. There would still be some private businesses. Within government departments and cooperatives, workers' democracy would mean that enterprise managers were elected or chosen by lot. 'Democratic planning needs to be part and parcel of the production process, such as in deciding what goods are needed and whether they are environmentally sustainable'.[15] This planning must take place 'at all levels'.[16] For example, should owners of private cars pay special taxes to subsidize public transport? A decision at the national level. Planning decisions at the national level set the terms for the economy. The elimination of jobs that contribute to emissions. The creation of new jobs in renewables and public services. A shift to 'green jobs' funded by 'public expenditures' that will require action by 'governments and government-directed programs.'[17] Beyond this, a world government. 'Socialist governments in various countries ultimately need to be part and parcel of a world government, with reduction of armies, police and prisons.'[18]

Democratic Socialism – What could go wrong?

I'm going to look at the economic and social problems that might arise in a democratic eco-socialist post-capitalism. Conservative commentators usually refer to this economic model as a 'command economy'. It's not the market that decides which goods and services are going to be provided, but the government exercising *command* of the whole economy. Conservative commentators attack Soviet style economies that were in no way democratic. It may be unfair to apply these critiques to *democratic* socialists, willy nilly. Yet some aspects of classic state socialist economies are still central to the democratic socialist model. Comparisons are not always a mistake.

My view is that this kind of system would be likely to end up with some of the same problems as a standard market economy. The problems with money would also infect the democratic socialist economy. That is not the end of it. There are other problems uniquely connected to *this* economic model.

Government departments and cooperatives

Democratic socialists mark their distinction from earlier state socialisms through their support for participatory democracy. In nationalized industries and government departments, a 'cooperative' manages economic units. Workers elect their own management. I am sceptical. A democratic socialist government sets up a national plan and government-owned firms and departments implement it. If workers are ambivalent, the government can bring them into line quite readily. They depend on government funding for their wages. Elected managements are au fait with this context. Workers would be crazy to elect a management that did not keep on the right side of government. A typical moral argument backs government authority. The government represents the 'people', taken as a whole, while the workers in any one unit are pushing their own barrow. In a monetary economy, a workers' committee, a cooperative, can go one of three ways.

1. It is a workers' *consultation* committee within a government owned department. The government implements their plan by making all the important decisions.

2. The cooperative receives government funding but acts as an independent NGO.

3. The cooperative is a piece of private capital owned by its workers – a market co-op.

In the first case the committee of the 'cooperative' is an apparatus for democratic national control of the economy. The workers are government employees. In the second case, the NGO sacrifices its independence as it is forced to implement government policy. Conditional funding pulls strings. In the third case, the cooperative is constrained by the market. Workers do not have full control over what they are going to produce and how to distribute it. The market decides a lot of that. To operate a democratic national plan, the government also regulates that market in detail. Setting a price on resources, setting prices for distribution. Compromising the market independence of the cooperative. The democratic socialist model works against the independence and participatory management promised by recent proponents of democratic socialism. The central plan and state ownership are pitched against any local economic actors.

The monetary assessment of efficiency

Let's assume you're a manager of a state-owned firm. You're competing with other managers to access government favours. To get advantages measured in money. For example, you might get a bigger enterprise and more government funding, more power as a manager. You might get to increase your firm's output. You could advance your political career. Or you might get private perks, such as a nice car, a holiday house.

So, how are you going to get that government favour? You're going to get it by demonstrating your efficiency. Now, what does efficiency mean? This is the interesting point. Efficiency means efficiency measured in money. That does not mean efficiency measured in any other way—looking after the environment, looking after your workers, distributing useful products to those in need. It just means you are making more goods worth more money and using less money to do that. For example, producing more widgets at a lower cost in labour, equipment, and resources. And those costs are going to be measured in money. So, your motivation as manager of the firm is to expand production. Reduce costs. And reduce inputs of labour—all measured in money. The effect is just like in a capitalist firm. Other values get sidelined. Your motive as a manager is to get government support. You get this support by demonstrating efficiency calculated in money.

So, we can look at an example of how this worked out in the Soviet Union. Very early on, the Soviet Union adopted assembly line production and the theory of management called 'Taylorism'. This method of management, invented in the US, cut workplace tasks into small, readily supervised fragments. Making work very boring. The point was to facilitate supervision. Why do this? Because the whole system depended on monetary incentives. Work was not a joy and creative pursuit, but a task set by the planners. Taylorism is an arrangement of workplace tasks invented to *control* an alienated workforce. Soviet managers embraced Taylorism—to increase production and cut costs. Getting state funding by demonstrating monetary efficiency. Turning workers into robots.

In 1932 and again in 1936, Trotsky wrote about the problems of the Soviet economy. He defends the view that money must be the measure of efficiency. The success of planned interventions cannot be assessed in any other way.

> The raising of the productivity of labor and bettering of the quality of its products is quite unattainable without an accurate measure freely penetrating into all the cells of industry—that is, without a stable unit of currency.[19]

And further.

> The plan is checked and, to a considerable degree, realized through the market. The regulation of the market itself must depend upon the tendencies that are brought out through its mechanism. The blueprints produced by the departments must demonstrate their economic efficacy through commercial calculation.[20]

The monetary calculation of efficiency is implicit in the democratic socialist vision—even if firms are workers' cooperatives. A cooperative could be hired by government to implement a part of the central plan. To be sure of being contracted next time, the co-op would have to maximize its efficiency, measured in money. If the socialist economy included market cooperatives, they would have to compete with other cooperatives—or go out of business.

Planning a nationalized economy

But it will be apparent, a democratic socialist model economy would not operate entirely like a capitalist economy. A critique of planned state-owned economies comes from authors who grew up in the Eastern bloc. Typical problems were waste, inefficiency and the failure to meet planned goals. In a capitalist system, firms that succeed in the market attract investor funding and use their profits to expand. In a Soviet style economy, government bureaucrats make decisions to fund production. Tactics to influence those bureaucrats make sense. Feher, Marcus and Heller make these points.[21]

The managers of state-based firms compete to get state funding because their own careers are tied to the success of their firm. What they want is more state funding for their firm. A common tactic is to promise big. They know their promise is over stretched. But if they can convince government, their firm will grow. They will say that what they are planning is a vital necessity. We need desperately to put in these electricity towers, or whatever. The point is to get initial commitment. Then it is hard for the state to back down, even when costs blow out. For example, you promise to produce Y tonnes of bolts for \$X of government funding. The government commits to Y tonnes of bolts and later realizes that you are going to need \$X + Q to produce that amount.

Let us see how this plays out when tactics like these are common. The people who are in the planning departments expect these tactics. Knowing this, they *discount* the bids across the board. They make a bureaucratic decision to assume that the firm will produce *fewer* bolts than they say and accordingly will need *less* inputs. How do managers respond to these typical counter moves? They put aside resources for a rainy day. The day in which the government does not provide what they need. Leading to even further inefficiencies, waste, and environmental damage.

The emphasis is on projects that guarantee promised results. The way James Scott describes it is to say that central authorities favour enterprises which are 'legible' and easily monitored—over enterprises that are complex and hard to supervise.[22] To make a career as a manager or in planning, it is not a good strategy to back projects that may not work out as promised. For example, a therapy strategy for addicts. You would be uncertain whether the project would work as well as promised. Whereas the company that comes in and says, we're going to make ten tonnes of steel rails, you go. That's right. That's the one we're going to fund. Creating an overemphasis on basic industry—as in the Soviet economy. Even contemporary China is afflicted by this problem. Despite considerable moves towards a capitalist economy. Faced by the huge downturn of 2008, the Chinese government responded by encouraging a boom in construction and infrastructure. State banks provided generous loans to construction companies to build apartment blocks and public infrastructure. An intervention with very quantifiable outcomes. But much of this building and infrastructure was unnecessary. Vast swathes of urban apartments were left empty[23]. Inefficiency and environmental problems because there's a lot of waste. The long-term outcome was that an oversupply of housing depressed the price. Families that had invested their savings in their house found the value of that security had plummeted. They were reluctant to spend on consumer goods. Just when the regime needed to boost the local economy and employment to deal with failing export markets.[24]

James Scott considers farming in the Soviet Union. Peasants were permitted to have a private plot and sell some of that produce, as well as working on the government owned collective farm. It was typical for the collectives to specialize in a monoculture. A crop easily monitored and very predictable, such as a cereal crop. The small peasant plots were more likely to produce fruit and vegetables, tricky crops depending on daily fine tuning.

In other words, a centrally planned economy is likely to prioritize things that are easy to monitor and supervise. Not necessarily the best choices for environmental reasons or to satisfy real needs.

White elephants

As argued in chapter two, the capitalist economies of the rich countries have been adapted to working class pressure. The effect has been to prioritize consumer goods that people are prepared to buy. In a state socialist economy, this minimal control can be absent. White elephants designed to deal with political problems can take precedence. The Chinese example shows how this can work. After the 2008 crisis, consumer demand in the rich countries (China's export destinations) dropped severely. Chinese workers who had been making goods for export were out of a job. The government funded a boom in apartment construction to solve this *political* problem. Environmentally, this was a worry. Using all that steel and concrete to soak up unemployment by building unnecessary housing. Economies with high levels of state ownership tend to end up with white elephant projects of every variety—dams, airports, housing, expressways. These projects are very showy and visible—and provide employment. The downside is environmental damage and meaningless use of people's time.

Let us think how this might play out with an eco-socialist government in charge. A large plant for pumped hydro would be showy and politically visible. With clear benefits in employment. A program to retrofit housing to stop drafts would be hard to police, quantify and assess.

Class conflict and purges

One of the effects of a monetary economy based on state ownership is class conflict. Government control on the economy is premised on monetary incentives. We will plan this project and then fund it. People are signing up because they need the money. The government rewards those who are helping them most by paying them extra money. People supervising other workers, ensuring that the government plan is being implemented. Paid for their loyalty. People whose technical expertise is essential. None of this is accidental. It cannot be ended by a decree of equal pay. Any such measure would undermine the government's capacity to implement the plan. So, there's a hierarchy of pay, which is very similar to the hierarchy of pay within capitalist economies. Where capitalists use monetary incentives to ensure that *their* wishes are implemented. Yet at the same time the ideology is all about we, the people, taking control and running the economy to suit our own interests.

The likely effect is that most people resent the upper middle class. What, Barbara and John Ehrenreich call the professional managerial class—the engineers, the teachers, the lawyers, even the media stars.[25] A violent purge of this class can be the outcome. The party decides they are getting too much influence. They allow popular resentment to find a scapegoat. The effect is waves of disorganization and upheaval as these class tensions play out—with no ultimate change in the system. This is what happened in Mao's China, with the Red Guards and the Cultural Revolution. The accounts of those who lived through these events make it really evident that hostility to the professional managerial class drove the purges.[26]

Adolfo Gilly is a Trotskyist who arrived in Cuba five years after the revolution. At that time, ordinary people were enthusiastic supporters of their revolution. Proud they had taken the means of production from the capitalist class. At the grass roots, they celebrated equity and comradeship. At the same time, people were becoming increasingly hostile to party bureaucrats.

> The term used is not always "bureaucrat." The workers also call them, for example, "the ones with the briefcases," because they always arrive in a great hurry with a briefcase under one arm, supposedly containing very important documents; they glance at the people working and leave again with the same haste. "The ones with the briefcases" is an allusion to an unproductive social group who, along with other special privileges, have that of deciding and leading in matters where the masses should be taking the initiative.[27]

Alienated labour

The democratic socialist economy depends on alienated labour. Democratic socialists often write about the workers 'taking control' of the means of production. How can you be alienated if you've got control of the means of production? Well, in your daily life, you don't have control of the means of production in a state socialist economy—democratic or otherwise. If you're in a nationalized firm, your firm is being instructed in what to do by the government. Told how to produce, what wages to set, how to distribute the product—to fit with the national plan. Democratic control through the national government *depends* on you having little control locally. The government sets goals, deadlines, and targets to fulfill the plan. Without this, the plan could never work. As an individual worker, you have little control. You are constantly being told what to do. The alienated labour of capitalism is maintained. You're not actually meeting with other people, deciding what to produce, how to produce it and how to distribute it.

As in capitalism, this alienated labour leads to political pressure for increased consumption. You are being ordered around at work, and you expect to be compensated. The joke is that the Soviet Union fell because people wanted jeans only made in America. There's a constant drive to increase resource use. We can see this operating in China now. The last thing the Chinese government can afford is for the growing provision of consumer goods to falter. The regime depends on the support of the mainstream middle and upper working class. Their experience has been increasing consumer well-being. It's a political necessity to constantly 'modernize' and 'develop' the economy. For example, to continue to expand electrical supply with coal fired power stations.

We can compare a capitalist company to a public department. There are structural similarities and also differences. Both are embedded in a market economy where labour is a commodity.

- In a capitalist firm, the means of production are owned by shareholders (the capitalists). In a department, the means of production (like a railway or hospital) are owned by the public, represented by its elected ministers.

- The private company recruits private investors, pays workers and builds capital. We might say that for a government department, the public buys capital through taxes. Taxes supply the money to build government owned capital. Or we might say that the government prints money, pays wages with that money and uses that work to create capital.

- The company buys labour on the market. The department also buys labour on the market. A hierarchical organisation implements the decisions of the owners and instructs the workers.

- The company then sells its products on the market. The owners receive surplus value because the monetary value produced by their workers is greater than the amount they are paying those workers. It is difficult to compare this to a government department. The combination of taxes, price setting, fees for service, and government control over money makes it meaningless to assess *monetary* surplus for a government department. Nevertheless, there is no doubt that these mechanisms make a surplus product available to governments. This surplus can augment the means of production in government hands or fund a state elite. Those who produce this surplus do not control it. Just like a capitalist business.

At all events, a government department, as experienced by its workers, is remarkably like a private firm.

Managerial elites

Another aspect of the state ownership model is the tendency to develop a wealthy management elite. Managers compete to get government support. Those who succeed become very powerful. They jockey for positions in the state bureaucracy. They end up displaying their wealth competitively. Buying expensive cars, going on long trips, using holiday houses. All these displays have environmental consequences. Of course, none of this is unique to a state-owned economy. It also happens in capitalism.

Authoritarian politics and the democratic socialist economy

The authoritarianism of regimes premised on this economic model is no accident. Democratic socialists vow to avoid such problems through a strong commitment to democracy. A commitment lacking in previous Soviet style socialisms. Yet it was not the original intention of these statist parties to stifle democracy. On the contrary, they aimed at an expanded democracy—that would also run the economy. What went wrong? Democratic socialists today still argue for a vanguard party, leading the masses to victory and taking control of the state. The members of the party can come to believe in their superior understanding, undermining democracy. Within workplaces, the party members become an unelected fifth column, representing the government. From the perspective of the party, they are ideally suited to monitor the implementation of the plan. But of course, that authority structure makes workplace democracy notional.

I hesitate to point to the authoritarianism of nationalized economies in practice. This is a key tactic in the most stupid anti-communist raves. At the end of the day, I would prefer to be a poor person living in Vietnam or Cuba than a poor person living in South Africa or India. The daily authoritarianism of capitalist society is never acknowledged in these 'anti-communist' diatribes. Nevertheless, this conservative argument does have a point.

The dictatorship in the Soviet Union did not immediately follow the revolution and was contested at the time. Lenin wrote as a supporter of democracy, following Marx. Most of those making the revolution expected democracy. However, within a few years, the Bolshevik state, with Trotsky leading the army, suppressed workers' control in the port of Kronstadt. In other words, eliminating a participatory form of democratic governance. Going on to defeat the Makhnovist anarchists in the Ukraine. The party subordinated and then eliminated popular councils and workplace assemblies.[28]

The intensification of the party oligarchy is often blamed on the civil war and the encircling attacks of capitalist powers. Be that as it may. China was equally disastrous. The 'great leap forward', an attempt to speed up industrialisation, was responsible for a famine that killed at least 30 million people. More than 30 per cent of the population in some rural areas.[29] The 'cultural revolution' was a vicious upheaval that achieved nothing.

Authoritarianism is not restricted to such extreme cases. Take Vietnam and Cuba as examples. Ordinary workers are cynical about the system. There's a lack of efficiency in planning, production, and distribution. At the present time, Cuba is facing a crisis of blackouts and failures in the provision of electrical power.[30] People are working hard at useless tasks and know it. There's an elite that everybody resents. It is a joke to think that these countries are on the way to a classless society. In an open election the communist party would lose. At the very least, ordinary people expect economic growth and consumer well-being as the payoff for obedience.

I will consider two examples to show how the economic problems of state socialism can push the party to authoritarian solutions.

The Bolsheviks and the Peasants

The early development of the Soviet Union is my first example. In the twenties, peasants owned much of the farming land in Russia. They ran their village affairs communally, even though they owned private plots and sold crops as households. Their market was national, and they also exported grain. Preobrazhensky, a 'left' Bolshevik, believed that to speed up industrialisation, the state needed an economic surplus. They could buy grain from the peasants at a low price and sell it at a higher price. Using the profit to finance industrialisation. Buying machinery from other countries and paying the industrial workforce.

Stalin attempted to carry out this policy in the late twenties by organizing a system of state procurement. However, peasants preferred to market their grain to private contractors at a higher price. The state was unable to buy enough cheap grain to create a surplus to pay the costs of industrialisation. More and more force was used to persuade farmers to sell to the state. A kind of taxation. Peasants responded by feeding surplus grain to their livestock—which they could still sell at market prices. Or by eating more grain. In the end by burning their supplies. Stalin responded with a forced collectivisation, between 1930 and 1934. The state seized peasant holdings and turned them into 'collectives'. State owned and party-controlled enterprises. The state could buy grain from these collectives at low prices. Agricultural production did not expand as hoped. Yields per hectare were lower than before the revolution.[31] But the state was certainly able to extract a surplus. The police killed those who resisted these changes. Others died in the famine accompanying this upheaval. Estimates of deaths range from 3 million to 20 million.[32] The agricultural sector lost about half the livestock that peasants had used to plough their fields—sold or killed. So, the state had to supply the collective farms with tractors. Another cost.

It is easy to condemn Stalin and the party for their ruthless hubris. Yet this episode also shows us how difficult it can be to reconcile state planning and a monetary economy. The options for resistance to central planning, the vested interests that flow from any monetary economy, the resentment and sabotage that comes with alienated labour. How attempts to implement a central plan can tip over into coercion.[33]

Chavez and Venezuela

As I have suggested, the leaders of socialist revolutions were often quite democratic in their intentions. The problems of the revolution in Venezuela are a good example of what can go wrong. Chavez was elected president in 1998. His party, the Fifth Republic Movement, intended to decentralize control and set up a planned economy based in workers' cooperatives.

Ferne Edwards explains what went wrong with one of these initiatives. An attempt to establish participatory urban agricultural collectives. The government wanted to set up market garden cooperatives, giving community work and local food provision to the urban unemployed. They funded these cooperatives and paid government employees to supervise. The idea was that community volunteers would supplement the work of the paid government staff. In time the gardens would make a profit. The volunteers would get an income—supplying food to the urban community. This strategy did not work. Ordinary members of the community were not participating. The paid functionaries were the only people maintaining these gardens. This apathy reflected market conditions. The new cooperatives were unable to compete in the food market that already existed. State-run ration stores, and private supermarkets.[34] Importing food cheaper than it could be produced in Venezuela.

Asa Cusack explains how problems like this affected the whole economy. The state funded cooperatives to compete against private companies. In most cases, the state owned fifty per cent. An attempt to reign in market competition. But in fact, incompetent political cronies often ended up in charge. Tapping the government's oil revenue. Almost all these cooperatives failed. To begin with, high oil prices allowed the government to fund social welfare by this method. When oil revenue declined, it became difficult to maintain this spending. The government fixed exchange rates to prevent capital flight. This measure was only partially successful. A black market in US dollars developed. Locally produced goods, priced in local currency, could not compete with imports smuggled in. Attempting to maintain government spending by printing more money kicked off an inflation spiral. The final blows were dealt by US sanctions, restricting oil revenue.[35]

After the death of Chavez in 2013, the new president Nicolas Maduro presided over an increasingly desperate situation. A million Venezuelans left the country. The huge inflation made it impossible for the poor to buy food. Maduro responded by clinging on to power.

...blocking a recall-referendum mechanism that was itself established under Chávez in 1999; installing a constitutional assembly without popular legitimisation; arbitrarily preventing prominent opponents from participating; and unconstitutionally scheduling elections to the ruling party's advantage[36].

This tragic episode shows the difficulty of running a market, monetary economy while also implementing state ownership, cooperatives, and government planning. It's very hard to put them together successfully. The party becomes increasingly authoritarian as it struggles to hang on to the gains of the revolution.

Democratic socialism as a monetary economy

In what I've said so far, I've given quite a few examples from Soviet Russia and China. This may seem unfair. These regimes are not what democratic socialists are promoting. Yet some of the problems of the Chinese and Soviet societies are tied to their economic foundations. New systems of political representation cannot jump over these economic structures. Representative democracy is a very inadequate form of 'ownership' of the means of production. The monetary economy is premised on alienated labour. Your ability to buy something depends on someone else doing what the market, or the government, requires. Money implies markets. At the end of the day, people make market decisions with their money, buying cheap and selling dear. Putting market pressure on decision making even in a nationalized company. There would be no point in a cake making department if no one would buy cake. These are not just ethical problems. They end up being environmental problems—consumerism as compensation.

Socialism, money, and the market are not a good mix. The democratic socialist model uses money to implement political control. The government allocates money to fund enterprises to carry out the central plan. These enterprises recruit people to work for a wage. They sign up, knowing that without money, they won't get goods and services.

The whole system runs upon monetary controls. And this implies alienated labour. I'm ready to buy something. To buy what someone else's alienated labour has made. They had to do a job that would earn them money. There's a connection between *your* use of money and *their* alienated labour. In the dream of the people *taking control* of the means of production, it doesn't make any sense. There's a mismatch.

Money implies a discourse of buying cheap and selling dear. It implies winners and losers. And that's what we see in state owned economies. Corruption is a constant problem. This competition drives the party feuds that end up with authoritarian purges. It is inevitable in a monetary economy. By owning money, you have privatized some of the community's wealth. The parts of the economy that the state owns can't be owned by the market. The parts of the economy that the market owns can't be owned by the state. There's a seesaw. They're always in competition. Competition for wealth because money implies ownership of private wealth, of the community's resources.

Democratic socialists of the present time generally recognize some of the problems with nationalizing a whole economy. They support a move towards a mixed economy model—state owned departments, market cooperatives, small businesses, and voluntary community work. But all these added extras can interfere with attempts to 'plan' the economy, creating economic chaos.

The unpopularity of the nationalized economy model

If we're looking at the rich countries today, democratic socialism is a very unlikely choice. Hostility to the nanny state is pervasive. To give an example. I was interviewing steelworkers in Newcastle, Australia, when there still was a steelworks. One of my interviewees told me two telling narratives. I was asking him about his views on 'burning off'. A common practice in Australian suburbs has been for the householder to take some of their rubbish into the backyard and burn it. My interviewee did this one day. He described the way the fire brigade had walked on to his property and told him to put the fire out. He was outraged at this invasion of his private space. The nanny state taking over. In many of my interviews at that time I heard the following narrative. The recent bushfires had happened because landowners had been banned from burning off the understory of plants on their own properties. This ban was because 'the Greenies' had stopped the burning off. In other words, an unrepresentative minority had got the ear of government and stopped people from exercising their age-old rights. A similar perspective informed this interviewee's thoughts on fishing. New rules were about to be introduced for Lake Macquarie to ban commercial fishing. He said, 'I like to fish. I go out in the tinny (aluminium dinghy) with my son. Yes, it's true that the fish stocks are down in Lake Macquarie because of the commercial fishing. But, you know, I don't think they should be banned. Those guys are making a living, we shouldn't be coming in telling them what to do.'[37]

This rejection of regulation is spread throughout the community. The Trump campaigns traded on that feeling. Likewise, Brexit. There's a widespread feeling in the community that we've had enough control—don't tell us what to do. Accordingly, democratic socialism is not a particularly likely choice if people are looking for a way out. I trace this all back to the authoritarian control of the workplace, authoritarian pedagogy of the education system, the puritan control of sexuality. These aspects of daily life engender resentment. You go to work every day and stupid bosses are telling you what to do. You go to school, and the stupid teachers are telling you what to do. The far right has a field day using this resentment to scapegoat state regulation. I cannot see any of this going away. As the environmental crisis ramps up, there will be increasing regulation and increasing resistance to it. Egged on by factions of the capitalist class that are losing out. It is hard to see a popular revolution demanding central planning and state ownership.

Final words on this

While I have been talking quite a lot about the Soviet and Chinese cases, there are clearly other examples. Cuba, Laos and Vietnam have been relatively successful. But what of the many cases where economic problems, civil war and outside interference have brought down socialist governments? For example, Nicaragua, Tanzania, Zambia, Angola, Mozambique, Chile. The revolution in Venezuela has not been a beacon of hope. Then there is North Korea. Not to mention Cambodia. In AA, they define insanity as doing the same thing over and over—and getting the same disastrous results. How many times do we need to try a nationalized, centrally planned economy—using money and attempting to implement democratic control?

This chapter should not be interpreted as a condemnation of public ownership in *current* society. Public ownership can be a barrier to the worst excesses of capitalism. For example, a public health service. It's also essential when the capitalist class cannot make a profit providing public goods. These days, the capitalist class is shooting itself in the foot. Cutting taxes on the rich, they starve the economy of necessary infrastructure. Public hospitals, bridges, energy supply. So, in this economy, I am a supporter of public ownership. But if you're talking about a post-capitalist economy, I do not think that public ownership of most of the economy is a viable option.

Endnotes

[1] Hans Baer, Merrill Singer, Debbi Long, Alex Pavlotski, *Introducing Health Anthropology, A discipline in action*, Lanham, Rowman and Littlefield, Fourth Edition, 2026, p. 297.

[2] Anitra Nelson, *Beyond Money: A Post-Capitalist Strategy*, Pluto Press, London, 2022; Jasper Bernes, *The Future of Revolution: Communist Prospects from the Paris Commune to the George Floyd Uprising*, Verso, London, 2025; Michael A Lebowitz, *The Socialist Alternative: Real Human Development*, Monthly Review Press, New York, 2010.

[3] Adolfo Gilly, *Paths of Revolution*, Verso, London, 2022, p. 62.

[4] Joel Kovel, *The Enemy of Nature: The End of Capitalism or the End of the World*, London, Zed Books, 2007, p. 264

[5] ibid, p. 270

[6] ibid, p. 272

[7] ibid, p. 273

8 ibid, p. 273
9 ibid, p. 275
10 ibid, p. 275
11 ibid, p. 274
12 ibid, p. 275
13 ibid, p. 274
14 Hans A. Baer, *Global Capitalism and Climate Change: The Need for an Alternative World System*, Alta Mira Press, Plymouth, 2012, p. 208.
15 ibid. p. 221
16 ibid. p. 221
17 ibid. p. 229
18 ibid. p. 216
19 Adolfo Gilly, *Paths of Revolution*, p. 176.
20 ibid, p. 175.
21 Ferenc Feher, Agnes Heller and Gyorgy Markus, *Dictatorship Over Needs: An Analysis of Soviet Societies*, Basil Blackwell, Oxford, 1983.
22 James C. Scott, *Seeing Like a State: How Certain Schemes to Improve the Human Condition Have Failed*, Yale University Press, 2020, p. 219.
23 Steve Chao, 'Inside China's Ghost Towns: Developers run out of money', *Al Jazeera*, 21 September 2016; Whenzi Zhang, 'Construction industry in China - statistics & facts', 2023, viewed on 3 September 2023, https://www.statista.com/topics/7728/construction-industry-in-china/#topicOverview
24 Laura Bicker, 'Xi's real test is not Trump's trade war', *BBC News*, 30 April 2025.
25 Barbara Ehrenreich and John Ehrenreich, 'The professional managerial class', in Pat Walker (ed), *Between Labor and Capital*, South End Press, Boston, 1979, pp. 5–45.
26 Lian Heng and Judith Shapiro, *Son of the Revolution*, Fontana, Aylesbury, UK, 1984; Jung Chang, *Wild Swans: Three daughters of China*, Flamingo, London, 1993.
27 Adolfo Gilly, *Paths of Revolution*, p. 24.
28 Voline, *The Unknown Revolution: 1917-1921*, Black and Red, Chicago, 1974; Maurice Brinton, *The Bolsheviks and Workers' Control: 1917-1921*, Solidarity, London, 1970.

[29] Jung Chang, *Wild Swans: Three Daughters of China*, Harper Collins, London, 1993.

[30] Reuters in Havana, 'Cuba hit by widespread blackouts after national energy grid collapses', *The Guardian*, 15th March, 2025.

[31] James C. Scott, *Seeing Like a State*, p. 203.

[32] ibid. p. 202.

[33] Paul R. Gregory, T*he Political Economy of Stalinism*, Cambridge University Press, 2004, pp. 22-48.

[34] Ferne Edwards, *Food Resistance Movements: Journeying Through Alternative Food Movements*, Palgrave, London, 2023, pp. 49-82.

[35] Asa Cusack, *Venezuela, ALBA, and the Limits of Postneoliberal Regionalism in Latin America and the Caribbean*, Palgrave, Macmillan, New York, 2019; Francisco Rodriguez, 'How Sanctions Contributed to Venezuela's Economic Collapse', *Global Americans*, 9 January 2023, viewed on 20 January 2023, https://theglobalamericans.org/

[36] Cusack, *Venezuela*, p. 48.

[37] John [Jenny] Gow and Terry Leahy, 'Apocalypse Probably; Agency and Environmental Risk in the Hunter Region', *Journal of Sociology*, Vol. 41(2) 2005, pp. 1–25.

Chapter 6
Pathways out of Capitalism: Radical Reformism

This chapter is on what I am calling 'radical reformism'. Radical reformism traces its origins to the 'steady state economy' conceived by the economist Herman Daly in the seventies.[1] But since then, left and environmental theorists and activists have created plans with very similar features in a great number of versions. Some acknowledge the roots of this perspective in Daly's work and others present their ideas as a new invention. I call this tendency in thinking and activism 'radical' because it aims at system change. The system that is being proposed is not capitalism. I call it radical 'reformism' because the proponents hope to use parliamentary democracy to bring in a set of measures that *reform*, rather than *abolish*, the market economy. It is like the welfare state on steroids. That will become clear as I explain it.

All versions of radical reformism current today embrace the idea that we need to *de-grow* the economy of the rich countries to achieve sustainability. Some use the term 'degrowth' in making this claim. Indeed, there are radical reformists who are participants and leaders in degrowth as a social movement.[2] Here, terms can be confusing. In France, the birthplace of the degrowth movement, the term 'decroissance' is readily translated into the English version 'degrowth'.[3] Likewise for other romance languages. However, in German this translation is awkward and the term post-growth or 'postwachstum' is used by participants in the German part of the de-growth movement.[4] Here, reality escapes categories in several ways. The term 'post-growth' can be used in English to characterize a 'growth agnostic' position that is certainly quite different from the very definitive determination to de-grow GDP that founders of the degrowth movement had in mind. In other words, post-growth because growth in GDP might continue in the economy, while there is a shrinkage of material resource use and energy use, at least for the rich countries.[5] The other escape from categories comes out of the de-growth movement itself. With wings of that movement promoting post-capitalist scenarios that are non-market socialist[6] or even democratic socialist[7] rather than radical reformist. Though radical reformism is still the dominant tendency of the degrowth movement.

Before I end this prelude, I should just say that within the degrowth movement the view that we need to cut back GDP has been and still is the dominant view. An end to growth is necessary, we can't have infinite growth on a finite planet. Economists usually calculate growth in relation to GDP (gross domestic product)—a measure of growth in the monetary value of transactions. The dominant wing of degrowth argues that this monetary growth inevitably comes along with a growth in the use of resources, the production of waste and environmental damage. That argument is certainly backed up by the history of actual GDP growth and environmental impact.[8] This view is also consistent with the views of radical reformists outside of the degrowth movement, such as Tim Jackson or Richard Heinberg.

In many ways this prelude is irrelevant to the central concerns of this chapter. I am interested in radical reformism as a version of post-capitalism. What are the ideas of radical reformism for the economy, the cultural and political structures of post-capitalism? Placing it in relation to wings of the degrowth movement is not my concern. Not to mention the fact that radical reformism includes authors who are not participants in the degrowth movement.[9]

Radical reformists aim at a peaceful transition in the context of a market economy rather than a revolutionary overthrow and seizure of the means of production. I like Tim Jackson's description.

> Is it still capitalism? Does it really matter? For those for whom it does matter, perhaps we could just paraphrase Star Trek's Spock and agree that it's 'capitalism, Jim. But not as we know it.'[10]
> (Jackson 2009: 202)

Other authors claim the proposal is to go beyond capitalism. For example, Serge Latouche, one of the founders of the degrowth movement, suggests that various aspects of the capitalist economy continue but they are to be animated by a new understanding and practice—that implies an end to capitalism.

> Getting beyond development, the economy and growth therefore does not imply abandoning all the social institutions that the economy has annexed; it means embedding them in a different logic.[11] (Latouche 2009: 92)

Some aspects of capitalism that radical reformists intend to keep are the market, wage labour, and private ownership of much of the economy.

As indicated above, radical reformists reject a common strand of optimistic pro-capitalist thinking. That it is possible to *decouple* economic growth from the growth in resource use. As economies 'mature', so goes the argument, they produce less as material goods (toasters and washing machines) and more as immaterial services (digital games and MP3s). Radical reformists point out that while this may well work in theory, the reality on the ground is that industrial goods are still being produced, but in the global South. Meanwhile the rich countries have appeared to enter the 'service' economy. None of these 'services' float free of resource use—in energy used to store data and devices used to read it. A huge growth of industrial production, with vast amounts of resource use and carbon dioxide emissions.

Accordingly, radical reformists insist, what we need is a *steady state* economy. A low use of non-renewable resources. With most recycled. A low level of production. Wastes produced only if they can be absorbed by the environment. A steady population. Renewables only to the extent that natural processes replace the resource. A constant stock of 'capital'—industrial machinery, farms, and the built environment. This steady state is maintained by a low rate of throughput—from resources at one end to wastes at the other. The steady state comes about because very few resources are being extracted, and few wastes are produced. These ideas were first developed by the economist Herman Daly in the seventies.[12] Current versions make the point that we have already exceeded planetary boundaries. We need to get to a steady state at a much lower level of resource use than we have at present.[13]

There is much in this analysis shared with other currents on the left. What is distinctive are the proposals for change advocated by radical reformists. Degrowth and the final steady state economy are to be achieved by state regulation and cultural change. The community, even including the capitalist class, comes to see the necessity for a sustainable economy. This cultural shift provides the parliamentary majority necessary for state regulation. It also alters daily life—the behaviour of economic actors, both firms and everyday consumers.

Before I go into it in more detail, let me just say that this viewpoint is *very* mainstream in the environmentalist movement now. Environmentalists—as in people who are seriously concerned about environmental problems. That we need to move to a sustainable society. Most people who believe that also think that the steady state is the way forward. Here are a few examples. Herman Daly is the founder of this perspective.[14] More recent writers are Paul Gilding, previously a chair of Greenpeace.[15] Richard Heinberg, from the peak oil movement.[16] Tim Jackson, an environmentalist economist.[17] Kate Raworth, the originator of the concept of 'doughnut economics'.[18] Naomi Klein, a 'socialist', who promotes a radical reformist program.[19] Jason Hickel.[20] A prominent author from the degrowth movement. While he recently identifies as a 'democratic socialist', his proposals for reform are all from the radical reformist playbook. Paul Mason, with his book on 'post-capitalism'.[21] In Australia, Haydn Washington, an ecological economist.[22] Even Robin Kimmerer, promoting a 'gift economy', recommends radical reformism.[23]

Restraining resource use

As you will know if you have read some of the books mentioned above, this is a very diverse collection of writings. The way I think of radical reformism, it is a cluster of ideas, a bag of tricks. Different authors select different packages. Many of these measures would also be endorsed as *transitional strategies* by people who might have quite a different end game in mind—democratic socialism or the gift economy.

Let's start off by looking at some of the measures to restrain environmental damage and to bring about a steady state environmentally sustainable economy.

Cap and trade as a measure to restrain the use of resources is an option suggested by Herman Daly.[24] There are cases of this legislative measure in place that show that it works. For example, with fisheries, set a cap—a weight of fish that can be caught in a month. Fishing companies bid for a certain proportion of this capped amount. The price is the effect of an auction. People bid more if there is more market demand. There must be policing so that when the fish are brought into port, their weight is measured by an independent authority. Another example is the auctioning of rights to water from a river, to be used for irrigation. The government sets a total amount that they think is consistent with sustainable use and auctions water rights from that amount.

So, cap and trade is that system. The government sets a limit to how much of the resource will be extracted and used in any given year (the cap) and firms bid for access to it (the trade). The price goes up if there's high demand and goes down if there's low demand. At the end of the day, the government can be confident that only a certain amount of the resource is being used. This system can be used to reduce carbon emissions. In the beginning, the cap is set at an amount equal to present usage. Then each year, the cap is reduced, forcing the price of fossil fuels to rise, and limiting their use. Eventually, we get used to using less energy or find an affordable substitute for fossil fuels.

A similar option uses ecological taxes to *reduce* resource use.[25] Or to set the tax so high that the resource ceases to be used. For example, with carbon emissions. Set the tax low to begin with so that businesses are not driven into bankruptcy. Then gradually increase the tax to the point where it is cheaper to use renewables—or necessary to reduce energy use. Use the resource tax to replace income taxes or to fund environmentalist re-structuring. Let's look at a resource that is hard to replace with an alternative. Phosphates. There are deposits of concentrated phosphates around the world. There is a limited supply that we can mine. We use phosphates to supply phosphorous—an essential element for plants. Deposits are running low. But so long as they are available, they will be mined—and sold at a low price despite the looming shortage. Because different producers are in competition with each other. Eventually, there will be a sudden collapse in supply and a drastic shortage of food. To avoid this disaster, governments could gradually increase the price of phosphates with a tax, growing every year. The tax would force agricultural producers to think twice about using phosphate fertilisers. They would develop farming systems using manure, a traditional source of phosphate. That would become the cheaper option.

In both these cases, cap and trade, and eco-taxes, the intention is to shift the behaviour of businesses by changing the market context. To phase out or reduce the use of a resource. An even simpler measure is banning or regulating. Most European governments have now legislated to end the sale of petrol and diesel cars by a certain date.[26] This is a ban. Falling short of a total ban are restrictions on sale. For example, only allowing gas to be used in industries that cannot be profitable without it. Aluminium plants but not cooking stoves.

How could measures like this end up with a zero-growth steady state economy? The argument here is that growth in GDP cannot take place without a growth in resource use. The measures being proposed are all measures intended to cut resource use. The effect must be to reduce GDP. Since GDP is a measure premised on monetary transactions, it tends to relate to other measures of economic well-being as that is generally conceived. For example, employment figures, taxation revenue, incomes for workers. The aim is not to keep reducing GDP forever. But down to a point compatible with environmental goals. To achieve a steady state by tweaking these measures—to allow the economy to function at this level. The reduction in GDP and the final steady state are not in fact the *primary* goals. The primary goals are to reduce resource use and reduce environmental impact. As Daly puts it, the aim is to have a constant quantity of resources and energy going through the economy. That at a low level to avoid environmental damage. To get to that we need to reduce population and the stock of machinery using energy and embodying material resources.

> we might define the SSE in terms of a constant flow of throughput at a sustainable (low) level, with population and capital stock free to adjust to whatever size can be maintained by the constant throughput.[27]

Declining GDP is a side effect, and the SSE an economic method to become sustainable.

Other economic measures

As explained, radical reformists do not believe that an economy can 'decouple' economic growth from resource use. Yet concrete proposals often mention a shift from industrial goods to less materially intensive service industries. Any industry has some material impact. But some have less impact than others, per unit of monetary value. For example, therapeutic services, cultural productions. These industries will expand and provide employment—while more damaging industries will contract.[28]

Radical reformists want strong government support for environmental technologies. Funding research and development.[29] Subsidies for sustainable technologies. For example, a taxpayer funded grant on heat pump hot water to replace gas systems.

Steady state proponents understand the way private companies 'externalize' environmental costs to increase profitability. To rescue key drivers of environmental damage from this market context, they recommend government ownership of some industries— energy, transport, even agriculture. As with democratic socialists, radical reformists see workers' cooperatives as more likely to operate sustainably. So, they favour government support for cooperatives.[30]

One measure is government management of money supplies. Using 'Modern Monetary Theory'.[31] MMT. In other words, the government funds what is necessary to construct a sustainable society. Not by taxation, but by printing money and allocating it to these purposes.[32] A more conventional proposal is taxing the wealthy. The rich pay for an environmentalist retrofit.[33]

Political support

Radical reformists see these government measures being backed up by a cultural shift. Changing economic behaviour and driving political change. For the wealthy, a shift to ethical investment options— investments in projects that do not damage the environment. Sustainable forestry, solar or wind power. Paul Gilding, previously a head of Greenpeace, writes about this with great enthusiasm. The capitalist class itself, along with the military and other elites will come to understand the environmental crisis and act accordingly.[34] Other writers in this vein are more likely to see popular pressure putting limits on market elites. People become ethical shoppers. They vote for parties that put the environment first. They make a choice to reduce, re-use and recycle.

Representative democracy is a key. The necessity to 'get the political will' to make these changes.[35] People will vote in governments prepared to make the necessary changes. These governments will collaborate with a global program of change. Imagine the COP summits on climate having more teeth because there's more popular support for drastic measures. This scenario seems more plausible for representative democracies. It seems less likely with more authoritarian regimes.

Social measures and redistributions

What I have been talking about so far are the changes in the economy. How it is regulated and how it operates in practice. Radical reformists also discuss a range of social measures.

Recent radical reformist writings propose a *degrowth* of the economy to reach a steady state—at a low level of throughput. For example, Serge Latouche and Tim Jackson envisage a cut in GDP to a third or even a quarter of what it is now in the rich countries.[36] This contraction would usually be called a 'recession'. With less value in total monetary transactions, there is less employment. People are buying less, there is less produced for the market, there are fewer jobs. Of course, some people are employed by the government in environmental restructuring. But in the economy taken as a whole, there's less money going around and less employment. The effects of unemployment can be dire. No money for housing, food, education, or medical expenses. People proposing a steady state economy are totally aware of that. They have several proposals to deal with this problem. All these work by redistributing the wealth of the affluent employed working class, the middle class and the rich.

One of the proposals most often mentioned is a universal, basic income (UBI). A UBI is universal because anyone getting less than the basic income can receive the UBI. Or it is universal because everyone is paid the UBI as a basic starting point. The aim is to provide enough income for living quite comfortably without a job. You are not even expected to look for a job. A recognition that the degrowth economy cannot find jobs for everyone. Less stuff is being produced and marketed so there is less need to employ people. We could have up to seventy per cent unemployed and, with the UBI, it would not be a problem. The UBI would be set at a level that allowed a comfortable living. People on the UBI would be enjoying their leisure or spending their time on useful but voluntary community work—community gardens, creative arts and drama productions, music festivals. A redistribution from the employed taxpayers, or from the rich—to those who are unemployed. Some of the work that in the old economy would have been making things for the rich would now be devoted to the needs of the unemployed. The total level of production would diminish but the unemployed would not feel the impact. They might be getting slightly less cash than employed people, but they would enjoy more leisure.[37]

How does this affect the wealthy? We could tax the wealthy to pay for the UBI. Or we could make use of the strategy suggested in

Modern Monetary Theory (MMT). The government prints money to pay the UBI. The effect is to direct the economy to producing things for those who are on the UBI. How does this affect the rich? Because we have a steady state economy—there is no extra piece of the economic pie being made available through MMT—we cannot grow the economy to produce *more stuff*, for those on UBI. Instead, the incomes and assets of the wealthy have less value in real terms. Their money can buy less. Taxation by the back door.

Another proposal to produce somewhat similar effects is a limitation of the working week. The available work would be parcelled out in equal shares. The economy would shrink—but we would *not* have some people with a 40-hour week, making a decent income—and other people scraping by. If the economy shrank to thirty per cent of what it is now, the government might restrict you to two days of paid work. A huge expansion in leisure. As in the UBI scenario, this time could be spent putting your feet up—or in community pursuits. Organizing dance festivals. Seasonal rituals. Wood carving. This is also a form of redistribution. Redistributing paid work, and with that income. Government provision of guaranteed employment. So, no one is out of a job. The cost coming from taxes or MMT, just as with the UBI. Another kind of redistribution.[38]

This model has implications for relationships between the global South and the rich countries. One of the most common critiques of 'degrowth' is that it cannot apply to the global South. Do people who are going hungry, have no clean water supply, no sewerage and no electricity need degrowth? Surely what they need is *growth*—in consumption and infrastructure. Responding to this charge, radical reformists advocate a policy of 'contract and converge'. The rich countries contract their use of resources—while the global South expands. Both ending up with a steady state at a much lower level of resource use than today. They go on to say that the rich countries must assist the global South with renewables.[39] In fact, this redistribution would be necessary to get political support for radical reformism from the global South.

A critique of radical reformists

As I have pointed out, some version of this package is very popular with environmentalists. I hate to be the party pooper. In the context of a largely capitalist economy, there is a lot in these ideas that I like. I just doubt whether a strong package of these reforms can work as envisaged by radical reformists.

If we look at what I describe in the second chapter, we can see why radical reformism is such an appealing idea and how it hangs together as a package. The first world bargain is the deal in which capitalism promises the people of the rich countries increasing affluence—and they give up on dreams of an anti-capitalist revolution. The environmental crisis puts that deal on notice. The cost of an environmental retrofit and the cost of environmental damage must reduce the standard of living for ordinary people in the rich countries. A possible consequence is a revolution. Radical reformists don't want that outcome. They equate a socialist revolution to terror and totalitarian dictatorship.

> There are those for whom revolution appears to be the answer ...
> Let's end capitalism. Let's reject globalization … But there are risks
> here too. The spectre of a new barbarism lurks in the wings. A world
> constrained for resources, threatened with climate change, struggling
> for economic stability: how long could we maintain civil society
> in such a world if we have already torn down every institutional
> structure we can lay our hands on?[40](Jackson 2009: 172)

What they want instead is a peaceful transition that will encompass an environmentalist re-structuring. They think that is most likely if we move towards something, that's not too different to capitalism. A welfare state on steroids.

This explains why all the redistribution measures proposed by radical reformists are considered to be necessary. They are *politically* necessary to enable environmental reforms. From a purely environmentalist point of view, we could cut resource use and just let ordinary people in the rich countries *cope* with high levels of unemployment, poverty, and economic insecurity—as most do now in the global South. That would not be an *environmental* problem. But it would quickly become a political problem. Political support for radical reformism would crumble.

I will argue that to be effective, the reforms proposed by radical reformism would destroy the market economy—with unpredictable consequences. You certainly would not end up with anything like what is proposed by radical reformism. A milder set of reforms would be unable to deal with the environmental crisis. They would not go far enough and full-scale capitalism, with all its problems, would come back.

To make this argument, I'm going to look at two key groups. One is business owners and the second is ordinary people—workers, in the broadest sense.

Business owners

For business owners, competition for market share and increased profits is not an option. It's a necessity. If you don't always try to get increased profits and an increased share of the market, some other firm will come along and take your market. Getting more sales, while your products just sit on the shelf. Your capital, your means of production, will be worth nothing because some other firm has grabbed your market. Your workers will end up without a job, your workplace will be lying idle. Pushing hard to make more money and more profits is absolutely necessary. It is a mistake to think of this pursuit of growth as a *cultural mindset*, something that could vanish if the capitalist class were converted to environmentalism. It comes out of the economic structure of a market economy, with competing firms owned privately. This applies to firms at every scale. Whether we are talking about huge multinationals, ma and pa corner shops or workers' cooperatives.[41]

In fact, it's this drive to compete and increase market share, which creates the efficiency that radical reformists want to retain. In praise of market efficiency Daly writes.

> Properly functioning markets allocate resources efficiently, but they cannot determine sustainable scale or a just distribution; those can be achieved only by government policy.[42]

But let's look at how markets might react to this government policy. Every firm is trying to find a cheaper way to do things—so they can increase their market share and their profits. But at the same time as the market drives this monetary efficiency, it also creates economic growth. People are competing to get more profits. They are doing this by producing more with less money, increasing the number of items they are selling and (in most cases) the resources they are using.

How would this play out in the economic system envisaged by radical reformists? The market continues to operate, and firms attempt to grow their market share. But the government steps in through cap and trade, through taxes and regulations to stifle growth by restricting resource use. You come up with a great new idea to produce more widgets and make more money. But the government moves in and increases the price of some essential ingredient. You end up unable to sell any more widgets than last year. From the firm's point of view, the government is constantly making it difficult for you to grow your income. Making you vulnerable to competition. For the people who invest in businesses, every investment is less likely to be profitable than in a growing economy. In a growing economy, you lend some money to a firm, and you've got a reasonable expectation of getting it back with interest. The debtor firm can grow their business because the economy, taken as a whole, is growing. When the economy is flat lining, that becomes more difficult. The typical reaction of investors is to keep their money in the bank, rather than invest it. The market has 'lost confidence' in the economy. With unemployment and poverty for ordinary people, and a downturn in taxable income.[43]

What can the radical reformist government do if this happens? Step in and fund projects to boost the economy and employ people. Moving away from radical reformism and ending up closer to a democratic socialist economy. The capitalist response is to pull out even more investments. The government takes over even more of the economy. With all the problems of the democratic socialist model. The opposite response would restore the confidence of the market— reducing taxes on the rich, reducing resource taxes and easing caps.

The business-as-usual solution. With all the typical environmental problems of capitalism. Just as likely, the government might muddle through, sticking to their caps and regulations. The market economy would fail, with social and political breakdown. The drastic alternative would be to abandon the market economy lock stock and barrel. Abolish money and invite workers to take over and run their businesses as gift cooperatives. The radical reformist model *itself* is not stable. It will not work in the long-term.

For the rest of us

I've now looked at the problems of radical reformism for business owners and talked about how they might be likely to respond. Let's look at the problems where ordinary people are concerned. The social measures that radical reformists recommend would undermine the market in labour. At present, the market functions because people need a job. They need a job, they become employed. They produce something which goes on the market. Other workers who've been paid, in *their* jobs, can then buy it. That's how it all works. If you undermine the necessity to get a job, you undermine a key pillar of the market economy.

Let us look first at the proposal for a universal basic income (UBI). The UBI must be enough to live comfortably. That is because it must help people to cope with the economic contraction consequent on de-growth. To give these changes continuing political support at the ballot box and in everyday life. Quite a lot of people will be unemployed—maybe even 70 per cent. We don't want that to become a political problem. So, we're going to pay people a comfortable income. You, as a worker, don't need to get a job. You can leave the paid workforce and live comfortably, spending your time in hobbies and voluntary community work.

In the worst-case scenario for radical reformism the UBI reform would spark off an instant general strike. Who wants to go to work? In a more likely scenario, those who did stay on in a job would find their bargaining power massively strengthened. Imagine you are one of the small number of people who are fully employed. You turn up at work and the boss says, 'We're going to do it this way.' And you and five other workers in that unit go, 'No, we're not. Now you can do it our way, or we'll just go and get the basic income.' This change in power relations would undermine the economic logic of the market, what it means for a market to be a market. The supposed owners of capital would lose the power of ownership. They would be unable to control how their workers were using the capital. They could not run their business to ensure a profit. There would be no work discipline.

This could go even further. Workers could end up challenging the market in a hundred other ways. Imagine a cooperative that decides *not* to sell their products to those with the money to buy them at a market price. Instead, they are going to mark them down for people who cannot afford them otherwise. Or for their friends and relatives. They are not worried that they are not getting a market price. They will just live on the UBI if their cooperative is not making enough to pay them adequately. Living comfortably while their cooperative makes decisions that make no market sense. Such behaviour could well be expected with the cultural shift radical reformists anticipate. To sociable generosity and away from competitive greed. The end result. Money would have no predictable value. The UBI itself—as a monetary payment—would end up being useless.

When radical reformists consider critiques of the UBI the one they most often engage with is this. What would motivate people to work when they can live comfortably on the UBI? The answers from radical reformists are always the same. People have an innate desire to express themselves creatively.[44] They like the public participation that work enables. This reply misunderstands the issue. The issue is not whether people like to work and do socially useful things with their time. It is whether people are willing to work under the conditions *of a market economy.* Working under a boss who is more interested in money than anything else—and must be to keep the business competitive. Marketing things that people want to buy and selling them to those prepared to pay the most. Running your enterprise to compete with other firms. Well, yes, people will put themselves under those constraints if (as now) the alternative is economic insecurity and stigmatizing poverty. But maybe not if the alternative is the UBI. Even if people do go to work, they cannot be expected to remain within limits that make a market function *as a market*. Who is going to behave like that when the UBI is available?

Quite a few radical reformists do not propose the UBI. Instead, they want paid work to be *shared* equally.[45] For example, the government might enforce a 10-hour working week. If you are out of work, there is a job guarantee. On the face of it, this seems to avoid the problems of a UBI. You must have a job to get income. But perhaps it is not too different. Everyone's working for only 10 hours. In the rest of the week, what are they doing? They're doing voluntary community projects. Community gardens, wildlife restoration, amateur theatricals, public sculpture or whatever. Hanging out with friends and producing things. Things which are generally useful. Things produced for free—making it difficult to sell the same goods on the market. Your community garden is growing a glut of lemons and giving them away. The local supermarket cannot make a cent out of lemons.

The huge preponderance of this voluntary community work reminds us every day that we do not actually need the market. The things we are doing in our paid work—obeying a boss, competing to corner the market, distributing to those with the money to buy. All of this is really beside the point. We could do better by just expanding voluntary community work to cover the whole economy. The restriction of paid work to ten hours a week invites people to experience voluntary work as a way of life—not just as a hurried snatched moment. Like the UBI, this situation undermines market discipline. Especially if joined to this, is a job guarantee. You can leave any job and expect to get another—or at least to be secure on a generous welfare payment. With reasonable prices for essentials, some of which are provided free by government.

The long and the short of it. The market economy depends on alienated labour. If you allow people to escape alienation, you undermine the market economy.

Bureaucratic overkill

Looking at the democratic socialist vision I talked about the difficulty of combining public ownership, democratic planning, and a market. In some ways the problems of a radical reformist economy are not that different. In the democratic socialist vision, the government owns the bulk of the means of production and provides money to carry out the tasks that the government sets. This turns out to be a lot more complicated than you might think. The money that the government provides creates incentives for people to interfere with the plan. Massive bureaucratic oversight is required to keep lining things up. In the radical reformist vision, the market has a lot more freedom—in theory. There is no central plan. Nevertheless, in any case where an issue of social justice or environmental impact is concerned, the government steps in and uses market incentives and regulations to guide the market to politically required outcomes. The basic premise is that the unregulated market understates the real value of social justice and environmental goods. A 'market failure.'[46] Accordingly, government must intervene to restore the supposed 'real' values and translate them into monetary incentives. That's a very fraught exercise, with complications that are not immediately apparent.

One thing. It's actually impossible to compare values according to some universal standard. There is no way a computer programme could answer these questions to the satisfaction of all concerned. For example, how much is a polar bear worth compared to twenty sleepless nights in a stressful job? These are both values, which we could consider, but, quantitatively, how would we measure this? It is hard to think of a production decision that does not have implications for social justice and environmental impact. How many kinds of plastic are in the world and how should we price these to avoid environmental impact? Which environmental impacts are the ones we should be worrying about? What are the social consequences of regulating these plastics? Remember that in the radical reformist vision, these decisions are all to be made democratically—if possible, through participatory democracy. Then, having decided, the government must pay for the necessary enforcement. In a market economy—where every player has an incentive to cut corners to stay ahead of the competition. Am I the only one who thinks this is a bureaucratic nightmare? We can adjust the market through measures like this on a small scale—and get away without a massive bureaucratic headache. But we are only scratching the surface of the problems. Look at the debates raging between environmentalists about renewable energy. One environmentalist is saying, every solar panel you buy has been produced by slave labour. Another is saying, we need to replace fossil fuels with renewables—to give working class men a job.

The effect of re-pricing and regulating resources, goods and services is that each of these re-pricing decisions produces a ripple of consequences, which are difficult to foresee in advance. Let us make an example of an issue that governments are taking up with varying degrees of determination. In the rich countries, one of the key uses of fossil fuels is for private transport. Driving to work in your own car is pretty well a necessity in suburbs built to be car dependent. Using public transport can mean you spend more than two hours a day commuting. Driving your own car can cut that in half. The logical approach for a radical reformist government would be to boost the price of petrol and diesel through a carbon tax. Or ban the sale of cars using these fuels. They could promise that EVs would replace petrol and diesel cars. The most politically palatable option. This is where the largely unpredictable effects of a market economy kick in. A global policy like this would see a drastic increase in demand for electric vehicles. With that, a steep increase in the price of the minerals for the batteries and motors.[47] Increasing the cost of EVs so most people could not afford them. Suddenly, the radical reformist government is in an untenable political situation. They have intervened to reduce the use of fossil fuels, promising the electorate they can still travel to work in their own car. But there has been an unexpected market impact—negating that promise. This example concerns just one little part of the current economy. In an economy seriously devoted to the environment and social justice, ripples like this would be endemic.

To constantly adjust for these effects, to predict them, to legislate, to impose market limits and to enforce these solutions. Mountains of red tape, paperwork, and costs to government.

To which I am sure some readers are saying, 'So what is the alternative?' The gift economy avoids this. A decentralized decision-making process with money taken out of the equation. That alternative *could* make these adjustments *without* bureaucratic overkill.

Conclusions

I have argued that radical reformism is not a viable long-term post-capitalist option. I can see why it seems to be a good idea. Everything radical reformism proposes is a version of something we have already done to regulate the market. These measures are just to be ramped up to the point where degrowth to a steady state takes place. What could go wrong? As I've explained, the minute you ramp it up to that extent, you destroy the market economy. The foundation on which radical reformism depends. Faced with this argument, many environmentalist activists respond like this. 'Your concern is that we will destroy the market economy. Why is that a problem?' Well, to begin with, that kind of thinking is gaslighting where the population at large is concerned. We are going to promote this idea, knowing it can never work. Of more concern is that the most likely outcome is that you do not have a peaceful transition at all. You create economic chaos—which could be followed by a revolutionary transition to the gift economy. Whoop whoop! But just as likely fascism or the return of business as usual—with collapse as the outcome.

At the same time, I recognize that this is the mainstream alternative coming from the environmentalist left. Even people who get labelled as 'socialists' are moving in this direction. For example, the 'Green New Deal' associated with the Bernie Sanders campaign or Jeremy Corbyn's campaign in the UK. Not to mention groups more readily identified as environmentalist—the Green parties, Greenpeace, the peak oil writers, permaculture activists and a large part of the degrowth movement.

I have very mixed feelings about this. It makes sense to propose demands that sound realistic. Pushing for small reforms we may get something better than nothing. That is certainly the strategy of the Greens in Australia. I can understand that. But I do not think that a host of these small reforms can be stitched together for a stable post-capitalist society. So far, some of these reforms get put in place and they're not strong enough to make a huge difference. Or they get wound back as the capitalist class pulls the usual strings. Julia Gillard was the Labor party prime minister in Australia between 2010 and 2013. Her carbon tax was a classic of how these things work out. I supported it, even though it was a minimal intervention—inadequate according to the science. The conservative parties scared people. The capitalist class spent lots on media campaigns. Australian industry cannot compete if we are hobbled by the carbon tax. You will lose your jobs. The electorate voted for the conservative coalition at the next election, and the new government scrapped the tax. Even now, twelve years later, the ALP is not brave enough to suggest anything similar.[48]

The radical reformist political strategy is based on this reasoning. Let's not scare the horses. We are not going to overthrow the market economy. Instead, lets engineer a peaceful transition through measures people can understand. But in fact, to get support for these measures we need a population prepared to go to any lengths. But a population angry enough to take such a drastic step would not stop at radical reformism. Ideally, I'd like to see growing recruitment to the gift economy perspective. At the moment, that seems extremely unlikely. But if I had to say what I think could *in fact work*, that would be it. Defending the radical reformist position, a common argument is this. We do not have the time to build a political groundswell to overthrow capitalism. Let's start with something within the Overton window.[49] To which my short reply is, we do not have time to try something that can't work. Nevertheless, many current projects of radical reformism make sense—even if your long-term objective is the gift economy. More on this in later chapters. In the next chapter I will consider the transition to the gift economy.

Endnotes

[1] Herman E. Daly, *Ecological Economics and Sustainable Development: Selected Essays of Herman Daly*, Edward Elgar, Cheltenham, U.K. 2007.

[2] Serge Latouche, *Farewell to Growth*, trans David Macey, Polity: Cambridge, 2009, Jason Hickel, *Less is More: How Degrowth Will Save the World*, London: Windmill Books, 2021.

[3] François Jarrige and Vincent Liegey, 'The French Origins and Pillars of Degrowth', in *The Routledge Handbook of Degrowth*, edited by Anitra Nelson and Francois Liegey, London, Routledge, 2025, pp. 55–68.

[4] Mathias Schmelzer and Barbara Muraca, 'Postwachstum: German roots and currents of degrowth, in *The Routledge Handbook of Degrowth*, edited by Anitra Nelson and Francois Liegey, London, Routledge, 2025, pp. 81-93.

[5] Giorgios Kallis, Jason Hickel, Daniel W O'Neill, Tim Jackson, Peter A. Victor, Kate Raworth, Juliet B Schor, Julia K Steinberger, Diana Urge- Vorsatz, 'Post-growth: the science of wellbeing within planetary boundaries', Crossmark, Crossref DOI link: https://doi.org/10.1016/S2542-5196(24)00310-3, 2025.

[6] Francois Liegey and Anitra Nelson, *Exploring Degrowth: A Critical Guide*, London: Pluto Press, Anitra, Nelson, *Beyond Money: A Post-Capitalist Strategy*, PlutoPress, London, 2022, Nina Treu, Matthias Schmelzer, Corinna Bukhart, *Degrowth in Movement(s):Exploring Pathways for Transformation*, London, John Hunt Publishing, 2020.

[7] See this recent conversion of Jason Hickel to 'democratic socialism'. Probably an outlier even if he is a leading figure in the degrowth movement. https://substack.com/home/post/p-170272249, the Break-Down Journal.

[8] Terry Leahy 'What is the Relationship Between Growth and the Environment? A degrowth critique of the 'contingent' position', *Journal of Australian Political Economy*, Jan 14th 2025; Haberle, H., et al. (2020) A Systematic Review of The Evidence on Decoupling of GDP, Resource Use and GHG Emissions, Part II: Synthesizing

the Insights, *Environmental Research Letters*, 15; Parrique, T., Bath, J., Briens, F. and Spanenberg, J. (2019) Decoupling Debunked. Evidence And Arguments Against Green Growth as a Sole Strategy for Sustainability. *A study edited by the European Environment Bureau*, July, EEB: Brussels, Belgium. https://eeb.org/library/decoupling-debunked/

[9] Timothy Jackson, Tim *Prosperity Without Growth: Economics for a finite planet*, Earthscan, London, 2009, Klein, Naomi, *This Changes Everything: Capitalism versus the Climate*, Penguin, London, 2014, Kate, Raworth, *Doughnut Economics: Seven Ways to Think Like a 21st Century Economist*, Random House, London, 2017.

[10] Timothy Jackson, Tim *Prosperity Without Growth: Economics for a finite planet*, Earthscan, London, 2009, p.202.

[11] Serge Latouche, *Farewell to Growth*, trans David Macey, Polity: Cambridge, 2009, p. 92.

[12] Herman E. Daly, *Ecological Economics and Sustainable Development: Selected Essays of Herman Daly*, Edward Elgar, Cheltenham, U.K. 2007.

[13] Jason Hickel, *Less is More: How Degrowth Will Save the World*, London: Windmill Books, 2021; Joshua Farley, Steady state economics. In G. D'Alisa, F. Demaria & G. Kallis (Eds.) *Degrowth: A vocabulary for a new era* (pp. 76-79). London: Routledge, 2015.

[14] Daly, *Ecological Economics*.

[15] Richard Heinberg, *The End of Growth: Adapting to our new economic reality*, New Society Publishers, Gabriola Island, BC, Canada, 2011.

[16] Gilding, Paul, *The Great Disruption: Why the Climate Crisis Will Bring on the End of Shopping and the Birth of a New World*, Bloomsbury, London, 2012.

[17] Jackson, *Prosperity Without Growth*.

[18] Kate, Raworth, *Doughnut Economics: Seven Ways to Think Like a 21st Century Economist*, Random House, London, 2017.

[19] Klein, Naomi, *This Changes Everything: Capitalism versus the Climate*, Penguin, London, 2014.

[20] Hickel, *Less is More*.

[21] Paul Mason, *Post-Capitalism: A Guide to Our Future*, Penguin, Random House, London, 2015.

[22] Haydn Washington, *Demystifying Sustainability: Towards Real Solutions*, London, Routledge, 2015.

[23] Robin Wall Kimmerer, *The Serviceberry: An economy of gifts and abundance*, Penguin, Random House, 2024.

[24] Daly, *Ecological Economics*, p. 18.

[25] Daly, *Ecological Economics*.

[26] Rob Harris, 'Wrong decision: Germany to defy EU plan to ban petrol cars by 2035', *The Age*, 22 June 2022.

[27] Herman E. Daly, 'A failed growth economy and a steady-state economy are not the same thing; they are the very different alternatives we face', *Sustainable Development Commission*, UK, 2008, p.3.

[28] Jackson, *Prosperity Without*, p.130.

[29] Jackson, *Prosperity Without*, pp. 140, 201; Heinberg, *The End of Growth*, p. 233.

[30] Heinberg, *The End of Growth*, p. 253; Gilding, *Great Disruption*, p. 245.

[31] Christopher Olk, Colleen Schneider, and Jason Hickel, 'How to pay for saving the world: Modern Monetary Theory for a degrowth transition', *Ecological Economics*, 2023, vol. 214, pp. 1-12; Stephanie Kelton, *The Deficit Myth: Modern Monetary Theory and How to Build a Better Economy*, John Murray, New York, 2020.

[32] Jackson, *Prosperity Without*, p. 178; Heinberg, *The End of Growth*, pp. 240, 242.

[33] Jackson, *Prosperity Without*, p. 155.

[34] Gilding, *The Great Disruption*, p. 239.

[35] For example, Washington, *Demystifying Sustainability*.

[36] Latouche, *Farewell to Growth*, p. 3; Jackson, *Prosperity Without*, Loc 3579.

[37] For example, Sam Alexander and Brendan Gleeson, *Degrowth in the Suburbs: A Radical Urban Imaginary*, Palgrave Macmillan, London, 2019; Andre Gorz, *Farewell to the Working Class: An essay on post-industrial socialism*, London: Pluto Press, 1982.

[38] Jackson, *Prosperity Without*, p. 134; Latouche *Farewell to Growth*, p. 40.

[39] Hickel, *Less is More.*

[40] Jackson, *Prosperity Without*, p. 172.

[41] Andrew McLaughlin, *Regarding Nature: industrialism and deep ecology*, State of NY Press, Albany, 1993.

[42] Daly, *Ecological Economics*, p. 18.

[43] Wolfgang Streeck, *How Will Capitalism End? Essays on a Failing System*, Verso, London, 2016.

[44] Tim Hollo, *Living Democracy: An Ecological Manifesto for the End of the World as We Know It*, University of New South Wales, Sydney, 2022; Hickel, *Less is More*; Alexander and Gleeson, *Degrowth in the Suburbs.*

[45] For example Jackson, *Prosperity Without*, p. 134; Washington, *Demistifying*, p.65.

[46] Robin Hahnel, *Green Economics: Confronting the ecological crisis*, Routledge, London, 2011.

[47] Rob Harris, 'Soaring prices for raw materials threaten acceleration of electric car sales', The Age, 23 May 2022; Nick Toscano, 'In race for EV metals, BHP casts wider net to locate copper, nickel', *The Age*, 30 January 2023.

[48] Hans Baer, *Climate Change and Capitalism in Australia: An Eco-Socialist Vision for the Future*, Routledge, London, 2021.

[49] Farley, J., & Washington, H. (2018). Circular firing squads: A response to 'The neoclassical Trojan horse of steady-state economics' by Pirgmaier. *Ecological Economics*, 147, 442–449.

Chapter 7
Transitions to the Gift Economy

This chapter is about the transitions to the gift economy. Chapter four explains the idea of the gift economy, and this chapter is about ways of moving to that goal. What we have today is a very complex networked economic system. It's global and people depend upon it. Predictability—knowing you can expect to get something you need or being sure that you won't—depends upon market forces. Do you have enough money to pay for it? We are very dependent for our livelihoods on the market economy. A gift economy has no money and works on agreements between voluntary collectives of producers and consumers. We must move to that with the least possible disruption. We do not want people dying in the streets because they are unable to access food, water, and heating—currently supplied through market transactions. It's very hard to say how all of this is going to work out. A certain amount of unpredictability and disruption could be unavoidable. We're at a situation now where *business as usual* is massively disruptive. Because of that, people will be prepared to take risks up to a point. This chapter is about mapping out a few plausible transitions. Recognizing the unpredictability of all this, lining up a variety of pathways, rather than recommending the 'one right way'.

Faced with these questions a lot of people are sceptical about whether a revolution to replace capitalism is even possible. How could we ever overthrow the capitalist class? In reality, the world has seen *lots* of successful revolutions. The problem is not—having a revolution and taking over. The real problem is *what happens next?* Are you able to nail down a classless society? To create a sustained egalitarian social order. The prognosis is not looking particularly good as far as that's concerned. A recent depressing example is Venezuela. They got the popular support and the necessary armed force. But the ambitious project of utopian social change withered away. With some version of class society maintained. With most of the population disillusioned and dragging their feet.[1] The other chapters of this book have more to say about those issues. For now, I am concentrating on the process of *achieving* a transition to the gift economy.

There are two broad types of transition that we might consider. The one that seems most obvious is transition by revolution. The institutions of the capitalist economy are dramatically abolished and replaced with the institutions of the gift economy. The second broad type is a transition by accretion. There is a *symbolic continuity* with aspects of the existing capitalist economy and a *real structural break*. Some symbols of the capitalist economy still seem to operate. Even money and the market. But the real content, the capitalist content, has been eviscerated. This is a very tricky argument. I'm not entirely convinced this pathway could work. But it's worth explaining because it informs the way a lot of people think.

Prefiguring projects

I want to introduce some concepts that are useful in conceiving a transition to the gift economy. The idea of 'prefiguring' is that you start to build institutions and practices *now* that create examples for a post-capitalist *future*. This prefiguring shows what you want to do, a propaganda exercise. It practices and deepens the culture on which a future society will depend. It also helps those who are participating to live better *now*. To escape from aspects of the market economy. I am going to talk about two kinds of prefiguring institutions. I will call the first 'hybrids of the gift economy and capitalism' because they include aspects of the market economy as well as features of a future gift economy. I will talk of the second prefiguring institutions as 'autonomous zones'—broadening out a concept drawn from Hakim Bey, an anarchist writer from the nineties.[2]

Hybrids of the gift economy and capitalism

A hybrid depends in various ways on the market economy. For example, it could use money, offer goods or services on the market, or pay wages. To give an example, we could consider a local community NGO operating in the global South. It's a community-controlled sustainable agriculture organization. The people of local villages have organised small face to face democratic assemblies. These assemblies elect representatives to direct their NGO and appoint professional staff. The NGO gets international donations and pays the staff. It uses this money to buy the equipment they need. For example, building materials, a car to visit local communities, laptops, phone services. Much of this works within the market economy—wage labour for the professional staff, ownership of the community centre as property, the purchase of commodities, the wage labour of the donors from the rich countries.

The other aspect of any hybrid is an ethical practice that departs from the usual operation of a capitalist firm. Some aspect of the gift economy. Looking after people or the planet. Participatory democratic control. The gift rather than market exchange. For example, the NGO in the global South facilitates community control through assemblies of local village communities. These organize applications to the NGO for assistance, and elect community representatives to the NGO board. The NGO enables workers' control through planning meetings that include the professional workers and community representatives. Just like what we would expect in a gift economy. The aim is not to make a profit, like a capitalist firm. Instead, the organisation aims to help local villagers to achieve food security. Caring for people. To make sure this is achieved through a sustainable agriculture. Caring for the planet. These aims are shared by the donors from the rich countries. They are spending their money to express their affection and solidarity. An ethical practice consistent with the gift economy. The NGO's strategies for food security are also departures from the market economy. Household food provision. Access to food without payment. For those who are familiar with writing on pre-figuring it may seem that my concept of hybrids equates closely to the proposals of Gibson-

Graham for the 'community economy' or Olin Wright for 'real utopias'.[3] How what I am talking about differs from their proposals will become clear in this and other chapters.

As the next few chapters will show, hybrids come in a great variety of forms. One more example. A community supported agriculture farm run by a workers' cooperative. The aim is to run a successful market enterprise and to get a wage income. But along with this, they want to relieve the alienation of wage labour. Setting up a cooperative where they make decisions, without a boss creaming off the profits. To get a market income but also to look after the environment. Using agroecology and permaculture, growing food sustainably. Selling food locally and reducing food miles. Their customers have similar mixed aims. To buy good food at reasonable prices. To buy food that has been grown sustainably and produced locally.[4]

Initiatives supported by governments can also be hybrids. The tax system takes a portion of the social product. In the best-case scenario, citizens vote to decide how to allocate their taxes. Initiatives can be directed to propping up the market system. But also, to undermining it. Or at least to supplementing the market in ways that could fit with a gift economy. Government support for an NGO through a grant. Allowing an organisation to survive despite market pressures. The most common example being funding for community arts. Government intervention to reduce environmental damage. Acts against air pollution. Subsidies for renewable energy. Payments to adopt organic agriculture. Payments for wildlife refuges. Sewerage. Public ownership of parks, railways, health systems. Funding for community services run by not-for-profit NGOs.

None of these government initiatives are an unmixed blessing. The use of money and wage labour to make the initiative happen. A paid police force protecting public assets. Attempts to make these hybrids a facsimile of a capitalist firm. Wage labour for government workers. Many of these initiatives are necessary to maintain the conditions for profitable business. Taxing citizens where the market will not go. Public education, roads, and bridges. At the same time, this is a shifting terrain. Governments can end up promoting the ethical values and practices of a gift economy. These initiatives point to an alternative economy. Or at least they can be seen in that light.

Taken in their many forms, hybrids enable a practice that survives capitalism but also alleviates it. While one or two hybrids make little difference to the capitalist regime, a multiplicity can undermine it.

Autonomous zones

Another prefiguring strategy is to set up organisations that attempt to *avoid* participation in the market and the state. To carve off a bit of economic life outside of the market, to escape state control. Hakim Bey (aka Peter Lamborn Wilson) talks about two kinds of situations like this—the 'temporary autonomous' zone and 'immediatism'.[5]

As Hakim Bey describes it, a 'temporary autonomous zone' (TAZ) occurs when a participatory egalitarian polity seizes a part of a state's territory. His term 'temporary' suggests there is no intention to hold this territory forever. Yet some of the best examples are rebellions which the state eventually defeated. For my purposes the term 'temporary' is misleading. Many of these uprisings and seizures aimed at a long-term transformation of society. For example, the Hungarian uprising of 1956 against the Soviets. The Rojava insurgency of the Kurds more recently. In several cases, the autonomous zone still carries on to the present day and may persist well beyond anything remotely temporary. The Zapatistas that I will consider in the next chapter are the key example.

In *Escape from the Nineteenth Century*, Wilson concentrates on examples that had less ambition to be permanent. Like the coup d'etat inspired by Nietzsche in Cumantsa, a town in Roumania in 1918. Setting up an autonomous government that lasted several years. Elias, one of the leaders of the insurgency wrote that any ordered society that has been established will have outside limits, where 'heroic tramps' will wander, 'who cannot live without planning ever new and dreadful outbursts of rebellion'.[6]

Wilson emphasizes such temporary polities to counter what he sees as a problem with the left. The left treats any revolution that is defeated, or succumbs to its own inadequacies, as a failure. We have failed to get rid of class society. Such an attitude is depressing. We should be counting our chickens. What has been achieved? What did participants get out of the rebellion? I am sympathetic to this critique. However, for the purposes of understanding prefiguring alternatives a more open-ended approach is most useful. As Hakim Bey himself acknowledged in a reflection on the concept of 'temporary' autonomous zones. Let us look at a variety of 'autonomous zones'[7] and call them that regardless of their long or short-term ambitions and their durations.

The Hungarian uprising of 1956 against the Soviets is a good example of such an autonomous zone. Huge popular demonstrations demanding workers' control started the uprising against the Soviet puppet government of Hungary. As people assembled at the radio station, police fired on the crowd. Workers in the arms factories distributed weapons. Most police and the army surrendered to the crowds. They destroyed a statue of Stalin. A revolutionary council of students and workers formed and remained in session. The Soviet Union sent tanks to crush the rebellion and fighting in the streets broke out. Some Russian tanks joined the uprising. Workers occupied their workplaces and formed councils. They demanded workers' management. Delegates linked up to form Revolutionary Councils. White collar workers, peasants and soldiers joined industrial workers. Peasants supplied the rebels with food. They redistributed the land of state-owned collectives or deposed their managers. A council of free trade unions demanded workers' management, free elections, and wage increases. A general strike paralysed all but essential services. In a second assault, the Soviets sent 5,000 tanks and pulverised the working-class heartlands of Hungarian cities. Up to 50,000 Hungarians died and the Stalinist bureaucracy was restored.[8]

One could see the early success of the Spanish anarchist movement in the revolution of 1936 as starting a TAZ. An anarchist federation of trade unions and popular assemblies took over Catalonia, a province of Spain.[9] More recently the Zapatista insurgency has taken over most of the Chiapas province of Mexico, starting in 1994. Running an alternative government and economy.[10] An uprising in southern Albania in 1997 began as a revolt against government corruption. The state ceased to operate. Decisions were taken by popular assemblies in the towns. Armed gangs defended the uprising. Eventually the UN stepped in to restore state control.[11]

A more localized and peaceful example is the Zone à Défendre (de Notre Dame des Landes) in France. Protestors occupied the area designated for a new airport, taking over 1650 hectares in 2007. They set up a local economy without money. Farmers whose land was to be taken for the airport squatted on their farms and were joined by activists. Together, they resisted the destruction of farm buildings and squatting constructions. A demonstration attended by 40,000 repelled the police. The occupiers constructed a small village with a community bar, a kitchen, a blacksmith workshop and residential quarters. They started up joint projects such as a community bakery and community gardens. In 2018, the French president shelved the plans for an airport. Attempts were made to remove the squatters, including police attacks with tear gas and stun grenades. Negotiations with authorities followed a stalemate. Many projects initiated in the occupation have sought legal recognition.[12] An exemplar of the *temporary* autonomous zone, as its *autonomy* was only maintained for thirteen years.

Another essay by Hakim Bey explains a similar concept, 'immediatism'.[13] The idea of immediatism is that people come together as a voluntary club, engaging in some common project— not mediated by money or by media. It could be a sewing bee making patchwork quilts. Or a voluntary working bee, set up to help a household with their food gardening – what is referred to as a 'permablitz'. The 'good karma' network that invites people to go online to find out how they might help someone in the network.[14] Organisations such as this are in fact quite common. They are rarely seen as 'political' or as prefiguring a new system.

I think it is fair to use the term 'autonomous zone' for both these concepts. The scale is the only difference. Autonomous zones suggest a whole territory reconfigured while immediatism carves off a bit of social space in the interstices. In either case, initiatives like this are a 'propaganda of the deed', giving people a glimpse of what a utopia might look like.[15]

Prefiguring initiatives are conceived differently within the two strategies for transition. Within the strategy of revolution, these prefiguring institutions prepare for the revolution. In the strategy of accretion, prefiguring institutions proliferate and link up. Without any decisive revolutionary break, they grow to constitute a post capitalist gift economy.

Transition by revolution

What I define as a transition by revolution does not have to be violent or illegal, though of course it could be both. The main thing is the relatively sudden switch from the capitalist economy to the gift economy. Parliament could even authorize a revolution. You get majority support for the Greens parties in several representative democracies. They come to power and finally work out that the market economy is the central problem. They invite people to take over their workplaces. To begin making compacts to run the economy, leaving money out of the picture. It would still be a revolution—a dramatic and decisive break. The Greens party would be saying, 'Come on, we are going to make a complete break and money will mean nothing. You might as well put it in your bottom drawer.'

Alternatively, a revolution could take the form which is more familiar. Massive assemblies on the streets in every urban centre. It becomes obvious that the status quo cannot continue. The police and the army refuse to follow orders. The powers that be negotiate a surrender.

If we are talking about a transition to a gift economy the following days might go like this.

Let us call this day after the revolution, day two. On day two, most employed people should come to work as they usually do, in their usual jobs. When they get to work, they form a committee. A democratic mini assembly of all the people they usually work with.

Units of twenty people. If the workplace is a large concern, they would also elect representatives to an assembly of the whole firm.

At this point these assemblies are faced by a key question. Is what we usually do in our work useful? Like growing wheat or repairing a bus. Or at least necessary right now to meet immediate needs. Like stacking a supermarket shelf. Or is it a task that has no relevance after the revolution? Like working in a bank or an advertising agency.

The aim would be for people to continue the useful parts of their work, at least in the short run. So as not to disrupt things too much. This would apply even in workplaces where the work was contributing to damage but was necessary to maintain services in the short run. For example, if you were repairing petrol cars, you might go on doing that. While voluntary teams of transport workers set up something more sustainable.

If your team decided their work was not necessary, they could dissolve their firm. They would volunteer to join another collective. Supplying workers to more useful projects. Teams of workers leaving these defunct industries would provide a floating labour force—relieving the pressure on those who are now overworked. For example, nurses. Or they would supply a work force for new projects to retrofit the economy. To work out where and how to volunteer, the floating workers would take advice from media organisations. The role of media collectives would be to expose gaps that needed filling. They would take advice from peak bodies for hospitals, schools, agriculture, housing, public transport. Communicating that information to the public at large.

A first task for these working collectives would be to set up arrangements to resource supplies and distribute their production. Today, administrators who handle these relationships contract supply and distribution through market arrangements. These monetary contracts would be replaced by negotiated agreements. The farmer would negotiate with the transport company, the transport company with the packing company, the packing company with the supermarket, the supermarket with the local community. In this transition, the more useful parts of the existing market economy would be maintained on a voluntary basis. Contracts would become compacts.

A lot of people who are working now are doing jobs that may be useful, but they are not the jobs they would prefer. To avoid disruption, they could stay in their jobs and train a new volunteer to take over. Any job that was hated by all and sundry could be eliminated or rostered—if the work was really necessary. If you had a job grinding stone bench tops, you would just stop doing that. No one would replace you. If your job was taking out the rubbish 24/7, you might be rostered on to continue, but only once a week. With other workers also doing their share.

This is about a first stage of implementing the gift economy. How we might do this without causing shortages, queues and worse.[16] In the longer term, we would see bodies set up to make deeper changes. For example, very large urban centres are unsustainable. If you bring foods to the city from long distances, the energy demands for transport become hard to manage with renewables. As well, we are running out of phosphates for agricultural fertilizers, sourced by mining phosphate deposits. It makes more sense to source phosphates from manure. But transporting human manure from urban areas to distant agricultural sites is energy intensive. Localising agriculture is the long-term solution. We could have rural towns linked by rail, with trains powered by renewables. Each town would be surrounded by a local farming zone, with donkey carts bringing produce into the town.[17] To create a reconstruction of urban life on this model would take time. Teams of builders could offer urbanites the opportunity to demolish their city houses and move to the country. The urbanites themselves could assist with the building work under the guidance of skilled trade workers. Other teams would be building new rail lines, to link rural towns and replace the long-distance road system.

In the context of settler colonial countries like Australia, Canada or the United States, this transition would have to be worked out in consultation with the Indigenous people. The people whose land has been stolen.

Against a staged transition

So far, I have been explaining how a revolutionary transition might work. I need to say why I have outlined *that* scenario and not something more gradual. The way I put it, the non-monetary economy begins on day two. This may seem a bit drastic. Why not continue to use money to smooth the transition? Paying for an environmental retrofit. Paying social welfare to those who are out of a job. Making sure people can put food on their table. Paying the armed forces to consolidate the revolution.

My view is that going for a staged transition after the revolution is a mistake. To explain this, I will look at two case studies. The Russian revolution of 1917 and the Spanish revolution of 1936. Neither of these revolutions aimed at a non-monetary gift economy. But they certainly aimed at a classless society. With ordinary people taking control of politics and the economy. Their history can help us to understand what can go wrong.

Revolutions generally begin with an effervescent popular participation. Hannah Arendt in *On Revolution* makes the point that in 'every genuine revolution' throughout the nineteenth and twentieth centuries, 'spontaneous organs of the people' appeared to enable participatory control of public affairs. Sticking to European examples, she mentions the sociétiés révolutionnaires of the Paris commune in 1870, the Soviets of the Russian revolutions of 1905 and 1917, the räte of the German uprising of 1918-1919, the councils of the Hungarian rebellion of 1956. These organisations sprang up outside of any revolutionary party and were entirely unexpected. For example, in Hungary 1956:

> The most disparate kinds of councils ... neighbourhood councils that emerged in all residential districts, so-called revolutionary councils that grew out of fighting together in the streets, councils of writers and artists, born in the coffee houses of Budapest, students' and youth councils at the universities, workers' councils in the factories, councils in the army, among civil servants, and so on.[18]

As Arendt notes, none of these exciting takeovers lasted to create a truly participatory democracy. To show what can happen next, I will consider my two key examples.

The Russian Revolution[19]

The Russian revolution commenced in February of 1917. Initially the Mensheviks were in government. Peasants took control of large estates and big commercial farms. Workers' committees started to take over industrial workplaces. The factory committees sometimes came to agreements with the owners, sharing power. In other cases, workers' committees took complete managerial control, expropriating the owners. Some owners closed their factories to prevent a workers' committee taking over. In October of 1917 a second revolutionary surge saw the Bolshevik party (the Communist party) take government. Initially they supported the factory committees as an expropriation of the capitalist class. Even in nationalized industries, they recognized them as legitimate bodies of oversight. The workers' committees set up congresses to coordinate their actions nationally.

As the factory committees gained more and more purchase, the Bolshevik leadership worried that these committees were hindering management by the state—the proper organ of workers' power. They were worried that independent market-based cooperatives would put their *own* interests first. Before the interests of the people. The party managed to get support from the Trade Unions—organisations that had pre-dated the revolution. Through a set of party resolutions and government decrees, the Bolsheviks established the unions as the legitimate organizers of 'workers' control'. In the trade union congresses, representatives of the workers' committees were a minority, Bolshevik loyalists the majority. Gradually, the party subordinated the trade unions to 'Vesenka', the government department organizing the economy. Where the membership had voted in someone who supported workers' power, the party replaced them with party loyalists.

Under the control of Vesenka, committees to run industry included a minority of worker representatives (mainly from the trade unions) with a majority of government members and technical experts. During the civil war, the party nationalized most industry. The plan of industrial production was to come from above. The party implemented 'one man management.' Leaving the workers' committees and the trade unions to discipline the workers and encourage commitment. These developments were contested by a faction of the party known as the 'Workers' Opposition'. The leaders of the party negotiated deals that would give this left faction some tokens of acknowledgement—while maintaining their own policies. Later they expelled them and closed their newspapers.

A creeping state control. The end of the participatory democracy. But what enabled the Bolshevik state to do this? The workers controlled the factories after the revolution. Why did they put up with this?

Before the revolution, these factories sold what they produced on the market. The aim of the workers' committees was to take over and run these plants as cooperatives. Selling goods to pay wages. However, this was quite difficult in the circumstances. The disruptions of the revolution, war with Germany and the civil war meant that firms often shut down. Preventing other factories from depending on what they produced. Later the capitalist powers banned exports to Russian industry, closing more factories. Even if a factory was producing and getting sales, it was difficult for their workers to buy food. The middle peasants who had gained land during the revolution were reluctant to sell their crops. They were not interested in the low prices being offered by the government. They hoarded grain or sowed less acreage. There was little point in growing and selling grain when they could buy nothing from a damaged industrial sector. Industrial workers jumped ship—going back to the country, where they had more chance of getting a meal.

Those who remained ended up depending on food supplied by the government. There was a system of food ration cards. The government deprived workers' committee activists of their ration cards. When the government nationalized most industry, they used monetary incentives to impose their control. Through piece work payment and bonuses.

Paying more to those who produced more. The trade unions excluded oppositional elements. Ultimately, government command was backed by armed force. The Bolsheviks were supplying the armed forces with food requisitioned from the peasants. It was armed bands, licenced by the party, that seized these supplies. It was the army under Trotsky that destroyed workers' democracy in the port of Kronstadt.

At the time, the theory of workers' management promoted by the anarcho-syndicalist minority was this. Workers would occupy nationalized firms and private enterprises. They would run them as cooperatives—selling goods on the market. To coordinate the economy, these autonomous committees would federate and make resolutions on prices, wages, and production. A democratic process. This approach was implicit in the actions of the workers' committees at the time. Recent anarchist writers also endorse it. For example, Maurice Brinton, writing in 1970 for the Solidarity group in the UK. In that analysis, this solution was stymied by the Bolshevik party.[20]

My take on this. The market system was the framework for the revival of class society under new managers. The people occupy the factories and farms. The factory workers envisage a classless society based in market cooperatives. In the aftermath of the revolution this dream cannot be realized. The market fails. The industrial workers cannot produce goods, sell them, and buy food. The state steps into the gap. It coerces a surplus from the peasants. Replacing peasant self-government with state power. It uses the food surplus to provision the army and paramilitary gangs. Control of food gives the state immense leverage with the urban workers. Step by step the state takes over the factories. A new ruling class replaces the old one. Throughout all this, monetary controls and direct coercion combine. For example, food is forcibly *requisitioned* from the peasants at a price below market prices. A kind of tax. Workers in nationalized industries get ration cards but also wages. The soldiers get a wage and can buy the food the state has requisitioned.

From the perspective of the gift economy, what was absent was any plan to run the economy *without money*. Making deals between factory workers and peasant farmers—exchanging produce by making agreements to supply and receive.

The Spanish Revolution

In Spain the revolution of 1936 followed the election of a leftist government. Local occupations accompanied the election and challenged the capitalist class. In response, Franco organized an army coup against the democratic government. While the Fascists took over some parts of Spain, the democratic government held out in other areas. Seizing their opportunity, the anarchist organisations and the local people occupied industries and took over farming land in much of Spain. They expropriated landlords and business owners. Replacing state authority with localized self-management. The whole province of Catalonia fell to this anarchist push. In the first days, local committees distributed essential supplies free of charge. In the longer term a patchwork of different arrangements organized economic life.[21]

In some rural areas, collectives ran farms and operated a local gift economy. They allocated food according to need. They sold the surplus production, using the money to pay for goods from outside the community. Also distributed in these communities without charge—according to need. In other areas, a local money was devised. In the urban areas, workers occupied government departments and took over many private firms. These co-operatives paid wages, charging customers, or getting government funding. For example, before the uprising there were 1,100 hairdressing salons in Barcelona. The assistants were on very low wages, and shops were not well maintained. The workers demanded a 40-hour week and a 15% pay rise. Many shops would not have been able to afford to meet these goals. So, all shops joined the union. They cut the number of shops to 235 and re-vamped them. All workers were paid the same, with wages increased by 40%. A collectivisation via the umbrella anarchist union.[22]

Murray Bookchin argues that the leadership of the anarchist federation/trade union (CNT/FAI) started to dominate these urban collectives.

Initially, nearly the entire economy in CNT/FAI areas had been taken over by committees elected from among the workers and were loosely coordinated by higher union committees. As time went on, this system was increasingly tightened. The higher committee began to pre-empt the initiative of the lower, although their decisions still had to be ratified by the workers of the facilities involved. The effect of this process was to centralize the economy of CNT/FAI areas in the hands of the union.[23]

After the participation of anarchist leaders in the Catalonia and Madrid governments, larger firms in Catalonia were 'socialized'. An elected committee appointed a manager. That manager was supervised by a government controller. Real decision-making power fell to the government. Factory councils had little influence. The 'Collectivisation Decree' of October 1936 established a 'General Council for Industry' with wide powers.

> Formulating a general program of work for the industry, orientating the Council of Enterprises in its tasks ... the regulation of total output in the industry, and of internal and foreign markets; to propose changes in methods of production; to negotiate banking and credit facilities.[24]

Tendencies in the Spanish anarchist movement had prefigured these developments. Santillan had argued for a central planning authority to coordinate production.[25] With *input* from the anarchist trade unions.

This centralisation was enabled by the economic context. The anarchist leadership had entered a coalition government with the Soviet backed communists and the liberals. The central Madrid government controlled the gold reserves. Given the hostility to the revolution, Spanish factories had to buy supplies from other countries with gold. The now 'nationalized' industries were forced to accept government control to get access. A government dominated by Soviet backed communists deprived the anarchist collectives of resources.[26] In the 'May Days' of 1937, the central government fought the anarchists in Catalonia, taking over the industries that had been occupied by workers. The anarchist armed wing was drafted into a Republican army. Organized in typical military fashion—a chain of command.[27] Franco defeated the Republic, a dictatorship lasting for 36 years.

This was a complex situation. Looking at its second stage, after the May days. The government nationalizes the workplaces and ends workers' control. In the nationalized industries, the government controls workers through their control of the money supply. This nationalisation followed the capture of the Republican government by Soviet agents—by Stalin. The Republican police and army defeat the anarchists in Catalonia.

But more interesting is the first stage of this process. According to Bookchin, it was the CNT/FAI—the national anarchist union and federation—that first undermined the participatory democracy of the revolution. The story of the hairdressers may give us some clues. To undo the chaos and inequity of capitalist hairdressing, the anarchist union steps in. Equalizing wages and conditions across all the barber shops. This move makes sense in the circumstances. Yet, it prevents hairdressing cooperatives from operating as independent firms in competition. Turning hairdressing into a facsimile of a government department. A bureaucratic elite takes control. Worker's control becomes workers' consultation—as the union makes rules for every hairdressing salon. The dream of independent market cooperatives controlled by their workers vanishes. Bureaucratic coordination and equalization replace market competition.

The perils of a monetary transition

The long-term failure of all these inspiring revolutionary moments is at least partly down to their failure to abolish money. A participatory takeover of the means of production cannot be achieved within a monetary economy. Money provides an opportunity for the state and social class to re-establish. It stalls any attempt at participatory governance.

The gift economy and the state

For the sake of a simple narrative let us assume that in representative democracies parliament (or some version of that) is the basic organ of the state. Parliament makes laws and the police enforce them. If necessary, the army may be called in. The police and the army must do what parliament tells them to do. Because they're in the police force or the army *as a job*. If they do not do what parliament says, then they'll lose their job. Why do they need a job? The same reason as anyone else. To get money. Why do they need to get money? To get access to the goods and services they need to run their lives.

After the gift economy revolution. People are being supplied by gifts. The workers in the various collectives are making their own decisions about where to distribute their gifts. You do not need a 'job'—because you do not need money. So, there is no body of people, needing a job. Keen to sign up to join the police force or the army. Ready to take orders and do what they are told. Regardless of whether they agree with those orders or not. Consequently, parliament can no longer operate *as a state*. It cannot maintain a monopoly of armed force, instructing it's armed wing to carry out *its orders*.

All states depend on alienated labour. People do not have ownership of the means of production and must obey orders in their working lives—to get access to goods and services. The army and the police are just examples of the condition of *every* member of the subordinated classes in a class society. If you get rid of alienated labour, you get rid of the state. A body that can centrally control the use of force and rule a whole society.

This is the basic argument to show why a 'state' could never exist in a gift economy. This argument has implications for parliament, and implications for the use of armed force.

So, let's look at it first in relation to parliament.

The state vanishes

A first alternative is that the whole operation of government could vanish and be replaced by networked decision making. There's no need for the political process. There's just networked agreements and compacts. Normally these agreements are worked out between the producer collectives and the communities involved. However, if something affects lots of different communities, they would arrange a joint meeting. A temporary talking shop. These could be international if the issue warranted that.

Parliament but not as we know it

A second alternative could be that parliament and some sort of representative democracy still happens. There are voluntary clubs charged by the community with organising elections. The members are supplied with their daily needs by gifts, just like everybody else. They organize voting, count votes, and send elected representatives to parliament. Likewise supplied by gifts, just like everyone else. Most people vote, seeing it as a civic duty. So, how do the votes of parliament count in a gift economy? Ultimately, what parliament decides is just advice. There's no coercive power in it. It represents what it is—the viewpoint of a majority of representatives elected by the community. Just that. Economic units may take that advice on board, or they might not. In the end, they are still in charge of their own affairs.

So, a voluntary network, an NGO, replaces the state. We can't call it 'a state.' It cannot enforce decisions with a paid police force or army. Nevertheless, it is an important advisory body. Many people get really worried by the idea that a gift economy could not have a state. That everything would be out of control. For these people, this 'talking shop parliament' proposal may be attractive.

The use of armed force

Now let's look at the use of armed force to implement the social rules of a gift economy. As I have explained, it is unlikely that armed force completely vanishes. Voluntary enforcer clubs would protect the community when required. They would be like any other voluntary club of the gift economy. The community would provide them with gifts, exactly as for other citizens. Their role would be to assist local community organisations to deal with problems of violence. Their continued good standing would depend on community support. Currently, police and armies are paid by a central state and can act without the support of the local community. In the gift economy, enforcer clubs depend for their material well-being on the communities they represent. Like a martial arts club, with community supervision. Communities might decide to roster this function. Rotations of training followed by work in the community. The police and the armed forces would join the revolution—helping to set up community enforcement. Handing their weapons to local community bodies. Where the police force is a hated presence, sympathetic police would pull out of those suburbs, leaving the community to organize alternatives.[28]

Transition by accretion

The idea of a transition by accretion is that the move to post-capitalism does not happen through a revolution but through small gains within the capitalist economy. These small gains link up and eventually we end up with something that can no longer be described as 'capitalism'. I'm not totally convinced this can work, but it's important to talk about it.

The strategy of transition by accretion is an idea popularized by three authors from the social sciences. Eric Olin Wright (sociology) and Julie Katherine Gibson-Graham (human geography—in fact two authors).[29] They envisage the transition as a deepening and extension of 'non-capitalist' market entities. Ethical businesses, cooperatives, NGOs, and government-funded citizen initiatives. They see a post-capitalist economy as a *market economy* regulated by a democratic state. Wright talks about 'real utopias.' Institutions that manage to survive in current 'real' conditions but also point the way to a new system. He provides criteria for distinguishing 'real utopias' from standard capitalist firms. In a similar vein, Gibson-Graham talk about 'the community economy.' Community economy organisations are not capitalist because they are not run by owners who are exploiting their employees. They work ethically to care for people and the planet.

I do not find this marketized post-capitalist vision or this marketized transition scenario likely. If a substantial number of firms *did manage* to behave in these non-market ways, they would end the power of money and the market. I call these alternative market arrangements 'hybrids of the gift economy and capitalism'. Their aim is to care for people and the planet. To sidestep the market to enable this. If hybrids became widespread and linked up, they would *undermine* the market and the state. The same with autonomous zones—where the departure from the market is even more extreme. An avalanche of hybrids and autonomous zones would *destroy* the market and the state. For me, that is the most likely scenario for a transition by accretion.

So, *my version* of system change by accretion is a bit different from versions popular in the social sciences. We have a pre-revolutionary situation where more and more economic units are hybrids of the gift economy and capitalism. Autonomous zones also take over large parts of the economy. Community gardens, food donations, free bike repair workshops. Transition by accretion takes effect when this avalanche of hybrids and autonomous zones undermines the market. For example, if you're in a cooperative that is distributing products according to need, rather than ability to pay top dollar, you are undermining the logic of money. The discourse of buying cheap and selling dear. If this kind of behaviour becomes widespread, then money ceases to have much meaning. The strategy of transition through accretion is that this happens more and more. To the point where money becomes merely symbolic. The parties to an agreement hand over money to signal the finalisation of the deal. But the real deal is going on in the negotiating rooms, working out the compact to supply and receive. Owning money does not give you predictable access to the things other people are producing. So, the African village has only got $800. But they can still buy $2,000 worth of steel. Along with that, top-down state control becomes increasingly difficult. The state pays the police force and the army to implement their decisions. But now, with an avalanche of hybrids, these forces are also receiving gifts and negotiating compacts. Getting some of their income as goods and services, rather than money.

In this scenario, accretion builds up to a tipping point to system change. There's a cultural shift. Even *being* a capitalist, who's just using their money to make the most profit, becomes stigmatizing. Trendy capitalists talk a different logic. Owners taking their property rights too literally find no one will do business with them. Their buildings get taken over by squatters. There could be a symbolic continuity. Capitalists still appear to own their property, but the community and workers make all actual decisions. The 'owner' is a figurehead only. The same thing could happen with parliament. Becoming a talking shop that could not actually enforce anything.

While a transition by accretion like that is possible, I doubt whether it is *likely*. The *most likely* strategy to get rid of capitalism *in the end* is a revolution. Why do I say this? I can see hybrids and autonomous zones beginning to create an alternative economy. But as they do this, it becomes more and more apparent that the one percent, the capitalist class, owns very significant parts of the economy. For example, mining, steel making, the internet, international shipping, farming land. The most likely scenario is that a revolution (of some sort) would declare these resources public property and start using them as such.

Preconditions for a gift economy

Developments in civil society must prefigure the gift economy that will follow. Some of these will go back decades, or even centuries. Hybrids of the gift economy and capitalism, as well as autonomous zones, large and small. A dense network of local organisation just prior to the revolution. Giving just one example. The Bolivian uprising of 2003 depended on community initiatives that anticipated and enabled the insurrection.

> Closures of streets and highways, neighbourhood councils on every block, volunteer vigils on every corner summoned by megaphones, barricades piled with stones, wire, and tires, independent radio stations broadcasting day and night, people's guards to prevent looting of stores, and assemblies held in the streets, trade-union offices, and parish churches.[30]

The global conditions for a turn away from capitalism and class society lie in the failure of the promises that have held capitalism together. The promise of development for the global South. The promise of increasing affluence and more leisure for the global North. The promise of a peaceful life. Instead, neo-liberalism and globalisation have led to wage stagnation, growing inequality, and economic insecurity in the global North. The environmental crisis looms large, and people are blaming big business. The threat of disasters to come undermines the legitimacy of the current order. The promise of development in the global South is compromised by the everyday disasters of climate change. In every part of the globe the local elite threatens war. To secure limited supplies of dwindling fossil fuels. To supply what is needed for a transition to renewables—when there is not enough to go around. To divert people's attention from more pressing problems.

These conditions are ripe for a revolutionary transition. But the far right could well make use of this discontent to take over.[31] To de-rail this trajectory, the left needs a feasible and attractive alternative. The gift economy makes sense as that. Democratic socialists and radical reformists are certainly part of the current resistance to capitalism. Yet these perspectives are not gaining traction more broadly. Contributing to the malaise of despair that the far-right exploits. What I look forward to is a breakthrough. The gift economy suddenly starts to gain huge support from *outside* the current left.

Revolutions can happen that are completely unexpected and have *not* been preceded by a long-term mobilisation and ideological consciousness raising. The gift economy could readily come about like that. Disillusion boils over and the end of money and the market are a consequence. The minute enforcements that support these institutions vanish. The conditions of an uprising eliminate their everyday foundations. Looting, occupations, rent strikes, illegal distributions, citizen assemblies, workplace meetings. This activism is so widespread as to confound any attempt to re-constitute the state and money. Instead, this activism becomes organized as a non-monetary economy, with compacts organizing distribution, with voluntary collectives organizing production, with communities running their own affairs, and with meetings to iron out conflicts.

The conditions for a post-capitalist gift economy

More of a worry is that a transition to an egalitarian polity will fade away after initial successes. Class society could re-constitute itself, using an agricultural surplus to fund a ruling class and their army. Consider the fall of the western Roman Empire. The invading tribes were egalitarian bands led by chiefs—with councils of warriors advising them. The empire they defeated was a class society, with slaves, citizens, the army, the aristocrats, the bureaucracy, and the emperor. But within 500 years, a new form of class society had re-established itself—with peasants, knights, lords, clergy, and kings. A patchwork of lordships and small kingdoms. How depressing.

What is different about the current conjuncture that could give us optimism? Agriculture has been the material premise of class society from forever. That is unlikely to go away. But what else could be different?

1. A strong feminist movement—augmented through the revolutionary transition. Necessary to eliminate the key psychological prerequisites for class society. To maintain a gift economy *after the revolution* we need that movement to succeed, a work in progress. That depends on maintaining some version of our current medical knowledge and low fertility rate.

2. The changes in child raising discussed in chapter four. A cultural shift to a more generous and less anxious approach to life.

3. Digital communication. To allow empathetic identification with people who are physically remote and culturally different. To enable long chains of production linking different communities in technologically complex enterprises. Where partners across different communities engage as friends—with shared interests.

4. Our knowledge of environmental science, the sustainable production of basic needs. Drawing on indigenous knowledge and recent science. For example, agro-ecology and permaculture. Ways to grow food that can be adapted to a geographical niche. That can produce an abundance without ecological damage.

I do not find this list of conditions entirely reassuring.

Late capitalism seems highly likely to end in collapse. A severe collapse might easily wipe out most of the current technological infrastructure (the poles and wires, the satellites, the undersea cables, the devices, the hospitals, the medical machines and pharmacies). Even the knowledge that animates these technologies. We could hope for a quick transition before collapse has gone too far. Current workers would re-constitute their operations as gifts.

As for the feminist reconstruction of the household and the gift economy reconstruction of childcare. These are projects in process now. Hardly a fait accompli. We must hope that these cultural shifts become mainstream—as political support grows for system change to the gift economy.

The next set of chapters will consider the topic of transitions in more detail. I start out with a chapter on the Zapatisa autonomous zone. The chapter following that looks at anarchist and Marxist takes on the role of the state in a post-capitalist mode of production. How do these discussions relate to my proposed 'gift economy'. Finally, two chapters examine 'hybrids of the gift economy and capitalism'. What is their role in bringing about a transition to the gift economy? How do they function now as political strategies?

Endnotes

[1] Asa Cusack, *Venezuela, ALBA, and the Limits of Post-neoliberal Regionalism in Latin America and the Caribbean*, Palgrave, Macmillan, New York, 2019.

[2] Hakim Bey, 'T.A.Z.: The Temporary Autonomous Zone, Ontological Anarchy, Poetic Terrorism', in The Anarchist Library, 1985, viewed on 24 April 2023, https://theanarchistlibrary.org/library/hakim-bey-t-a-z-

the-temporaryautonomous-zone-ontological-anarchy-poetic-terrorism; Hakim Bey, Immediatism, AK Press, Chico, California, 1994.

3 Julie Katherine Gibson-Graham, *The End of Capitalism (As We Knew It)*, University of Minnesota Press, Minneapolis, 2006a; Julie Katherine Gibson-Graham, *Post-Capitalist Politics*, Minnesota, University of Minneapolis Press, 2006b; Eric Olin Wright, *Envisioning Real Utopias*, Verso, London, 2010.

4 Terry Leahy, *The Politics of Permaculture*, Pluto Press, London, 2022.

5 Peter Lamborn Wilson, *Escape from the Nineteenth Century and Other Essays*. Autonomedia, New York, 1998.

6 Wilson, *Escape*, p.167. For a similar take on anarchist strategy see the perspective of the Sydney 'Libertarian Push' of the fifties and sixties. Anne Coombs, *Sex and Anarchy, The Life and Death of the Sydney Push*, Ringwood Victoria, 1996.

7 Hakim Bey, *Permanent TAZs*, Talklingmail 5, Winter 1994, https://dreamtimevillage.org/articles/permanent_taz.html, Accessed 31 August 2025.

8 Andy Anderson, *Hungary 56*, Solidarity, London, 1964; Rod Jones, 'The Hungarian revolution 1956', in *The Anarchist Library*, 1984, viewed on 20 April 2023, https://theanarchistlibrary.org/library/rod-jones-the-hungarian-revolution-1956; Hannah Arendt, *On Revolution*, Faber and Faber, London, 1963; Syndicalist Workers' Federation, 'The Hungarian Workers' Revolution', in *The Anarchist Library*, 1957, viewed on 24 April 2023 https://theanarchistlibrary.org/library/syndicalist-workers-federation-the-hungarian-workers-revolution.

9 Vernon Richards, *Lessons of the Spanish Revolution – 1946-1939*, Freedom Press, London, 1972; Sam Dolgoff (ed), *The Anarchist Collectives: Workers' Self-Management in the Spanish Revolution*, Free Life Editions, New York, 1974; Gaston Leval, Collectives in the Spanish Revolution, Freedom Press, London, 1975.

10 Dylan Eldredge Fitzwater, *Autonomy Is in Our Hearts: Zapatista Autonomous Government through the Lens of the Tsotsil Language*, PM Press, Oakland CA, 2019.

[11] A Few Anarchists, 'Albania, laboratory of subversion', in *The Anarchist Library*, 1999, viewed on 24 April 2023, https://theanarchistlibrary.org/library/anon-albania-laboratory-of-subversion; Military Wiki, 'Albanian rebellion of 1997', in *Military Wiki*, 2023, viewed on 18 April 2023, https://military-history.fandom.com/wiki/Albanian_Rebellion_of_1997

[12] Camille, What is the ZAD? https://zadforever.blog/about/, viewed on 9 April 2025; Isabelle Fremeaux and Jay Jordan, *We Are 'Nature' Defending Itself: Entangling Art, Activism and Autonomous Zones*, Pluto Press, London, 2021.

[13] Bey, *Immediatism*.

[14] Myfan Jordan, *Women's Work in the Pandemic Economy: The Unbearable Hazard of Hierarchy*, Palgrave, London, 2023.

[15] Guérin, Daniel, *Anarchism: From Theory to Practice*, Monthly Review Press, London, 1970.

[16] For similar accounts of the post-revolutionary scenario see Michael Velli, *Manual for Revolutionary Leaders*, Black and Red, Detroit, 1974; Pëtr Kropotkin, *The Conquest of Bread*, theanarchistlibrary.org, 1892.

[17] Terry Leahy, 'A degrowth scenario: Can permaculture feed Melbourne', in *Food for Degrowth: Perspectives and Practices*, Anitra Nelson and Ferne Edwards (eds), Routledge, London, 2022, chapter 14.

[18] Hannah Arendt, *On Revolution*, Faber and Faber, London, 1960, p. 270

[19] This account draws heavily on these two sources. Maurice Brinton, *The Bolsheviks and Workers' Control: 1917-1921*, Solidarity, London, 1970; Edward Hallett Carr, *The Bolshevik Revolution 1917-1923*, Volume Two, W.W. Norton, New York, 1952. See also Ida Mett, *The Kronstadt Uprising 1921*, Black Rose Books, Montreal, 1971; Voline, *The Unknown Revolution: 1917-1921*, Black and Red/Solidarity, Michigan, Chicago, 1974.

[20] Brinton, *The Bolsheviks and Workers' Control*.

[21] Guérin, *Anarchism*.

[22] Souchy, 'Collectivisations in Catalonia', p. 94.

[23] Murray Bookchin, 'Introductory Essay' in ibid., 1974, p. xxxii.

[24] Richards, *Lessons of the Spanish*, p. 108-109.

25 Guérin, *Anarchism*, p. 124.

26 Anna Funder, *Wifedom: Mrs Orwell's Invisible Life*, Hamish Hamilton, London, 2023; Vernon Richards, *Lessons of the Spanish Revolution – 1946-1939*, Freedom Press, London, 1972.

27 Richard, *Lessons of the Spanish Revolution*.

28 Piepzna-Samarasinha, Leah Lakshmi and Ejeris Dixon (Eds), *Beyond Survival: Strategies and stories from the transformative justice movement*, AK Press, California, 2020.

29 Wright, *Real Utopias*. Julie and Katherine Gibson-Graham, *The End of Capitalism*; Julie and Katherine Gibson-Graham, *Post-Capitalist Politics*.

30 Adolfo Gilly, *Paths of Revolution*, Verso, London, 2022, pp.138-139.

31 Pam Nilan, *Young People and the Far Right*, Palgrave, Singapore, 2021.

Chapter 8
Zapatistas: A State that is not a State

A question often comes up when I am talking about a non-monetary post capitalism. Can you show us examples where this is already being done? A pure case, where people are running their whole lives and their communities without the use of money. Not like a hybrid where people use money and commodities to prefigure a gift economy. Not a small localized non-monetary organisation, like a community garden.

To find a whole region of the world organized in a non-monetary way is a big ask. Chiapas where the Zapatistas have been dominant is the closest case. It makes sense to explore how this has been working. It is not a fully realized example of a gift economy. Nevertheless, the ambition to do without money has been defining.

In relation to the discussion of the previous chapter I will call the region controlled by the Zapatistas an 'autonomous zone.'[1] A participatory egalitarian political system established by seizing a territory previously controlled by a state.

In 1988, an organization called the FLN, the national liberation forces, established a front in Chiapas. This was a Mexican leftist grouping inspired by Che Guevara. They aimed to be the cadres of a revolutionary vanguard, a Marxist-Leninist party. To inspire the Indigenous peasants of Chiapas to rise in revolution. Then the revolutionary state would take control of the means of production. There would be representative democracy, wage labour, state ownership. The democratic socialist platform.

Working in Chiapas as an underground movement, they gradually changed their approach. They renamed their organisation as EZLN

– Zapatista Army of National Liberation. They came to believe that organizing had to come from the grassroots. The revolutionary army had to take instructions from local people. In 1994 at the same time as Mexico was entering the free trade agreement with United States and Canada (NAFTA), they started a revolution to take control of Chiapas. The Mexican government sent in armed forces, acting with great brutality. In reaction huge demonstrations opposed this crackdown in the cities of Mexico. International support came from leftists in Europe and other countries of the global North. The armed struggle lasted for only 12 days and was concluded in a stalemate. So, the EZLN had used the armed struggle to mobilize nationally and internationally. To force the government to a truce.

In these early days the Zapatistas took over large tracts of land. Landed estates owned by absentee landlords or local magnates. These landlords had forced the indigenous peasants into a status close to slavery. Paying them minimal wages and tying them to the estate through debt peonage. The local people, with the support of the Zapatistas, appropriated these estates, taking more than 500,000 hectares. They set up an autonomous and parallel government.

To an extent the stalemate continues. More on the current situation at the end of this chapter. While the government does not send its 'army' to re-conquer the Zapatista territory, they secretly fund paramilitary gangs. These paramilitaries sometimes kidnap leaders of the Zapatista movement. Occasionally, they launch attacks on Zapatista towns, killing civilians. The EZLN responds with force. Usually, these confrontations end with negotiations brokered by sympathetic priests.[2] Within the Zapatista region, businesses and market relationships continue, alongside alternative economic structures. Not everyone living in these areas has joined the Zapatistas. Members are allocated tasks and must sign a declaration supporting Zapatista principles. The Zapatistas open their alternative government services to *all* community members, including those who are not members or supporters.

My detailed account is based heavily on *Autonomy in our Hearts*, by Dylan Eldridge Fitzwater.[3] Fitzwater is a United States visitor to

Chiapas. He is a fluent Spanish speaker. In Chiapas he attended a Zapatista school for foreign sympathizers. Where he was learning about the struggle of the Zapatistas while also learning the local Tsotsil language. His book argues that concepts from Indigenous languages are central to the Zapatista movement. The aim of the movement, as expressed in the local language, is the coming together of a big collective heart. Another slogan is that they want to make life good for everyone. The foundational text is the revolutionary law of the Zapatistas.

The aim of the Zapatistas is to maintain this egalitarian polity into the long-term future. The dramatization I will describe later makes this very clear. Puppets represent sperm and eggs, the future seeds of the Zapatista people of tomorrow. They reap the fruits of the revolution, continuing the work of their forebears today, their now dead ancestors. The Zapatistas also connect their autonomous zone back in time to their ancestors, the egalitarian horticulturalists who replaced the Mayan empire. Their connection to time goes as far back as that. The Zapatistas aim to become an ally of similar but diverse movements elsewhere. In the end a global revolution against capitalism. A 'pluriverse'—to use the word coined by post-development authors:[4]

The Zapatista region as a hybrid

The framework of 'hybrids of the gift economy and capitalism' explained in earlier chapters can work for the Zapatista region. Beginning with some of the market aspects.

The region is host to market relations linking organisations to Mexico as a whole and to the global market. People may have jobs in Mexican or international companies still operating in the Zapatista territory. Money authorized by the Mexican government is still local currency. The Mexican state still runs some towns and villages in the region. In other words, a mixed or parallel government and economy. The Zapatistas receive donations from international organisations that rely on the global market. For example, supplying dry composting toilets or medical equipment. The Zapatistas have also set up local market cooperatives to assist ordinary local people to get an income and provide needed services. For example, agricultural cooperatives, bus services, community banks, community shops. Attempts to establish market cooperatives lead to some typical problems of international aid work. Projects funded by donors may not be able to establish themselves as long term successful businesses.[5] To control the market the Zapatistas have set up commissions to set prices and wages. For example, to set equal wages for women.

The non-market aspects of the Zapatista region are equally significant. The ZPA has a de facto commitment to non-market non-monetary provision. Manifest at the local level as community food production and more extensively in non-monetary supply of goods and services for community purposes—hospitals, schools, the political system of the Zapatistas.

To start with, one family cannot own more than 50 hectares of farming land. So, there is no possibility of large capitalist estates, employing people at dirt wages. Owners of these small farms are feeding their own families through subsistence (non-market) agriculture. Village and town agricultural collectives are doing the same. Marketing a small surplus while most production goes to the collective. Some collectives operate on what used to be large estates. The former peons gather every day to go to work on the community plots. Allocating their harvest as equal shares at the end of the day.

Neighbourhood committees decide on requests for housing. Based on need. The market in real estate has gone. Zapatista hospitals deliver free services. Education in Zapatista schools is free, and not just to the children of Zapatistas. The Zapatistas have established radio stations to connect communities. They are rolling out the supply of electricity to communities that are not connected.

A very significant innovation is that the Zapatista communities do not pay their governing authorities, their democratically elected representatives, a wage. They are paid in kind directly. Communities volunteer gifts to make it possible for the elected representatives to suspend their work at home, while they are in office.

As an autonomous zone

These intensive non-monetary aspects of their economy and authority structures are sufficient to nominate this region as an 'autonomous zone' and not merely a hybrid of the gift economy and capitalism. Though it is important to keep both these aspects in mind.

Dylan Eldridge Fitzwater spent a lot of time in one of the local communities. He describes the pattern of work and subsistence.

> Every day I was there all the men, women and children went together to work in their fields, with all tasks being shared equally by men and women. In the kitchen, everyone also worked together, with men and women both participating in making the meal. By far the most important source of resources in a Zapatista community is that community's own trabajos colectivos [workers' cooperatives].

For example, in the community where Fitzwater was staying, there was a community maize field of twelve hectares. Workers from each municipality were rostered on to work on this field. To provide food for the workers at the Zapatista hospital. They sold their surplus to fund other collective projects.

Before we look at the structure of governing authority in the Zapatista territory, it is useful to consider the way the Zapatistas deal with some typical problems.

Dealing with conflict—an example

One is the tension between wealthy and poorer regions of their territory. A frequent objection to a stateless post-capitalism is that inequalities between groups would magnify—without a democratic state allocating resources fairly. For example, sub-Saharan Africa versus Europe. The Appalachians versus New York. The Zapatistas face a problem of exactly this type. Their region can be divided into the highlands and the lowlands. The people living in the highlands do not have a lot of fertile agricultural land. In the period before the Zapatista uprising, they would supply migrant labour to landed estates in the lowlands. Following the Zapatista rebellion these large estates have been taken over by people from the lowlands. The lowland communities now use this land for their subsistence, and for cash-crops. With less employment and more poverty for highland people.

The first initiative of the Zapatistas was to encourage highlands people to migrate and take over some lowland estates. This initiative was not successful. The highland people were unwilling to stay in the lowlands. They would return to their highland villages and to poverty and malnutrition. The next initiative was to market maize to the highlands at a low subsidized price. This was also patchy in its effects. The lowlands farmers were selling only the worst of the maize crop to the highlands communities—the ears of corn that had gone mouldy. So, the Zapatistas intervened to try to remedy this. At the present time, this is a work in progress.

No central body attempted to solve this problem with a top-down decree, imposing a 'fair' solution. Instead, there were ongoing negotiations between autonomous Zapatista authorities—elected in their different districts. It was up to these bodies to come to an agreement on how to move ahead. The reader may take these events as a failure to solve a real problem. From the Zapatista perspective, all parties retained control of their own productive efforts.

Patriarchy and the Zapatistas

The Zapatistas are committed to gender equality. As argued in earlier chapters, it is unlikely that a classless society can be maintained without this. The formal commitment to gender equality is an element in the Zapatista revolutionary law. Aspects of traditional patriarchy are illegal within this constitution. Women are not to be forced into marriage. They have the right to decide how many children they want. They are to be protected from assault and sexual violence. They have a right to a just salary and to education. Zapatista members must abstain from alcohol. Men spend can spend their cash income on alcohol, worsening family poverty. Domestic violence and alcohol abuse go together. The Zapatistas attempt to forestall these problems. The revolutionary law is foundational. To sign up to become a Zapatista is to agree to these principles.

The Zapatistas stipulate quotas for women in governing authorities. Fifty per cent for every elected body. As Fitzwater notes, this is rarely implemented fully. The figure is usually closer to 30%. Women are often reluctant. They may not have enough time, given their domestic responsibilities. Their husbands may not support them.

These measures, and the problems in implementing them, relate to local culture. The power of men in families. The division of labour in the home. Men's better access to the cash economy. Grounded in traditional land ownership—passing land from father to son. The Zapatistas have proposed to change this inheritance framework, but these measures have not been passed by their governing bodies.

The Zapatistas have supplemented their more legislative interventions with economic support. To set up women's cooperatives. For example, weaving, embroidery, sewing, providing food at parties, agricultural collectives to grow cash crops. Fitzwater found that local women often despaired of changing the division of labour with their husbands. But they were committed to bringing their sons up to do an equal share of the housework.

Summarizing we can say that the demolition of patriarchy is ongoing. The Zapatistas and the people of their region have made some important inroads. This is a complex scenario. To become a Zapatista member, you must sign a set of principles that includes aspects of gender equality. Yet it would be a mistake to think of these as 'laws' to be implemented by a Zapatista state. The governing bodies of the Zapatista region are nested autonomous entities in charge of their own affairs. The implementation of these general principles relies on these autonomous bodies. A general principle can require fifty per cent of governing bodies to be women—while in practice there are closer to 30 per cent.

Zapatista justice

The system of justice operating in the Zapatista territories embodies local participatory control. An abolitionist paradigm case to a certain extent[6]. Recent reports note that a 'community safety commission' may intervene to imprison people who interfere with community processes—for a short time. One of the dramatizations presented at a recent gathering told of this incident. Two men got drunk in the council offices and were rude to the women who were there. The community safety commission were called. They arrived and put them into prison—till they calmed down and apologized.

In more serious cases, justice is via a system of community mediation, organized by elected governing authorities. The aim is to find a solution and get both parties to agree. For example, reparations to injured parties and their families and communities. That can be through a payment or work duties. However, to complicate this picture, the EZLN, the Zapatista army, uses force when necessary to secure the territory. When paramilitary thug squads attack, the EZLN responds with force. While that does not make them a police force, their function is certainly to police the territory. To respond to violence with violence. The paramilitary forces are treated as 'bandits' infringing on the rights of the community. The EZLN also negotiates truces with the paramilitary forces, brokered by local church mediators.[7]

The Zapatista army

Let us now look at the EZLN and consider whether it operates as the armed wing of a Zapatista state. Giving the state a monopoly of legitimate force. Weber's classic definition of a 'state'.[8] This is not an easy question to answer. The Zapatista occupation came out of an armed struggle. The Mexican state negotiated a truce because the EZLN was a credible military force. The Zapatista regime depends on their army. Yet the Zapatistas do not intend their army to become the instrument of a centralized Zapatista state—ruling over the population. Instead, their role is making it possible for the people to govern themselves. To clear the space so that other armed bodies do not take over. The EZLN responds to *requests* for action coming from the local elected bodies. For example, in 2021, a paramilitary thug gang kidnapped local Zapatista leaders. The EZLN 'took the necessary steps to free those who were kidnapped and to detain and sanction those who committed the crime'. In time a truce was negotiated with the support of parish priests.[9]

At the same time, the EZLN acts *internally* much the same as armies controlled by states. There is a hierarchical chain of command. This duality has a parallel in pre-colonial stateless societies of this part of the world. As Clastres pointed out, local war leaders have authority as commanders on the field[10]. But their authority is temporary. Recruits to war parties are volunteers, they are not drafted by their communities. The war chiefs have no power of command at home, where a participatory democratic polity runs affairs.

As part of the foundational 'revolutionary law' of the Zapatistas, the army makes no independent decisions to use armed force. They only respond to requests from the civil authorities. It is these authorities that have the power to raise funds for the EZLN. Whether money taxed from private businesses or contributions from local people in kind. In a typical state, armed force is commanded by the state. This armed force provides the leverage to tax the population. Pay up or else. These taxes fund the army. Giving the state a monopoly of violence. Here, these arrangements are altered substantially. The army does not step in on behalf of the state to coerce taxation. That is not their role. There is no police force to do this either. Instead, the funds provided to the Zapatista territorial organisations are gifts from the communities. Donations of money (war taxes) or goods in kind. The role of the army is to clear the space so these communities can run their own affairs. In doing this, they take instructions from the elected representatives.

To further complicate this picture, the EZLN is not the sole agency of legitimate armed force in the Zapatista territories. Regional councils also have the right to set up their own local militia.

Structures of governing authority

To understand the context, we need to look at the structures of governing authority set up since the Zapatistas took over.[11] The parts of Chiapas run by the Zapatistas are divided into five regions (*caracoles*). Each of these regions is further divided into municipalities. Each of these municipalities is made up of autonomous communities. Towns or smaller villages. At each of these levels of authority, they choose representatives for the next level higher up. At the village level, they choose representatives for the municipal level. At the municipal level, they choose representatives for the regional level. For the whole of the Zapatista territory, the five regional councils meet together.

The process of election is a bit different from that in rich world representative democracies. There's an assembly of the relevant electoral body. So, in electing municipal councillors, the relevant body is an assembly of all the people in a village, electing their municipal councillor. These representatives from each village constitute the municipal council. In electing the regional council, the relevant bodies are assemblies of each municipal council. To give a typical example of how these elections proceed. The electoral body will begin by nominating five candidates for each position. Then they will vote—deciding by a majority vote which candidate gets the position. Candidates cannot nominate themselves and cannot stand as representatives of any Mexican political party. Instead, the five potential candidates are nominated by their peers. Nomination is not sought. It is not perceived as an opportunity to wield power but as a responsibility to your community—to work on their behalf. A duty understood as being very taxing. For example, representatives must leave their homes during their period of office and walk from place to place, seeking the guidance of the relevant communities.

This is just an example. Each of these communities, municipalities and regions makes its own rules about the electoral process. So, there are minor differences within this general framework.

The revolutionary law of the Zapatistas stipulates seven principles for the civil authorities.

- Serve others, not oneself.
- Represent not supplant.
- Build not destroy.
- Obey not command.

- Propose not impose.
- Convince, not defeat.
- Go below, not above.

The fourth of these points summarizes their approach and is expressed in this slogan. The people rule and the government obeys. There are two main ways in which this slogan is implemented in practice.

1. The governing authorities can believe that a particular problem is causing trouble in their territory. For example, a municipality might be faced with a set of disputes over land ownership. A councillor could propose an agreement to deal with the problem. They would discuss this matter in the council and develop a promising approach. The next step would be for the councillors to take this proposal back to their communities. They seek opinions and meet again as a council to consider the responses. The aim is to adjust the proposal to achieve a consensus that all the communities will accept. What comes from this process are negotiated agreements. The municipality facilitates the making of agreements to solve problems in the communities. This applies at all levels of government. A regional proposal would be taken back to the municipalities to get agreement. And so on.

Once an agreement has been made, the role of the relevant authority is to monitor the agreement. So, in the example above, the councillor in each community would attend to the implementation of the agreement in their community. To find out whether the agreement is being implemented. If there is a community where the agreement is not implemented, the councillor would take this issue back to the council. Then the whole process would be repeated. The council would propose a further agreement to deal with the problems in implementing the first agreement. Then this would go back to the communities.

This process illustrates the way in which the autonomy of each governing unit is maintained. An agreement has no force to coerce the recalcitrant governing unit into line. It only continues to operate if the constituent units continue to abide by it. Otherwise, it must be re-negotiated. Here, governing authorities act like the production units of a gift economy. In the gift economy, autonomous bodies create 'compacts' to coordinate their economic activities. Here, the territorial units facilitate agreements between autonomous parties for issues that concern that territory. For example, how land disputes are to be resolved. How communities relate to international NGOs. How a road is to be maintained. How the local hospital is to be provisioned. And so on. We may reflect on this to review the issue of provisioning for the army. No territorial unit will be forced to provision the army, according to a majority decision of a higher governing authority. Instead, each territorial unit will work out its own agreement to supply funding and implement that agreement. Meaning that the funding is a gift, rather than a tax.

2. A second kind of governing by obeying is like this. Citizens in one or more communities ask their governing body to provide a particular project. For example, for their regional authority to provide local hydro power plants. The 'good government council' of the region will meet with local councils and community committees. To investigate the request and consider why citizens are asking for this. What is the nature of the need? What is the cheapest way? What international bodies might help? If the regional authority is convinced that this is a good idea, they will initiate moves to implement it. This procedure deals with a typical issue in a way that can be democratic and fair. Proposals from a particular constituency are considered by an elected body from the whole of the territory—so that resources owned by the whole territory may be applied to the problem. The government obeys—puts proposals into action—while the people rule—make proposals that the government implements.

A crucial policy is that elected representatives are not paid a wage. Instead, local bodies provide them with assistance in kind. Most usually this is food. In their period of office, the representatives cannot work on their fields. Someone from their local community volunteers to take on their agricultural work. At the heart of their system of political authority is a non-monetary economy. Voluntary gifting enables the political authority to operate.

Governing authorities secure funds for projects in a variety of ways. To pay for items that cannot be sourced locally. For example, cement for a hydro dam. One method is a ten per cent tax on Mexican or international businesses operating in their territory. Another method is to ask the community cooperatives set up by the Zapatistas to pay money towards community projects. For example, a coffee cooperative selling coffee on the international market. The governing authorities can ask them to use some of their profits to assist a local project requested by the community. Another source of funds for projects is donations from international NGOs supporting the Zapatistas. To avoid resentment between communities, the Zapatista authorities insist that all such donations are organized through their elected higher assemblies. So, a particular locality cannot enjoy largesse from an international NGO— while other localities miss out. To ensure that funded projects are those the whole community wants. This patchwork of practices is quite a bit different to a state using armed force to secure taxes. The closest thing to a tax is the demand that externally located businesses pay a levy on Zapatista lands.

A further practice prevents governing authorities from becoming a permanent elite, separate from the communities. This is a system of rotation. The elected representatives do not serve every day of their term of office. Instead, they serve for an allocated period and then return to their normal life. While another representative on the roster serves in their place. For example, a municipal councillor might be in office for two weeks, back in the village for three weeks, back in office for another two weeks and so on—for a three-year term. So, people in government are also going back into their communities to participate in local life.

The Zapatista economy

The Zapatistas are committed in many ways to a non-monetary economy, and yet they are unable to implement that in full. Their economy, taken as a whole, is another hybrid. Showing how difficult it is to set up an autonomous zone that is totally non-monetary—when your local region depends in part on an external market economy. Hospital equipment. Generators and turbines. Cement. Vehicles. Weapons. There is a limit to the high-tech goods that a small agricultural economy can supply. The Zapatistas get money for these commodities in two ways. The territory hosts many local private businesses that earn money—and can purchase goods from outside. Some are branch offices of national and international companies. The second source of externally derived commodities is purchases enabled by donations from international NGOs—funnelled through the peak territorial organisations. The Zapatista governing authorities also provide funding to kick start cooperatives, marketing products both inside and outside their territory.

This hybrid economy works to a certain extent, but it is not without problems. As explained, the market economy can readily expand and undermine a hybrid. Families can make cash crops their priority, at the expense of the subsistence crops. Market incentives can undermine community control. Fitzwater describes the problems with a health bank. The purpose was to provide community members with loans if they needed expensive pharmaceuticals. The municipal authority was meant to supervise this. So that people received loans for a genuine medical purpose. Yet some municipal authorities started to allocate loans to friends starting up a business. This corruption illustrates the intrusion of the market—a constant threat in any hybrid.

Depending on NGOs for assistance to acquire high-tech goods

can be a problem—if those NGOs start to set the agenda. Fitzwater shows how the Zapatistas have faced problems like this. Cooperatives funded by NGOs for a bus service, a rice husking service, a shoe making business and a bike factory all failed. All these cooperatives depended on a donation of some high-tech machinery. In the end, the cooperatives found it impossible to maintain the machinery. It can be hard to put aside money to maintain high tech machinery. To save for a rainy day—when members of the cooperative are living on the bread line. NGOs from outside and local people themselves may favour projects which suggest a high-tech lifestyle. With technologies that may not actually work locally. The household where Fitzwater was staying was waiting on electricity to power up donated water purification filters. A water supply technology that is probably not apt for that context.

The most successful cooperatives made use of already existing skills and equipment. Grazing beef cattle. Growing coffee. The downside of such projects is that they do not help the Zapatista region to become autonomous and independent.

These problems point to the difficulty of maintaining an autonomous zone—when you must depend on high-tech products from the global economy. Even items like fencing mesh, guttering and cement. The solution adopted by the Zapatistas makes sense in the short run. To avoid burdening local people with the impossible task of producing everything they need locally. Ideally, we would internationalize the gift economy and provide high-tech goods through a network of producer clubs.

The state and the gift economy – lessons from the Zapatistas

A key question for this chapter is the issue of the state and the non-market economy. As indicated, there is an argument that there can be no state in a gift economy. A representative state depends on a body of paid enforcers who implement the will of the majority—as defined by their elected representatives. The police and army of the state. A gift economy makes it impossible to operate a system like this. Even if you wanted to. People are supplied by communities. Their 'income' is in the form of gifts. Either, in the form of self-provisioning. The household or community garden. Or through negotiated agreements with other producer units. A chair making collective. A health service. A bus service. So, no one has any need or motive to serve as the paid enforcer of a state. To carry out the will of the state and exercise violence on command.

Zapatista practice shows us how government of a territorial region may work without a 'state' in that sense. It's a state that's not a state— an un-state. Zapatista systems of governance constitute this as an un-state. The aim of the elected representatives is to develop agreements that get consensus between different territorial units. Related to this, their role is to monitor existing agreements and facilitate adjustments when agreements are not working. If we think of the territorial organisations as units in a gift economy, then the role of governing authorities is to mediate 'compacts' between smaller constitutive territorial units. At each level, a territorial unit handles matters that pertain to that territory, taken as a whole. For example, the roads used by all the people residing in a municipality.

We can think of two kinds of compacts in a gift economy. One pertains to a particular *territory* because everyone in the territory is affected. The proper concern of the territorial authorities. Another is a compact between organizations, which may not be the concern of these territorial authorities. For example, we may have a network of railway clubs in different municipalities. For the most part, they liaise with each other to provide rail as a community service. They do not need oversight via a democratic authority. Instead, as producers, they operate as a voluntary club, making compacts with other producer organisations and with their consumers. On the other hand, certain decisions relevant to the railway might be worked out in consultation with a territorial authority. Like *where* the rail line in each municipality is to be established.

The Zapatistas have various ways of ensuring that the governing authorities do not become a state, exercising coercive power over the population. There is one kind of taxation that is coercive – taxes levied on Mexican and international businesses. Aside from this, there is no 'taxation' backed up by armed force. Instead, gifts in kind allow the territorial authorities to do their work. We can think of these governmental authorities as just another voluntary producer club. The members are funded by their own work (self-provisioning) and by free donations in kind. This status has a parallel in the arrangements for the army. The army is not at the disposal of the central governing authority – the meetings of the five regional authorities. Instead, it responds to requests from local democratic bodies. In other words, the army is a club. Its actions are worked out in compacts with other clubs – the local democratic authorities. Central authorities do not (for the most part) fund it by raising taxes. Instead, local bodies provide voluntary contributions in kind.

I find this a very interesting way of looking at the Zapatistas. It may be that my description of their army and governing authorities is an idealisation. That further research will undermine my picture. Or that we will see the return of a more conventional state. But for now, the account in this chapter is a defensible interpretation. We can see how a democratic territorial organisation might work in a gift economy. We have an example of an autonomous zone that has occupied a significant part of a national territory and maintained their alternative governing structure. The Zapatistas are attempting the tricky task of starting up a non-monetary economy—without isolating their region completely from the global economy.

Hot off the Press – the Zapatistas today

I first wrote about all this in 2022. At that time, Fitzwater's book (2019) was a great guide to what was going on in the Zapatista territories. From the perspective of 'System Change for a Liveable Future', his description is an account of an autonomous zone that had taken over a whole region of the state of Mexico. That was beginning to implement a non-monetary economy.

According to *Jacobin*, a US democratic socialist journal,[12] the Zapatista region of Chiapas has been undermined by a new armed force. That of the criminal gangs bringing drugs through from Guatemala, into Chiapas and from there to more northern parts of Mexico and the United States. These gangs are allying themselves with the paramilitary thugs who represent the older rancher order of Chiapas, and with sections of the government of Mexico. These want to re-claim the Zapatista territory and regain state control. A shifting of the military balance.

The stalemate that allowed the Zapatistas to function as a parallel government joined together many local people, the leftist community (locally and internationally) and the EZLN (as an army) on the one side. With the Mexican government (acting sotto voce) and the paramilitary thugs (funded by the capitalist class) on the other side. The crime lords shift this balance. Their funding comes from the very lucrative business of selling drugs to the disaffected and depressed populations of the rich countries. Not unlike coffee or sugar. The Zapatistas are not taking them on in a direct confrontation. Likewise, the drug gangs are not taking on the Zapatistas in a full-scale attack.

I do not find all this particularly surprising. I do not see it as demonstrating the impossibility of a gift economy. What it shows is that any revolution must be prepared to defend itself by force. That it's long-term success will depend on doing that. We need revolutions in lots of countries. The point of an autonomous zone is to create a wonderful life for those involved for as long as the zone lasts. To be a model for how we might re-make our joint future. The Zapatistas have certainly done that. We should watch this space.

I will now give a detailed account of a recent Zapatista gathering. This account is based on the report of a member of a recent Australian delegation to Chiapas. Explained to me with phone messages, videos and photos. Along with a long phone interview. I took notes.

A Visit to the Zapatista territory in Chiapas – August 2025

People

A branch of the Australian Latin American solidarity network (LASNET) attended the Zapatista gathering in August 2025. Affiliated Australian leftists joined the LASNET party. About eight to ten from Australia. There was a handful of Spanish speakers in the group.

Including the member of the Australian delegation who gave the following account. A central purpose of the gathering was to host visiting delegations, so the Australian contingent was one of these.

In Chiapas, the delegations took part in a festival that lasted several days. An *encuentro* (or gathering). Many of these visitor delegations were from Mexico itself. There were also delegates from a variety of international supporters and their organisations. For example, from Germany, Denmark, Italy. Many visitors camped in tents—as did local participants. The visitors generally purchased food at designated community cafes. They also volunteered their help for bathrooms and kitchen rosters. Washing up and chopping vegetables. A familiar arrangement for activists.

- About 1500 local people drawn from 6 *caracoles*—municipalities of the Zapatista territories. These were elected delegates from their villages and Zapatista members. While a reader may imagine that the Zapatista villagers, as rural and Indigenous, were in some way distinctive in dress, this was not the case. The dress of the young people who attended the *encuentro* is typical of that worn in Mexico more generally. For example, jeans and shirts for men and women. Older villagers were more likely to wear more traditional clothing – with dresses for women. Most participants from the villages wore a black face mask used to protect from Covid and to signify Zapatista identity. Some wore the balaclava associated with the Zapatistas in the media. It was common for the men to wear a red bandana around their neck. This bandana is called the *paliacate* and has been taken up since the Zapatista uprising as a sign of Zapatista identity. The red bandana has a history in revolutionary struggle going back to Emiliano Zapata and Francisco Villa. Most participants had mobile phones. The young Zapatistas were participants in social media. They took photos on their phones to post to their favourite sites. It was these village Zapatistas who staged the plays that were a central feature of the gathering. They also did most of the work of running the camp. The *encuentro* used systems of rosters to provide this cohort with free cooked meals. Their rostered shifts were long, usually a whole day. Cooking for themselves and for all the other villagers. And for the visitor delegations.

- A leadership group at the *encuentro* consisted of about twenty people. It is unclear whether this group consisted entirely of EZLN members. Or instead included representatives from regional and zonal assemblies of Zapatista civilian bodies (see below the CGAZ and the ACGAZ). This group always wore full balaclavas at the *encuentro*. On more formal occasions, women from this group wore a traditional Indigenous ensemble. A long black skirt with embroidered panels and a white blouse. Participating in chairing sessions, they wore typical Mexican women's clothing. This group took a leadership role at events, usually by chairing meetings and introducing speakers. Rarely in the role of giving speeches themselves. A prominent member of this group was subcomandante Moisés, from the EZLN, who often spoke from the chair. He was a participant in a delegation of Zapatistas to Europe in 2022.

- The Zapatista EZLN. Their army. For the *encuentro*, they appeared on the opening morning in a military formation, in lines in separated groups. They wore the full balaclavas and full military uniform. They entered the space along a road, in formation, coming from all directions. This was a display of strength. They were marching close together in strict time. As they marched, they struck their batons to add to the rhythm. Each soldier had a long baton and a bow across their shoulder, with a quiver of arrows. They carried small Palestinian flags, poking above their back packs. As a sign of support for the Palestinian resistance. One cohort in this display was for women soldiers only. After this dramatic entrance the army withdrew to camps nearby, organizing protection for the *encuentro*. The Zapatistas believe that an army is necessarily a hierarchical structure of command. While the civil authority can be organized as a participatory democracy. Accordingly, as Fitzwater explains, the army takes instructions from the civil bodies. This viewpoint is displayed in the symbolism of these events. The army arrives in hierarchical guise and later removes itself to create a zone of protection for the gathering.

The Venue

A number of long-standing facilities adjoined the site, For example, a radio station, a health clinic and some housing, making up a dispersed community or *caracol*. The *encuentro* itself took place in a cleared space specifically designed for community events of this type. There was a flat arena like a small football field. Around the edges were small shops. Both visitors and local participants attended these shops, chatting and buying food. Fresh food and cold drinks. There were kitchens and community dining—free of charge—for the local participants.

Local Zapatista villagers supplied all the food that was served at the *encuentro*. Eggs, and freshly killed meat. Chickens, beef, and pork. Vegetables, maize kernels and maize flour. A huge logistical exercise. Tamales depending on the time of day. With chicken. A large part of this food was *given* by the villages to the *encuentro*, rather than being bought from village suppliers.

Further back and defining the space were two large open halls. Allowing the day to be divided into activities in each of these halls. The flat roof of each hall is supported on concrete pillars. The halls are about twice the height of a normal suburban house room—twenty metres. The floor is a cement slab. Rows of chairs fill most of the floor space—with a small rostrum for speeches and performances. There is copious space behind and next to the seating. Participants stand and chat together while events are taking place.

Daily activities

The day started at about 6:30. There were often announcements on the loudspeakers addressed to groups of the local participants, informing them of tasks. Calling for volunteers and rostered work parties. For the bathrooms, toilets, cleaning, fixing a pipe. These rostered tasks were chosen by participants as volunteers. I choose to be in the kitchen and so on. Breakfast was at the small shops selling food or more usually from the free supplies from the community kitchens. Each villager delegate brought their own cup and plate to these community meals.

A key activity of the daytime hours was a set of plays staged by local people and by visitor delegations. A group from a particular village or a delegation would start up a play in the street or the arena. Typically, the plays concerned some issue in operating an egalitarian participatory polity.

For example, the community had decided to found a health clinic. Delegates from the community were charged to liaise with building companies to get supplies. The delegates secretly cut a deal. The companies would appear to charge the community higher than the going price for their supplies. When the community paid this elevated price, their delegated representatives would pocket the difference. Between the prices that the companies in fact required and the price that the community was paying. This narrative is identical to one told to Fitzwater before 2019. In the narrative told to Fitzwater, it is the pharmacies that take part in this corruption. They appear to charge the community a higher price, secretly passing the profits on to their friends who had been appointed by the community to make the purchases.

A drama on political representation. Elected representatives fail to show up as expected at the assembly. Because they had to sell a cow or tend to a sick child. This patchy commitment is untenable over time. Some in the assembly say they should have a penalty like one day's work on a hard job. Because the person missed the meeting.

But then they decide this is replicating the authoritarian pyramid of capitalism and they will work out a better way. A dilemma that relates to negotiation of the monetary sphere. Selling a cow has priority. The proposed solution is a non-monetary one, but it replicates the authority structure of a monetary fine.[13] As alienated labour.

Another drama featured a local case of sexual assault. The assault had been reported to the Zapatista justice organisation in the village. The family of the perpetrator ensured that the matter was heard by the Mexican government legal system. Rather than the Zapatista community mediation. Using a bribe, their aim was to downplay the seriousness of the offence and to avoid a harsh penalty being placed on their family member.

The common theme of these plays was that the construction of community is an ongoing process, there is no ultimate resolution. Typical themes were long live the commune, protecting mother earth, the seven principles of the Zapatistas.

An optimistic street performance had the players dressed up as huge white sperm and pink eggs, paper and wood human size puppets. They represented the next generation of Zapatistas after the current generation has died. How these future Zapatistas might look back on the Zapatistas of today. The ongoing work of carrying the revolution forward.

Another typical daily event took place in the large halls. These were presentations by the visitor delegations, those from Mexico and the international ones. The coordinating group of the *encuentro* were seated on the stage next to a table. They chaired the event but did not speak on their own behalf. They called on the delegations to present to the community, explaining their interest in the Zapatista cause. In the hall, the visitors sat at the front of the hall with local participants at the back. These events were well attended and there was a spill of people standing at the back, milling about as the talks went on. Local people were listening to the talks or chatting, napping, using their mobile phones to take photos, taking notes and so on.

Some examples of groups that spoke were as follows. A women's collective. Activists for the people who have 'disappeared'. Activists against water privatisations. A Palestine solidarity group. A group representing Italian squatters. The National Indigenous Congress of Mexico. This was just one of the Indigenous organisations speaking. In general, they preferred the term *los pueblos originarios* for their identity.

The Australian delegation presented three topics. The Latin American Solidarity organisation—LASNET. Indigenous history and movements in Australia. Environmental activism in Australia.

Later there were more performances. From about 7:30 to 9 pm local people performed musical numbers. Each caracol (Zapatista zone) would stage some performance, whether a play, a rap performance, or singing with a band. There was a woman rap singer, as well as male rap performers. These performances were politically charged, exalting the Zapatista way of life and excoriating capitalist hierarchy. The topics were never those typical of pop music even though the musical forms derived from pop. Often the performers were wearing traditional dress and singing in local languages. Many local participants took videos of the performances, perhaps for posting to social media or for sharing with friends and family. Later a band performed for dancing, and this went till 2 am in the morning. Dancing was in couples for the most part. Local people explained the importance of an *encuentro* in enabling social contacts between local groups in their villages. Through these social activities the *encuentro* likely provided a way for young people from different caracoles to meet and make new social connections outside their immediate communities.

Two special events

During the *encuentro*, a large wooden pyramid featured as the centre piece of a special street performance. It was two stories high, a pillar culminating in an apex. On its sides, the wooden frame supported a canvas art space. A dominant slogan on each side represented one of the four aspects of capitalism and hierarchy that the Zapatistas reject. What they refer to broadly as 'the pyramid'. For example, *Desprecio* = Contempt. *Explotación* = Exploitation. Surrounding this bold text were cartoons and slogans with similar themes. A poster nearby proclaimed – the Commune has no property! After a theatre performance, a concluding ceremony set the pyramid alight and burned it to the ground. An effervescent party atmosphere included the singing and chanting of revolutionary slogans.

Another special event was a performance by the army in formations, a staged play explaining their support for the Palestinian cause.

Observations and comments

The most crucial was probably an observation from one of the European delegates who had been with the Zapatistas when they visited Europe in 2022. They had gone to Cyprus, an area where Greek and Turkish communities were separated by a no-man's land, a patch of territory where neither state had authority. What had happened here was that local people from both communities cooperated to work this land together and share the produce without monetary payment. The Zapatistas translate the local phrase for this land as *Tierra de Nadia*. The land of no-one. It is an apt metaphor for their own polity as an autonomous zone. Their experience here encouraged them to consider what it means to 'own' land and *exclude* non-owners. In a strategy of inclusion, the Zapatistas have reached out to villages where local people are not members of the Zapatistas. To constitute these joint meeting zones as border regions between the Zapatistas and other communities more like the *Tierra de Nadia* witnessed in Cyprus. To share the land together rather than parcelling out new ownership arrangements. The beneficiaries must be those without land, not land-owning families.

Incursions by the drug gangs in Chiapas are real and are a growing problem for the Zapatistas in the last five years. The gangs often affiliate themselves to the paramilitary thugs that have always dogged the Zapatista experiment.[14] They give those thugs an effective backing. In other cases, the Mexican government has been funding paramilitaries to control the drug gangs. In communities where the cartels have taken over, they run services for the community and buy support with drug money. They recruit young people into their operations. Encouraging farmers to grow drugs rather than food crops. They are heavily armed. There is a stand-off and neither side sees advantage in a knock down conflict. Instead, the drug cartel and paramilitary will do things like torch a school in a Zapatista village or drive through a village dropping a head from a Zapatista corpse in the road.[15]

One effect of these incursions has been to make it difficult for villages to link up across the whole territory. The Mexican government of previous presidents and regional governors funded these paramilitary enemies of the Zapatistas. The Zapatistas antagonized the landlord class of Mexico by appropriating large portions of their land. These oligarchs have been working with the Mexican government to fund the paramilitary thugs. From day one these forces have allied themselves to the drug cartels, with previous Mexican governments turning a blind eye to these alliances. Or actively fostering them. For example, the government of Rutilio Escandón allied itself to 'narcotraffickers forcing indigenous communities to create their own self-defense groups, as the government did nothing to protect the life, liberty, and property of the population. It not only protected the narcotrafficking gangs, but also encouraged, promoted, and financed paramilitary groups like those that constantly attacked communities in Aldama and Santa Martha.'[16]

The welfare policy of this and the previous government have been hailed by the international liberal press. A welfare state payment has been organized to pull the very poor out of poverty. This payment takes the form of a rations card that can only be spent at authorized supermarket chains owned by big companies. This arrangement directs monetary support to large powerful capitalist forces with their headquarters outside Chiapas. It makes it difficult for the Zapatistas to pursue a strategy of local provisioning, whether through small local businesses or non-monetary provisioning. A related problem infects a recent government initiative to provide micro loans. The poor end up in debt, further hooked into a global market economy that can never serve their needs. Based on some conversations with visitors at the *encuentro*, it seems that the Zapatistas are angry that so many of their leftist supporters in Mexico City have become supporters of Claudia Sheinbaum Pardo. She is a social democrat who was elected president in 2024. Leftist allies of the Zapatistas in urban Mexico have supported her despite her clear failure to give space to the Zapatista economy—or to reign in the drug gangs that threaten them.

The event itself, the *encuentro*, displays some of the politics relevant to this. This is an impressive show of force. A peaceful conference of Zapatista delegates from a wide area. Hosting international guests who are given no reason to think that they may be subject to any kind of violent confrontation. The Zapatista army presents at the event as a credible force. Another way to look at this event is to say that the international guests protect the proceedings for the Zapatistas. No faction in Chiapas sees any advantage in attacking delegations of leftists from the metropole. It would be very damaging to be seen as a group that attacked an unarmed civilian delegation.

The New Governing Structures of the Zapatistas

In 2023, the Zapatistas responded to demands from their local bases of support. The following account is based on ENLACE, an internet page set up by the Zapatistas. Along with Instagram posts that relay the same information. Supplemented by the accounts of those who have recently attended the *Encuentro* described above. The key change is to increase the number and scope of operations for the local bases of Zapatista governance. The local autonomous government or GAL. Whereas before there were 'a few dozen MAREZ, Zapatista Rebel Autonomous Municipalities, now there are thousands of Zapatista GALS'[17]. These GALS are varied in terms of how they are conceived locally. For example, a people's assembly, a community, a place, neighbourhood, ejido, or colony. They are coordinated by local Zapatista members and are subject to the decisions made by the assembly of the town. Compared to the previous arrangements, each GAL has considerable autonomy to make decisions for their local situation. For example, a group of eight families might have authority to allocate land. Each GAL controls its autonomous regional resources (such as schools and clinics) and the relationship with neighbouring non-Zapatista sister towns.[18]

Meetings organized at regional and zone level are portrayed in Fitzwater's account as 'governing bodies' of the Zapatistas. Not in the sense of bodies with the power to command obedience and enforce agreements. But bodies that coordinate and discuss proposals coming from more local bodies. Much of this seems unchanged in the account given in ENLACE. These coordinating bodies respond to *requests* to sort out problems referred to them by the GALS.

The GALS send representatives to the regional level. Collectives of Zapatista Autonomous Government, [CGAZ]. Here discussions are held, and agreements are proposed on matters that interest the convening GALs. For example, on Health, Education, Agroecology, Justice, Commerce. Proposals are discussed and approved or rejected. The coordinators of each area are at the CGAZ level. Their role is to ensure that the work decided on by the CGAZ is carried out. For example, preventive medicine and vaccination campaigns, campaigns for endemic diseases, courses and specialized training (such as laboratory technicians, x rays, ultrasound, mammograms), literacy, sporting and cultural events, traditional festivities. Each CGAZ has its coordinators. They summon assemblies if there is an urgent problem or one that affects several communities.

The CGAZ represent themselves at the zone level. The assemblies of collectives of Zapatistas Autonomous Governments. ACGAZ. The ACGAZ convenes and presides over zone assemblies – when necessary, according to the requests of GAL and CGAZ. It is based in the caracoles (the twelve Zapatista headquarters) but moves between regions. So, this umbrella assembly is mobile, according to the people's demands for attention. It moves its operations according to the requests of regional and local bodies.

Conclusions

The experience of the *encuentro* must put in brackets the account presented in *Jacobin*. There is a stand-off between the increased drug cartel presence and the Zapatistas. Their harassment is of a piece with threats that the Zapatistas have always dealt with. The threat is certainly intensified and has forced the Zapatistas to decentralize to the local level to a greater extent. On the other hand, the organisation and sophistication of the event management of the *encuentro* speaks to a very healthy broader community process. The Zapatista region as an ongoing autonomous zone. Which is amazing considering it has been going since 1994. For me the closest parallel is the Zimbabwe Chikukwa land care project—chapter 11. Another autonomous zone with amazing persistence.

Reflections on the autonomous zone strategy

What the story of the Zapatistas shows is the difficulties inherent in the autonomous zone strategy. That an autonomous zone struggles to continue against the forces of global capitalism. The Zapatista autonomous zone has been compromised by a branch of the global capitalist machine. Running on money, funnelling global South products to global North consumers. The whole gangster operation depends on money and fits into the global system.

In a gift economy, drugs like cocaine would be grown and distributed as gifts. We could expect them to be used to celebrate special occasions. Addiction and harm from drugs are a symptom of the stress and trauma caused by a capitalist economy. A self-medication. The punitive legal regime that funds the business model of the drug cartels expresses the culture of capital in the rich countries. Work hard, avoid indulgence and become successful in the meritocracy. The view being promoted is that there is nothing wrong with the system. People who succumb to addiction are just 'losers' and should be punished for their failures. None of these aspects of current culture would make it into a gift economy. Drug cartels would be as irrelevant as gas guzzling SUVs.

I like Hakim Bey's defence of the autonomous zone strategy for what it can do. But I also think it should not be elevated by the left as the only effective politics. While an autonomous zone always shows us how things could be radically different, it is also a target. Recuperation and defeat of such a zone is just breakfast for the capitalist class. The danger is that we will experience these defeats as failures. Hybrids are a less risky strategy, though they achieve a less dramatic change in the lives of the participants. People readily walk away from a problematic hybrid and start a new project. Without being knocked over the head with the *failure* of their alternative. There is always something that can be done. The *danger* in hybrids is that they will be perceived as 'just a kind of market enterprise'. A fatal complacency that sees the system as open to reform.

In following chapters on prefiguring hybrids, we will see how the global system makes alternative economic forms difficult. The problems of the Zapatistas with gangsters are not that different to the headaches of the Chikukwa project in Zimbabwe that I will describe. Local participants are drawn into new capitalist enterprise. International players undermine local solutions with entrepreneurial options. They are not unlike the problems that Mondragon faced with globalisation. Or a Welsh CSA faces with the price of land and competition from big food companies.

In all such cases, the ambitions of the participants can never be realized in full. Until we have a new mode of production. We need a new *system* that backs up each individual initiative—rather than surrounding it with sharks.

Endnotes

[1] Hakim Bey, 'T.A.Z.: The temporary autonomous zone, ontological anarchy, poetic terrorism', in *The Anarchist Library*, 1985, viewed on 27 March 2024, https://theanarchistlibrary.org/library/hakim-bey-t-a-z-the-temporary-autonomous-zone-ontological-anarchy-poetic-terrorism

[2] Subcomandante Insurgento Galeano, *Communique from the Indigenous Revolutionary Clandestine Committee-General Command of the Zapatista Army for National Liberation, Chiapas on the Verge of Civil War*, September 19, 2021, https://enlacezapatista.ezln.org.mx/2021/09/20/chiapas-on-the-verge-of-civil-war/ Accesssed 19th April 2022.

[3] Dylan Eldredge Fitzwater, *Autonomy Is in Our Hearts: Zapatista Autonomous Government through the Lens of the Tsotsil Language*, PM Press, Oakland CA., 2019; Carlos Lucio and David Barkin, 'Postcolonial and anti-systemic resistance by indigenous movements in Mexico.' *Journal of World Systems Research*, Vol 28(2):293-317. 2022.

[4] Ashish Kothari, Ariel Salleh, Arturo Escobar, Federico Demaria and Alberto Acosta, 'Finding Pluriversal Paths', in *Pluriverse, A Post-Development Dictionary*, Ashish Kothari, Ariel Salleh, Arturo Escobar, Federico Demaria and Alberto Acosta (eds), Tulika Books, New Delhi, 2019, pp. xxi-xl.

[5] Terry Leahy, *Food Security for Rural Africa: Feeding the Farmers First*, London, Routledge, UK., 2019.

[6] Piepzna-Samarasinha, Leah Lakshmi and Ejeris Dixon (Eds), *Beyond Survival: Strategies and stories from the transformative justice movement*, AK Press, California, 2020.

[7] Galeano, *Communique*.

[8] Max Weber, *From Max Weber: Essays in Sociology*, Hans H. Gerth (trans), Routledge, London, 1948, p.78.

[9] Communique from the Indigenous Revolutionary Clandestine Committee-General Command of the Zapatista Army for National Liberation, *Chiapas on the Verge of Civil War*, September 19, 2021.

[10] Pierre Clastres, *Society Against the State: Essays in Political Anthropology*, Zone Books, New York, 1987; Pierre, Clastres, *Archaeology of Violence*, Semiotext(e), Los Angeles, 2010.

[11] I am concentrating on the description of these structures as described by Fitzwater. Recent changes do not compromise this general account of the rationale and procedures of governing set up by the Zapatistas.

[12] Kurt Hackbarth, 'Violence is Overwhelming Chiapas: An Interview with Leonardo Toleno, *Jacobin*, https://jacobin.com/2024/02/chiapas-mexico-violence-cartels-zapatistas.

[13] Personal communication with Lily Leahy visiting Chiapas, August 2025.

[14] Galeano, *Communique*.

[15] Galeano, *Communique*.

[16] Galeano, *Communique*.

[17] *Ninth Part: The new structure of Zapatista Autonomy* Nov 2023, https://enlacezapatista.ezln.org.mx/2023/11/13/ninth-part-the-new-structure-of-zapastista-autonomy/, Accessed 10 Sept 2025.

[18] *The new structure of the Zapatista Autonomy.*

Chapter 9
The State and the Gift Economy: Anarchist and Marxist approaches

This chapter was prompted by a friend. He had been listening to my podcast series. He wondered why I was so insistent on getting rid of the state if it was so difficult. Why not accept the inevitable? Learn to live with the state and get reforms using the state. So, this chapter is intended to consider all that. I will begin by looking at two views of the state from foundational sociological authors. Not in chronological order!

Weber's definition of the State

Weber is associated with the usual definition of 'the state':

> *a state is a human community that (successfully) claims* the monopoly of the legitimate use of physical force within a given territory.[1]

The term 'legitimate' and the term 'human community' are both puzzling. They suggest that a state only exists when the *whole* of society endorses the coercive actions of the state. I doubt whether all 'states' are 'legitimate' like that. It is unlikely that the slaves of ancient Rome saw the Roman state as 'legitimate'. That they saw themselves as part of the 'human community' that monopolized violence. If we are aiming to describe society as it is, Weber's definition should be revised. A state is an organisation that has an *effective* monopoly of force. The state can ultimately win in any violent conflict with another part of society. As well, a state is an organisation that monopolizes force on behalf of some *part* of society. We do not call it a 'state' if *everyone* has the legitimate use of physical force. As in Indigenous pre-colonial societies.

Marx and Engels on the State

Let us now turn to Marx's ideas on 'the state'. Marx and Engels take for granted a definition of the state that is closer to the way I am using it. The state is a special body in the population that commands a monopoly of force. In a well-known passage of the Manifesto, they have this to say:

> The bourgeoisie ... has at last, conquered for itself in the modern representative state, exclusive political sway. The executive of the modern State is but a committee for managing the common affairs of the whole bourgeoisie.[2]

The 'executive' is a body that *makes plans* for the whole class—that manages the affairs of the bourgeoisie. They can do this because they have the 'political' power vested in the state. The power to coercively enact these plans. This was written in 1848, a time when only members of the upper classes had any political representation. In Marx's *Paris Manuscripts*, 'political' power follows from the alienation of people's innate sociable nature. Within class society, conflict is an inevitable effect of economic structures. The economy forces people into antagonistic conflict, stifling more sociable instincts. To enable social life to continue, the state intervenes to control violence. It does this on behalf of the ruling class. To enforce the exploitation of the subordinate class, whether slaves, serfs or wage workers.[3] These central ideas are also elaborated in Engels' later book on the origin of the state.

This analysis informs the description of the coming communist revolution. Because the proletariat needs to overthrow the bourgeoisie, it must come to dominate the bourgeoisie—becoming a ruling class. This is the definition of 'political' and *implies* a state—because the proletariat achieves a monopoly of force to control and defeat the bourgeoisie.

The first step in the revolution by the working class, is to raise the proletariat to the position of ruling class, to win the battle of democracy. The proletariat will use its political supremacy to wrest, by degrees, all capital from the bourgeoisie, to centralize all instruments of production in the hands of the State, i.e. of the proletariat organized as a ruling class.[4]

In so far as the proletariat takes the means of production from the bourgeoisie by force, they constitute a state. A body that controls a subordinate class. Marx and Engels conclude by predicting the demise of the state once the bourgeoisie have been defeated. The proletariat 'sweeps away' the exploitation of labour. Doing this, it sweeps away 'the conditions for the existence of class antagonisms.' There is no exploitation—so no ruling class and no subordinate class. The state, an organ of class power, can no longer exist.

What takes its place? Here Marx and Engels are a bit vague. The public power 'will lose its political character.' In other words, the organisation of society by the public will not enforce the domination of one class over another. Instead, 'we shall have an association, in which the free development of each is the free development of all.'[5] An anarchist might find nothing objectionable in all this. So long as we are using the definitions that Marx and Engels use themselves. Anarchists might well agree that 'the state' is a body that employs coercion to maintain the power of a ruling class. They would then agree that the revolution must defeat that state power. They would agree that the vast body of the population, the proletariat, would use coercive power, when necessary, to take the means of production out of the hands of the capitalist class. They would likewise agree that once this process had been completed, no class would coercively control another and organize society through that.

Where they would differ is that they would not use the term 'state' to refer to the coercive power of the proletariat—organized to take control of the means of production. Consequently, they would *not* see the 'conquest' of the state as 'seizing' the state for the proletariat. Instead, they might talk about 'defeating' the state. Appropriating the means of production by force. Setting up *an association* to run society. Both versions of this are committed to some idea of a 'transition'—a period in which the proletariat is taking over the means of production. It is starting to sound like the supposed difference between Marxists and anarchists is a mere verbal quibble.

If the difference between Marxists and anarchists is not here, where is it? The logical place to look next is the detail about what this period of transition might look like. 'Democratic Socialists' draw heavily on what Marx and Engels say about this in their *Manifesto* and in *The Critique of the Gotha Programme*.[6] Summarizing this. The working class is organized into municipalities and work councils. They elect delegates to a national government. This central government runs an army to suppress the capitalist class and appropriate the means of production. The representatives decide on an economic and industrial plan. A monopoly over distribution enables the government to implement it. Distributing to workers who are executing the plan. The government sets wages and prices and distributes the products of the nationalized industries. Wages are paid relative to hours worked. While this may seem like wage labour, it is not—because there is no extraction of surplus value by a ruling class. Democratic socialists sometimes claim that we cannot regard this payment as *money*. It is just a certificate that allows the worker to withdraw products from a government store. But clearly it is a universal quantitative measure of value. It is paid proportionally to hours worked and can be used to buy things according to 'prices' set by government.

This picture of the transition is implicit in a great range of detailed proposals. For example, in the *Manifesto*.

> *A heavy progressive income tax.*
> Implying a monetary economy.
> *Abolition of property in land.*
> A first step in taking over the means of production. In other words, a public ownership. People nominated to lease land pay a rent to government that is used for public purposes.
> *Equal liability of all to labour. Establishment of industrial armies.*

In other words, conscription of the proletariat by their state.
Extension of factories and instruments of production owned by the State.
Gradual appropriation of the means of production as state property.
The improvement of the soil in accordance with a common plan.
In other words, a common plan worked out by a body of representatives. By a State invested with coercive authority.
Centralization of credit in the hands of the State ... a national bank with ... an exclusive monopoly.
The proletarian state directs the economy through credit.
Centralize all means of production in the hands of the State.
The summary of what is intended.[7]

In chapter five I have explained what I think is problematic in this. The unintended consequences of attempts to implement this programme. How these attempts fall short—if the aim is to create a classless society. But here, I am interested in what anarchists make of this program. Also, what they propose as an alternative.

Bakunin on the State

Bakunin is one of the early anarchists. His writings have had a huge influence. The conflict between Bakunin and Marx split the early socialist movement. A key concern is that the state implies a despotism, a top-down command structure. Even if representatives are elected.

> Because under the pretext of representing the will of all it will bear down on the will and free impulse of each of its members with all the weight of its collective power.[8]

Bakunin envisages the transition of the *Communist Manifesto* as a new mode of production. A new form of dominion and exploitation run by a technocratic ruling class. This government,

> not content with governing and administering the masses politically, will also administer them economically, by taking over the production and fair sharing of wealth, agriculture, the establishment and development of factories, the organization

and control of trade, and lastly the injection of capital into production by a single banker, the State. All of this will require vast knowledge and lot of heads brimful of brains. It will be the reign of the scientific mind, the most aristocratic, despotic, arrogant and contemptuous of all regimes. This will be a new class, a new hierarchy of real or bogus learning, and the world will be divided into a dominant science-based minority and vast, ignorant majority.[9]

A barracks regime for the proletariat, in which a standardized mass of men and women workers would wake, sleep, work and live by rote; a regime of privilege for the able and clever.[10]

So, what is Bakunin's alternative? There are four key points. A bottom-up federation of associations plans the economy. There is no state, no organisation that commands obedience. Violence must be used to defend the revolution—but there is no standing army, no authorized (legitimate) coercion. Autonomous money-making cooperatives constitute the economy. These key points raise a few issues.

1. A federation of collectives.

A federation of autonomous collectives will organize society.

> The political and economic organization of society must therefore not flow downwards from high to low, and outwards, from centre to circumference, as it does today ... but upwards and inwards, on the principle of free association and free federation.[11]

The language here maintains the metaphor of centre/periphery and high/low. Not a distributed network but a central clearing house. The federation stands in place of the state that has been abolished. Autonomous social units send representatives to a federated think tank, that then works out the 'political and economic organisation of society'. Implying one of two possibilities. That people obey these decisions because the federation has legitimacy as a duly constituted authority. We're doing this because this is what the federation has decided. Or, that the decisions of the federation are so finely tuned to the wishes of the people that no part of society wants anything different. We're doing this because the federation, as usual, has decided to do what we want.

While Bakunin stipulates the 'absolute freedom of individual, productive association and commune', it is hard to square this with the detail. To organize a complex society, he suggests, the federation must impose laws and command through sanctions. The detail implies a monetary economy. The federation uses its financial power to secure compliance.

> The [provincial] parliament will modify provincial legislation in terms of both the respective rights and duties of individual associations and communes, and of the forfeits to which each shall be liable in the event of infractions of the laws it establishes. The communal legislatures, however, will retain the right to deviate from provincial legislation on secondary but never on essential matters.[12]

Having your cake and eating it too. Much of what the provincial and national federations will legislate is necessary to running a monetary economy—while ensuring social justice. It is difficult to see much leeway in the following. The parliament will decide the commune's share of national and provincial taxation. The federation will ensure equality in a child's maintenance, upbringing, and education. Implying federation funding. The federation will prevent people from exercising a right of inheritance – meaning that the federation will confiscate family wealth. Everyone will get equal development of their faculties and a job to enable that. Also implying funding and regulation. In the longer-term Bakunin envisages a global expansion for the federation. Free productive associations will:

... expand beyond national frontiers. They will form one vast economic federation, with a parliament informed by precise, detailed statistics on a world scale ... and will both offer and demand to control, decide and distribute the output of world industry among the various countries so that there will no longer ... be commercial or industrial crises.[13]

In other words, the global federation will take over distribution and the allocation of capital to industry. Accordingly, the associations (cooperatives) will lose their power to make these decisions.

2. Absolute freedom of action – no state command.

A second theme is that after the revolution people, associations (cooperatives) and communes (municipalities) are totally free to follow their own decisions. People are slaves if they must obey the decisions of a state. Instead, after the revolution:

All individuals, associations, communes, provinces, regions and nations have the absolute right to dispose of their own fate, associate or not associate, ally with whomever they please and break off alliances.[14]

Reorganisation of each region, taking as its starting point the absolute freedom of individual, productive association and commune.[15]

How can this be reconciled with the vision of the federation I have explained? The federation has many tasks to maintain an egalitarian and supportive society. Much of this work requires control over money—taxation, funding for social services, redistribution, the allocation of capital. While people may see the necessity for all this in the abstract, they are unlikely to welcome it when it disadvantages their own household, cooperative, or municipality. This is a post-revolutionary culture where 'command' is not legitimate. Where these constituting local organs are free to do the opposite of what the federation asks. How can this organisation of the economy, along with the sanctions required to manage that organisation, work in that context? Or considered from the opposite angle. How can these bodies be free to do what they will—while the federation can impose 'forfeits'—if they break federation laws?

3. No standing army or police force.

The next key point is the organisation of armed force. As explained, a State relies on armed force to ensure compliance. A police force and a standing army. The anarchist federation does not intend to command—so neither of these organisations are required. On the other hand, armed force will be necessary to make a revolution.

So, the revolution is to begin with the 'abolition' of central administration, state bureaucracies, 'standing armies and State police'.[16] While there will be no standing army 'every able-bodied citizen must, if necessary, become a soldier in defence of his home or liberty'.[17] The revolution itself will not be peaceful. Instead, a war of 'extermination' is inevitable. The duty of the revolutionary is to 'sacrifice his repose, his well-being, his vanity, personal ambition and often his personal interests.'[18] So, the revolutionary volunteers to fight the necessary battles to defeat the ruling class. This certainly endorses the use of force to seize the means of production. It is not clear whether force may also be used after the revolution. But perhaps this is implied. The statement that communal legislatures retain the right to deviate from provincial legislation *except on essential matters* suggests sanctions. What if we had an anarchist federation today? How would a national federation respond to a communal legislature that decided to instal a nuclear reactor? I am guessing that this would be regarded as an essential matter. If necessary, armed force would be used to block the project.

I will put Bakunin's vision for the state like this. In an anarchist society there is no special body of the population *invested with the authority* to monopolize the use of force. Moreover, there is no special body with *the capacity* to monopolize the use of force. While this is a good broad brushstrokes picture of the intention of Bakunin's view of the state, the fine print suggests something else. A federation that *does* have effective powers of coercion.

4. Market cooperatives are the economic units.

So now I come to the last key point. This is a move which very much defines the difference between the post-capitalism promoted by Marx and that of Bakunin. Marx envisages a transitional stage to full communism. In the transition the state owns the means of production, employs workers, and makes decisions about distribution. Bakunin by contrast intends that during the revolution, ordinary workers take over the means of production and run each unit as a cooperative. A market economy. Each association sells products and pays wages to the members of their cooperative. This program seems so obvious to Bakunin that he usually *assumes* it. He reveals this *context* as he comments on more detailed matters.

Bakunin usually describes these work collectives as 'productive associations.'[19] He is aware of workers' cooperatives, banks of mutual aid, workers' credit unions, and trade unions being established in England. He celebrates these as footsteps on the path to the revolution.

He recognizes the necessity for the post-capitalist federation to step in to enforce contracts. Given that cooperatives are organisations that function in a market economy, selling what they produce.

> … associations legally recognized as collective bodies will … have the right to bring charges against all individuals, whether members or outsiders, as well as all other regular associations defaulting on commitments to them.[20]

For example, if you pay another cooperative to supply a carton of spare parts and they never arrive, you could charge them with breaking their contract. It is unclear how the federation establishes this legal process and imposes sanctions. What is very clear is that we have a competitive market economy. The economic units are legally registered cooperatives.

The federation is supervising and enforcing the proper use of money—ensuring through legal sanctions that money means something.

There will be no coercion to force people to enter these cooperatives. They can continue as sole traders. So why would people become cooperative members? Because:

> It would miraculously increase the productive energies of each associate member ... who will earn a great deal more in less time and with far less trouble.[21]

In other words, for exactly the same reasons the capitalist class replaced the cottage weavers with factory employees. More monetary value per worker. This reveals much about the assumed economic context. The workers in any cooperative depend on sales to earn a living. So, they are as vulnerable as any capitalist employee to market competition. Their cooperative must seek the highest possible profit—or risk going out of business. The 'freedom' of the worker is the freedom to do what the market requires.

Describing the anarchist programme for the revolution, he advocates the establishment of a market economy of cooperatives in somewhat confusing terms:

> Confiscation of all productive capital and means of production on behalf of workers' associations, who are to put them to collective use.[22]

Here, he means taking control of these means of production and running them as market *collectives*. The means of production are to be used collectively—in other words, *by collectives*—to make money.

This context informs everything Bakunin has to say about the federation. No wonder the federation needs to tax, needs to supply social services, needs to enforce contracts. The economy is a market monetary economy. Each enterprise competes to hang on to its place—and may fail. Throwing the members of the cooperative into poverty. The federation must intervene to mediate this competition, to enforce the rules of the market game, to back up the monetary system, to supply public services. But, on the other hand, anarchist principles dictate that there is no state to enforce these sanctions, the forfeits, the taxes, the charges in court. Really?

Kropotkin

Kropotkin is the first well known anarchist writer to promote a non-monetary post-capitalism. He describes his vision as 'communism'. In many ways identical to Marx's vision of a post-transitional fully realized communism. His major departure from Marxism is that he has no time for a transitional stage. Kropotkin, like the other anarchist founders, does not envisage a statist transitional period – a dictatorship of the proletariat with state ownership. It is typical of Kropotkin to talk about the 'abolition of the wage system' rather than the abolition of money.[23] Yet everything he says about this shows that he does not intend to continue with money.[24] In a clear break with Bakunin, Kropotkin sees market cooperatives as *prefiguring* experiments. Not as a *model* for the constituting units of the post-capitalist society.[25]

Kropotkin creates his own 'communist' position as a close analogy to Marx's vision of 'communism'. Communism is common ownership with allocation based on need. What Kropotkin rejects is Marx's transitional stage—after the revolution but before communism. In that model, the *state* (as a 'collective') allocates goods and services *through a wage* related to hours of work. Kropotkin refers to this model as 'collectivist'. For both Marx and Kropotkin, the possibility of 'communist' distribution is the abundance that modern industry permits. Accordingly, the dispute between 'communist' and 'collectivist' may end up like this. Have we got to a point where we can produce so much that we can allocate according to need? Kropotkin, writing in 1892, thinks we have.

Okay, so what is Kropotkin's vision of anarchist communism?

1. All means of production, including housing, land and even clothing, are owned in common.

> private individuals should control neither the instruments of labor (tools, machines, factories), nor the places of cultivation of raw materials (the earth), nor the raw materials previously stored up, nor the means of storing and transporting them to particular places (the means of communication, warehouses, and so on), nor the means of existence during work (the supplies of the means of subsistence and housing).[26]

2. People choose what do from any field of work that is considered necessary. They bind themselves to work five hours a day between the ages of 20 and 50. Leaving another five hours for tasks not deemed necessary.[27] Because the workers themselves organize production, they make sure their work is enjoyable, avoiding boring work and extreme divisions of labour.[28]

> men, women, and children will gladly turn to the labour of the fields, when it is no longer a slavish drudgery, but has become pleasure, a festival, a renewal of health and joy.[29]

3. Modern technology allows us to produce a more than sufficient abundance.

> it is ... certain that mankind in general, aided by the creatures of steel and iron which it already possesses, could already procure an existence of wealth and ease for every one of its members.[30]

In other words, 'modern' technology as realized in Kropotkin's day. A common view is that this argument is only magnified by recent developments of technology. An alternative view is that the environmental consequences of all this modern technology are so severe as to jeopardize Kropotkin's project.

Distribution is egalitarian. So, frivolous over consumption by a minority does not deprive the rest of us.

4. Distribution is according to need.

> no stint or limit to what the community possesses in abundance but equal sharing and dividing of those commodities which are scarce or apt to run short. If this or that article of consumption runs short, and has to be doled out, to those who have most need most should be given.[31]

Kropotkin refutes the argument that distribution ought to be allocated in proportion to hours of work. All products are the outcome of the work of a vast multiplicity of producers. It is impossible to quantify these inputs. By what right does any one person claim a certain proportion of the ownership? In cases where there is more than enough to go around, people will just take what they want from a common stock. A scarce resource will go to those with greatest need. Or be parcelled out in equal shares. After the revolution, these forms of distribution will be implemented by parties of volunteers, handling different parts of production and distribution. For example, a collective manufacturing ploughs for peasant farmers. The same principles of distribution apply to agricultural land, factories and housing. They are to be allocated equally and according to need.

5. There is no state and no state enforcement. An anarchist society is one in which people are never motivated by fear of coercion.

The state is one issue. More on this later in the chapter. On the topic of coercion. I doubt you can sustain *any* specific version of social order without the *option* of coercion. That does not make coercion a favourite strategy. Nevertheless, if it is an option, there must be occasions when someone has a second thought about what they are intending. Because they fear coercion.

Kropotkin and the gift economy

The gift economy, as I have described it in earlier chapters, may be viewed as a detailed scenario of how Kropotkin's anarchist communism could work. Many of Kropotkin's examples fit the concept of the gift economy quite exactly. The people who go out to sea in lifeboats to rescue mariners. They do not expect compensation from those they rescue. They do not ask first, 'Can you pay me for this service?' The gift is for those in need, and it is calibrated exactly to their need.

Kropotkin considers the problem of food provision immediately after the revolution. After previous revolutions in France, the peasants stopped selling their grain. Even though the revolutionary authorities threatened to execute them. The peasants did not trust the currency. The urban workers starved. Kropotkin suggests this solution. Voluntary work committees will make agreements to supply the peasants directly with what they need. To organize production to cater to the real needs of the peasants—for tools, machinery, clothing. The peasants will just come in to the workshops to collect their requirements. In return, the peasants will agree to supply the grain the workers need.[32] To supplement this arrangement, parties of urban volunteers will take over land around the cities. Land the rich now use for their parks. They will turn this land over to agriculture.

A similar strategy is suggested for the distribution of clothing after the revolution:

> Groups would spring up in every street and quarter to undertake the charge of the clothing. They would make inventories of all that the city possessed and would find out approximately what were the resources at their disposal. It is more than likely that in the matter of clothing the citizens would adopt the same principle as in the matter of provisions—that is to say, they would offer freely from the common store everything which was to be found in abundance and dole out whatever was limited in quantity.[33]

In other words, authority over distribution would go to a voluntary collective of clothing distributors. Likewise, the food crisis likely to follow a revolution.

The well-intentioned citizens, men and women both, will form themselves into bands of volunteers and address themselves to the task of making a rough general inventory of the contents, of each shop and warehouse. In every block of houses, in every street, in every town ward, bands of volunteers will have been organized. These commissariat volunteers will work in unison and keep in touch with each other. An immense guild of free workers, ready to furnish to each and all the necessary food. Give the people a free hand, and in ten days the food service will be conducted with admirable regularity.[34]

There is a jump between the broad theoretical position and the examples. Broad overview. The whole population owns everything, and distribution is by need. In the examples. Self-constituted voluntary groups take control of parts of the means of production and distribute to groups they themselves nominate. The term 'gift economy' captures the spirit of this jump. A slogan that shows *how* ownership by all and distribution by need might be put into practice.

The division in anarchist thought

While anarchists are agreed on the topic of the state, they differ on economic matters. I will call it a split between 'market anarchism' and 'non-market anarchism'. Some recent anarchist texts lean towards market anarchism—while they also acknowledge that anarchists have different opinions on money. Sam Buchanan [1999] defines anarchism in accord with Bakunin's first and second points. 'Anarchists see any use of force or coercion, or any constituted authority, as illegitimate. The organisation of society must be by voluntary agreement.'[35] He endorses the use of money, because it is 'so fantastically useful that it will always turn up in some form or other. Money only gets dangerous when it is allowed to accumulate and can be used to get power over other people. The only way of stopping this is to change what is socially acceptable.'[36] Nicolas Walter [1977] describes anarchist federalism like this. 'Members of such councils would be delegates without any executive authority ... the councils would have no central authority, only a simple secretariat.'[37] He acknowledges a range of options where money is concerned. 'There might be equal pay for all, or pay according to need, or no pay at all. Some associations might use money for all exchange, some just for large or complex transactions, and some might not use it at all. Goods might be bought, or hired, or rationed, or free.'[38] Yet the emphasis is on market cooperatives.

> A society organised according to the principle of anarchist mutualism would be one in which communal activities were in effect in the hands of cooperative societies ... Economic mutualism may thus be seen as co-operativism minus bureaucracy, or as capitalism minus profit.[39]

Non-market anarchists in recent times

Market anarchism has not gone without challenge. The example of the Spanish anarchist revolution is hard to ignore. In some rural areas, communities provided goods and services according to need, dispensing with money. In the early days of the revolution in the cities, the workers supplied people with necessities without payment. For the most part, anarchists cite these examples to show that anarchists have a variety of perspectives on money, suggesting this is not a defining issue. Recent versions of non-market anarchism come out of anarchist and ultra-left critiques of alienation. While capitalism offered the working-class affluence, it could not relieve alienation. In the fifties, Paul Cardan [first 1959] nominated alienated labour as the central contradiction of current capitalism.[40] In the seventies Murray Bookchin, took up this theme [1971].[41] They celebrate the revolt against boring work as a revolutionary impulse.

The Situationists of France in the sixties drew the implications of these writings where money and the market are concerned. If people were free from alienated labour, they would want to be free to distribute their work. In a typical passage, Vaneigem [1967] remarks:

> The crumbling away of human values under the influence of exchange mechanisms leads to the crumbling of exchange itself ...

new human relationships must be built on the principle of pure giving. We must discover the pleasure of giving; giving because you have so much. What beautiful potlaches the affluent society will see – whether it likes it or no – when the exuberance of the younger generation discovers the pure gift. The growing passion for stealing books, clothes, food, weapons or jewellery simply for the pleasure of giving them away, gives us a glimpse of what the will to live has in store for consumer society.[42]

Anarchist takes on anthropology were influential. Stateless societies of the past did not have money and markets. Marcel Mauss [1925] named 'the gift economy' as a typical form of non-monetary distribution.[43] Marshall Sahlins [1972] argued that these were the original affluent societies. Hours of work were minimal.[44] Pierre Clastres [1974] claimed stateless societies of the Amazon actively blocked state formation. The role of chiefs was to mediate—to facilitate a consensus. 'Command' was unknown, and autonomy expected.[45]

A later anarchist author in this tradition is Peter Lamborn Wilson [1998]—aka Hakim Bey. He celebrates Fourier as a founder of his thinking on post-capitalism. Let's have work that is also play, ritual and art. He investigates pre-class societies of the archaeological record to confirm Clastres' ethnographic report. To give one example.

> Money originates and emerges in history as debt. But it has a "pre-history" as appropriation. The egalitarian economy of the Gift—which does not know money—can be shattered only by the economy of surplus and scarcity ... some few will enjoy surplus, the rest must experience scarcity. Slavery, tribute, and debt are all forms of scarcity.[46]

Meaning that class society creates scarcity and with it surplus. These are not primordial givens for the human species. In these recent versions of non-market anarchism, the absence of alienated labour implies the absence of money and the state.

The Gift Economy and the State

The first two sections of this chapter have looked at Marxist and anarchist views of the state and post-capitalism. The 'gift economy' is a non-market anarchism. Non-monetary post-capitalism is a tendency newly promoted in recent years. Yet its roots go back to some of the authors mentioned above, and especially to Kropotkin. Recent writers with this perspective do not usually describe themselves as anarchists. The term 'non-market socialist' describes their political location well.[47] I use the term 'gift economy' as a convenient shorthand, following the Situationists.

A key insight is the following. Gift economy socialists emphasize control of the means of production through voluntary collectives. Operating to provide goods and services to communities directly—without monetary payment. As either gifts or self-provision. Views on the state flow from this central premise. As argued in previous chapters, the state is impossible in a gift economy. This is because every person is being supplied with goods and services by other producer collectives. These other collectives operate independently and control the distribution of their product. A state means a monopoly of the control of violence. The state must reliably command an army or police force to implement its decisions. In a gift economy no one has any motive to put themselves in that position. To be the willing servant of state directives and wield violence accordingly. Nobody needs a 'job' paid in money to access goods and services. Nor are they looking to get a privileged position, supplied with good rations. Vis a vis a broader population of impoverished slaves. We could also say that 'the state' is expected to control, or at least supervise, the economy. This becomes impossible in a gift economy—where producers' collectives independently make decisions.

From this perspective, anarchist attacks on the state often miss the point. They treat 'the state' as a moral problem—coercion, hierarchy. Looking for a moral solution once everyone can see that the state is not required. I look at it more like this. The gift economy is run by voluntary producer collectives, controlling their own distribution, depending on other voluntary bodies for supplies. Participation becomes a necessity when working groups are constituted by volunteers. Likewise, cooperation and mutual aid, when these voluntary groups coordinate their actions to serve the needs of the community. By contrast, participatory control at the grass roots is impossible for any kind of market economy. Whatever the system of political decision making. In a market economy, whether radical reformist, state socialist or anarchist, the people must attempt to regulate the market through decisions made by representatives. Using monetary incentives. This top-down control blocks local participatory democracy. By contrast, in a gift economy social justice, economic planning and environmental restraints must come from the independent decisions of voluntary producer collectives. Earlier chapters have explained why this is quite feasible.

Territorial organisation in a gift economy

Foundational anarchist texts talk about two types of organisations for a post-capitalist society. Workers' associations and communes. Associations are workers' collectives. In a gift economy these would operate without monetary exchange. Through networks. Associations with a common purpose would federate to exchange ideas and work out strategies. For example, transport collectives running bus services. These associations would also operate through agreements to supply and receive. To construct chains of production. The second kind of organisation that these texts refer to is a 'commune'. This term refers to a municipal level territorial organisation, run by assemblies of citizens living in the municipality. What these early anarchist authors envisage is a 'federation' constituted by delegates from these communes. In other words, an overarching territorial organisation.

Whether such territorial organisations are necessary in a gift economy is debatable. For example, we might think of sewerage as a service provided by a local commune that requires territorial supervision. Alternatively, we might imagine a club of sewerage providers operating in chapters in each locality. Linking up with other associations to supply their needs—pipes, compost bins, cement or whatever.

In *Beyond Money*, Anitra Nelson envisages 'Yenomon' as one version of a territorial organisation in a post-market community mode of production.[48] Yenomon is pretty much like the 'Twin Oaks' intentional community that she describes in other writings.[49] The assembly of Yenomon sets up working committees. They allocate work rosters to ensure that all members are participating fairly. People can choose what work to do, from a list of tasks set up by the assembly. The community ensures fair distribution based on needs. The committees assess the needs of members for goods and services that can be produced locally—almost all of what is necessary. They liaise with other similar communities to source goods constructed outside their own community.

Nelson makes it clear that this is just *one way* of organizing a post-money society. There might be a plurality of models. Her example suggests at least one function for a territorial organisation. That is to ensure fair distribution of products in the community. For my favourite example, fencing mesh. The association producing fencing mesh would likely have a factory in one community and distribute into a whole bioregion. Rather than distributing mesh to each farming unit across this whole landscape, they might prefer to rely on local communities to undertake that. A local territorial organisation that could assess the needs of each community garden, farm and residential backyard.

What I would like to consider is what kind of territorial organisation could make sense in a gift economy. The 'un-state'. As argued, it could not be a state, with the powers of command that a state can exercise. So how could a territorial organisation operate? I am going to draw from the strategy of the Zapatistas, explained in the previous chapter. Taking some of that into a more general framework.

We can think of the un-state as a territorially focused gift economy club. The bioregional un-state helps to facilitate agreements between communities in a whole bioregion. The municipal un-state helps to facilitate agreements between community members at a more local level. For example, agreements about land use. Agreements about distributing products—after they have been supplied by associations from other communities. These territorial clubs could be stacked in a nested set of federations—municipal, bioregional, national. Altogether this is the un-state. The municipal level sends representatives to the regional level, which then sends representatives to the national level. We could imagine international meetings to discuss issues relevant to several nations at once.

The intention of such a territorial organisation is to facilitate compacts on issues that are particularly relevant to a *territorial* unit. For example, the use of water from a river that runs through a bioregion.

There is no intention to take the power of distribution away from workers' associations. There are compacts that are not a concern of the territorial organisations. For example, the train service. The people making rails need to communicate with the people who are laying the rail line, and they need to communicate with the people who are planning the route. These are compacts, which link a chain of production across different territorial units. There are also federations of clubs, which are independent of the relevant territorial organisation. For example, a regional federation of lifesaving clubs.

On the other hand, these producer associations would on occasions need to make agreements with territorial units. Let's assume that the federated railway clubs might like to offer a new service for a set of towns and villages. With new stations and rail lines. Anybody residing in that region would want to have a say. The regional un-state could be the organization where coordination between the train clubs and the residents could take place. Facilitating an agreement.

In detail, how might this federated un-state operate? Starting at the municipality. Residents nominate several candidates and then vote to elect a selection. In the municipal assembly, the representatives nominate candidates for the regional assembly and so on. Elected representatives are expected to see their role as a duty, rather than an opportunity to dominate. You might elect three times the number of required representatives—and rotate them. Two thirds of their time back in their communities, continuing their usual work and community commitments. One third in office. There would be a right of recall if the elected representatives were not acting in good faith.

One role of these territorial organisations at each level is to propose agreements for their territory. The next step is to take their proposal back to their communities and see if there is a consensus. If not, they suggest an alternative and go through the same process. Until finally an agreement is reached. Or not as may be the case.

Once an agreement is reached, the role of the representatives is to monitor this compact—to discover whether it is being implemented. They are not expected to *enforce* that agreement—they have no authority and no capacity to do that. If they discover that the agreement is not implemented, they notify their assembly that there is a problem. The whole process starts again. The assembly attempts to develop a new agreement that everyone's going to be happy with.

Another role is to respond to a request for an agreement on a particular matter. People in the municipality might approach the un-state and say, 'Well, we've got a problem with this proposed train line here, and we want to talk about it in our municipality. Let's come to an agreement that's going to work for everybody.'

How is such an un-state supplied? Well, not by taxes enforced by the courts and a police force! That is not how the gift economy works. Instead, the un-state must be supplied like every other club. By donations of goods in kind. To give an example of normal process. The people who are in the birdwatching club are supplied by their local communities with food and do their share of the housework and agriculture. Their community is supplied with goods from other communities through chains of production. This is how the birdwatchers receive food, and also cement, wire, binoculars and solar panels. It would be exactly the same with the elected officials of the un-state. They also get gifts from the community. Donations produced and distributed by the workers' associations.

I offer this picture of the un-state to give readers a sense of what the options may be. However, I am not sure that I advocate it. It might be that all the functions of a territorial organisation could be carried out through producer clubs. For example, the railway clubs might approach the residents in a bioregion. Inviting them to a set of forums to consider their needs. To arrive at a consensus about what might work. A territorial organisation for a particular set of issues. Likewise with fencing mesh. The village producer association with the factory could invite communities in their bioregion to set up fencing mesh committees—to estimate needs for fencing mesh. A federated bioregional committee could consider these in combination to develop a bioregional plan. After which, the producer association would make and supply fencing mesh according to this plan.

Conclusions

This chapter has considered three approaches to the state in a post-capitalist society. Marx and Engels make a distinction between the transition and full communism. In the transitional period the state ensures that the working class, through its representatives, controls the means of production, plans what is to be produced and ensures fair distribution. This is a monetary economy. The workers' state owns the means of production. The state's control of money enables planning and distribution. In the market anarchist account, workers' cooperatives produce and sell goods and services, paying their workers accordingly. The state is absent—there is no authoritative command. This is somewhat difficult to reconcile with another foundational idea in market anarchist texts. That the federation plans production, allocates capital, determines distribution, and restrains competition. A third approach is that of the gift economy. In the gift economy approach, the absence of the state is *an effect* of the economic arrangements of non-market socialism. With no money, voluntary clubs produce stuff and distribute gifts. The State is impossible. On the other hand, some form of territorial organisation could occur. So long as it works like other economic units of the gift economy—as a voluntary club with members supplied by gifts. Whether or not an un-state is *necessary* is a moot point.

Endnotes

[1] Max Weber, *From Max Weber: Essays in Sociology*, Hans H. Gerth (trans), Routledge, London, 1948, p.78

[2] Karl Marx and Friedrich Engels, *The Communist Manifesto*, Penguin, Harmondsworth, 1967, p. 82

[3] Karl Marx, *Early Writings*, trans. T.B. Bottomore, C.A. Watts & Co. London, 1963; Leahy, Terry, *Humanist Realism for Sociologists*, Routledge, London 2017; Friedrich Engels, *The Origin of the Family, Private Property and the State*, Penguin, Harmondsworth, 2010.

[4] Marx and Engels, *The Manifesto*, p. 104.

[5] ibid, p. 105.

[6] Karl Marx, 'Critique of the Gotha Programme', in Karl Marx and Frederick Engels, *Selected Works in Two Volumes*, Vol. 2, Foreign Languages Publishing House, Moscow, 1962, pp. 18-37.

[7] ibid., pp.104 – 105.

[8] Michael Bakunin, Selected Writings, Arthur Lehning (ed), Jonathan Cape, London. 1973, p. 139.

[9] ibid, p. 266

[10] ibid. p. 259.

[11] ibid. p. 64.

[12] ibid p. 72.

[13] ibid. p. 83.

[14] ibid. p. 88.

[15] ibid. p. 67.

[16] ibid. p. 66.

[17] ibid. p. 75.

[18] ibid. p. 92.

[19] ibid. p. 67.

[20] ibid. p. 70.

[21] ibid. p. 82.

[22] ibid. p. 170.

[23] Pëtr Kropotkin, 'Communism and Anarchy', Graham Purchase (ed), in *The Anarchist Library*, 25 February 2009 [1901], viewed on 25 November 2023, https://theanarchistlibrary.org/library/petr-kropotkin-communism-and-anarchy, p. 4.

[24] Pëtr Kropotkin, 'The conquest of bread', in *The Anarchist Library*, 15 February 2009 [1892], viewed on 25 November 2023, https://theanarchistlibrary.org/library/petr-kropotkin-the-conquest-of-bread, p.87.

[25] ibid., p.8.

[26] Peter Kropotkin, *Peter Kropotkin: Anarchism and Revolution*, Freedom Press, London, 1969, p. 3.

[27] Pëtr Kropotkin, 'The conquest of bread', p.60.

[28] ibid. p. 70.

[29] ibid., p. 47.

[30] ibid, p. 10.

[31] ibid, p. 40 – 41.

[32] ibid. p. 45.

[33] ibid, p. 56.

[34] ibid, p. 39.

[35] Sam Buchanan, *Anarchy: The Transmogrification of Everyday Life*. Committee for the Establishment of Civilisation, Wellington, NZ., 1999, p.7.

[36] ibid. p. 31.

[37] Nicolas Walter, *About Anarchism*. Freedom Press, London, 1977, p. 15.

[38] ibid. p. 20.

[39] ibid. p. 15.

[40] Paul Cardan, *Modern Capitalism and Revolution*, Solidarity, London, 1974 [1959].

[41] Murray Bookchin, *Post-Scarcity Anarchism*, Ramparts Press, Palo Alto, 1971.

[42] Raoul VanEigem, *The Revolution of Everyday Life*, Donald Nicholson-Smith (trans), Left Bank Books and Rebel Press, London. 1983, p. 59.

[43] Marcel Mauss, *The Gift: Forms and functions of exchange in archaic societies*, Trans. Ian Cunnison, Routledge and Kegan Paul, London, 1970.

[44] Marshall Sahlins, *Stone Age Economics*, Tavistock, London 1974.

[45] Clastres, Pierre, *Society Against the State: Essays in Political Anthropology*, Zone Books, New York, 1987.

[46] Peter Lamborn Wilson, *Escape from the Nineteenth Century and Other Essays*, Autonomedia, New York, 1998, p. 31.

[47] John Holloway, *Hope in Hopeless Times*, Pluto, London, 2022; Anitra Nelson, *Beyond Money: A Post-Capitalist Strategy*, Pluto Press, London, 2022; Friederike Habermann, *Ecomony: UmCare zum Miteinander*, Ulrike Helmer-Verlag, Sukzbach, 2016; Nelson, Anitra and Frans Timmerman (eds), *Life Without Money*, Pluto Press, London, 2011.

[48] Anitra Nelson, *Beyond Money: A Post-Capitalist Strategy*, Pluto Press, London, 2022, pp. 46-58.

[49] Anitra Nelson, *Small is Necessary: Shared Living on a Shared Planet*, Pluto Press, London, 2018, pp. 222-226.

Chapter 10
Prefiguring the Gift Economy: First Bite

What I intend in this chapter is to discuss a particular kind of institution that we might create now, that *prefigures* a gift economy. What I call 'hybrids of the gift economy and capitalism'. These hybrids are not a new invention—but it is new to think of them as a strategy of transition to the gift economy. I will begin with a summary of capitalism and the gift economy, as explained in previous chapters.

In a capitalist mode of production, the means of production, like factories or land, are owned by members of the capitalist class. These owners of the means of production pay their workers in money and the workers use that money to access goods and services. So, most people must work for a wage to live. The means of production are themselves commodities. They can be bought and sold on the market. These means of production are used to make money by producing goods for sale. The capitalist invests a certain amount of money, then employees work and produce things. Then the capitalist sells these products. Capitalists compete to make a profit. If they fall behind their competitors, they are likely to lose market share and investor support. What consumers do is to buy the cheapest available product to satisfy their needs and desires—and suitable to their values.

So, this is the outline, the rules of the game, if you like, of the capitalist mode of production.

Now let's look at the gift economy. The gift economy is an envisaged mode of production. There is no money so there's no payment of wages. People work as volunteers. There is no state organizing everything and paying an armed body of enforcers. People provide for themselves. For example, a community garden providing food for the gardeners. Or they distribute their products as gifts. For example, a train service that serves many. The people making the trains, producing the rails and driving the trains are producing their train service as a gift.

In a gift economy, 'compacts'—formal written agreements—are promises to provide goods and services. People make a promise to produce a specified quantity of goods or services and deliver them to particular people at a certain time. These can be exchanges, or one-way donations. For example, the people who operate the railways are making a compact with the community at large to provide a train service. Ultimately there is a generalized reciprocity in the production and receipt of gifts. People are *receiving* gifts as well as providing gifts. But there is no expectation of reciprocity in relation to any one *particular* gift.

The gift economy runs through a set of cultural presumptions. It takes care of people by making sure everyone has meaningful work. Compacts make decisions about who gets goods and services from a production group. So, workers directly express their care for other people by providing them with their needs. The gift economy allows people to care for other species, too. Partly out of self-interest. We don't want to live on a destroyed planet. But also, out of love and aesthetic appreciation of the living world. The gift economy allows people to be involved in a productive task that looks after the global commons and their bit of it. People gain status by looking after the natural world in their work.

Predictable market behaviour in capitalism

We can think of capitalism as a set of legal rules, and structures, like ownership. If you take something that someone else owns, that's 'theft' and you get into trouble with the police. These are *structures*. But also, capitalism operates according to a set of cultural *presumptions*, that make the market economy work. Capitalism is not just a set of laws or regulations but it's also about predictable market behaviour.

Let us describe two key aspects of this behaviour.

Consumers maximize private satisfactions for the least cost. You're being paid in wages. You go out to buy something. The aim is to buy what you want. That's useful to you for the least cost. If some other identically useful thing comes along at a lower cost, then you'll buy that. That's the bare bones, the minimum assumption that makes the market economy work. The second key behavioural assumption is that capitalists maximize profits. Their aim is to make the most money out of selling stuff. They'll sell things at the highest price that the market will bear or drop prices to increase their market and get more profits that way. So, these are assumptions about behaviour that make a market economy work.

Hybrids of the gift economy play on this line. On the one hand, what they are doing is not (usually) illegal, it does not defy the formal structures of the market economy. On the other hand, what they are doing breaks with typical assumptions about market behaviour. A hybrid uses some typical aspects of market practice and at the same time implements some of the ethical assumptions of the gift economy—embodying some of the practices that will animate a gift economy. For example, control by the workers. Like a cooperative. Workers together decide how to produce stuff. Unlike a typical capitalist firm or government department—where the workers are told what to do. Or some control by the community at large. Perhaps the customers have some input into what's happening in the production process. Like a community supported agriculture farm (a CSA). Customers make a choice to spend money on *that* farming product—to have an influence on the way agriculture is being done. Unlike a typical supermarket purchase, where customers just look at the product and choose the cheapest food that looks ok. Purchases that do not buy the cheapest product. Like buying timber that is forest stewardship certified—certified to be from a sustainable timber operation. A gift to the natural world. Or there may be some distribution that does not follow the normal market practice of making the highest possible profit.

Like charging a low price for the unemployed. And these forms of distribution are aimed at benefiting particular people, animals, or plants.

These alternative gift economy practices are combined with some aspects of the capitalist market economy, like wage labour. So, for example, the people working in a hybrid may be working for a wage, producing goods, and selling them on the market, just like in any normal capitalist firm.

Now, how do hybrids work to bring about the gift economy? Well, they operate by undermining the cultural pre-suppositions of the capitalist economy. People are not behaving according to the cultural assumptions that make the market work. That make money work. Like the presumption of buying cheap and selling dear. They are undermining this even if only to a slight extent—while also making use of capitalist economic forms, like wage labour, private ownership of the means of production, money.

If a hybrid is going to work, continue and sustain itself, the people involved must pay attention to their gift economy practices as well as paying attention to their capitalist context. They would regard their project as a failure if they were unable to implement some of their gift economy goals. For example, a community supported agriculture farm. If they did not look after nature better than the ordinary commercial farm, what would be the point? So, they must look at their gift economy side. But also, they must work in the market. They're producing a market product. People must want to buy it. They must pay adequate wages.

This combination can work, but it's also a situation with tensions and difficulties. The hybrid pays a price for defying the logic of the market. There are market sanctions against that. Those sanctions do not come out of a top-down conspiracy. They operate through the structures of the market economy. You cannot expect it to be easy to establish a hybrid in the capitalist economy. I'll explain that by talking about examples.

I will begin by just listing some hybrids. To give a sense of what I'm talking about.

— Margaretta's belly dancing school in Eastern Australia. A business for Margaretta but one that donates services to the community and relies heavily on the voluntary work of its students.

— Purple Pear. A CSA (community supported agriculture) farm in Australia.

— Oxfam as a donor organization. It donates free of charge to clients. But also pays wages to its staff and solicits money from middle class donors. The donors have earned their income in paying jobs.

— Fair trade coffee. The aim is to benefit impoverished farmers from the global South by charging a premium price to consumers from the global North.

— Government subsidies for solar panels. Voters aim to help to save the environment by tweaking market prices for energy services.

— Government labour legislation—like the 8-hour day. Such legislation undermines the presuppositions of the capitalist economy and puts a brake on capitalist firms. To secure the real needs of people, rather than allowing capitalists to extract maximum exchange value.

— Wind power collectives in Denmark. People get together and put in their money to provide their own wind power.

— Agricultural co-ops in the Philippines, run by smallholder farmers to market their produce. A partial collectivisation of privately owned farms.

— Community gardens. Often the land is lent by the council. Sometimes there's a paid coordinator. So that is a market aspect of some community gardens. Goods and services must be bought to make the community garden run. People are buying seeds to start their plots. Or buying fencing material and tools.

— The Mondragon collectives. A set of workers' cooperatives in Spain. Selling white goods while ensuring that profits go to the workers themselves.

— Ethical investment. People aim to make money by investing. But only in certain things. What comes first is to make sure that the money's invested in ethical projects.

We can see from this that there is a multiplicity of hybrids. This is not a new development. It's not owned by the left or environmentalists. Hybrids are not necessarily driven by ideology. Nevertheless, there are various ways in which the capitalist market economy—taken as a structural force—is undermined. I do not imagine that hybrids are an equal player in the current economy. Capitalist firms and ownership by the wealthy, the market as the structuring principle of economic life. This is what is dominant, as previous chapters indicate. Nevertheless, hybrids exist, are important and are significant for a transition out of capitalism.

In writings that are quite popular in sociology and human geography, organisations of this kind are theorized quite differently from my analysis. Let us mention the work of Gibson-Graham from geography and Olin Wright from sociology.[1] These authors envisage a transition out of capitalism in which 'alternative market' institutions or 'real utopias' come to dominate economic life. What these authors think of as the 'standard capitalist firm' is a firm run by owners and investors to make the most profit regardless of human or environmental considerations. Ethically guided alternative market institutions depart from that model. After a transition, these alternative market institutions come to dominate the economy. There is still a market, and the state exercises a role of benign supervision, funding state-owned alternatives and regulating where necessary. My analysis differs on the following key points.

- If these hybrid organisations came to dominate the economy, the market and money would be untenable.

- Hybrids *undermine* a market economy rather than constituting a new kind of benign market economy.
- These organisational forms are not easy to introduce into a market economy. They struggle to operate within the market.

Let's start looking at some examples in more detail to explain what I mean. I will start off with an example from my recent research into permaculture as a social movement.[2] As part of that research, I interviewed permaculture activists doing projects inspired by permaculture.

A CSA farming cooperative in Wales

Alice was a member of a community supported agriculture cooperative in Wales, an organic vegetable farm. They had 31 acres of land and 10 of these under cultivation. There were eight members in their cooperative. Most of the work was being done by these eight cooperative members—who were also living at the farm. The cooperative organised the following arrangement. Members of the community signed up for a month of vegetables. Every week the members would come out to the farm to collect their box of vegetables. They would pay in advance, for a whole year or a whole month. When they came to collect, they would get a box of assorted vegetables—depending on what was in season and being grown on the farm. The farm would also sell some produce to restaurants.

Let's go through the various market aspects of this project. First, they're selling vegetables. That instantly implies that they're in market competition with other vegetable sellers, certainly other farmers selling organic vegetables. If their vegetables were eight times as expensive as supermarket vegetables, that would limit their customers. This market in vegetables is the sea that they swim in. The second aspect of the market economy is that the land they farm is privately owned. By the parents of one of their members. The eight members of the cooperative could not afford to *buy* a farm like this. So close to a town—where they can sell their vegetables. If the parents die, then the land goes to their estate. That might include another sibling who says, 'Well, I'd like to sell this farm and take half the money'.

Another market aspect is that they are joint owners of that business. They own it together. It's a private business. No one else can come along and say, 'Well, you know, I wouldn't mind some of the money that you're making from these vegetables. Give it to me'.

In many ways, even though they run the farm as a cooperative, they're typical wage labourers. They exist in a market economy where they must earn an income. Their CSA income must allow them a standard of living not wildly different from a more typical job. The competitive market economy. If they're not paid enough and other jobs are much more lucrative, they might have to leave their CSA.

Now for the non-market aspects. The co-op members control their own work. It is not your standard example of alienated labour. They decide together as a cooperative what work they're going to do. And how what they're doing is ethical work. They get a benefit that they would not get by taking any random job. Instead, they have an ethical job—because it's organic agriculture, because it's taking community control of land and because of the cooperative work process.

So, as distinct from a typical capitalist firm, run by a boss and, making the most money possible, decisions are made by consensus—by the eight members getting together and having a meeting. They rotate leadership roles. Like accounting or running the poly tunnels. Everybody has a leadership role so nobody's the boss of this project. Volunteers also do some of the work. So, these extra hands are giving *their* work completely for free. Which may be exploitation from the perspective of the market. But can also be seen as a gift to support an enterprise that might struggle otherwise. The motive of the volunteers is partly to learn about community supported agriculture and agricultural techniques. To that extent, it's an apprenticeship. But also, for ethical reasons, they want to involve themselves in organic agriculture and producing food through that. A gift.

Customers are getting some control of the means of production. They're saying, 'I'm not going down to the local supermarket. That's unethical. The supermarket chains exploit workers in Poland and then bring the carrots from Poland to the UK using fossil fuels. And then they put the carrots into plastic bags and store them with refrigeration powered by fossil fuels. So instead of that, I am going out to the co-op to get my cardboard box. I am sourcing local vegetables produced without long term toxic impacts.'

These customers are using their vegetable shopping money to support this ethical project—despite what it is costing them in time and organisation. A *gift* of time and convenience. They are not following the market norm of buying the most useful product at the cheapest price. They're getting an assorted box of vegetables. Rather than being able to look through a recipe list and go, 'I'm cooking this on Monday and this on Tuesday. I'm going to the supermarket and buying what I need for that.' So that means more housework, working out what recipes will fit with the vegetable box you *get*. It also means more housework, going out to the farm to collect the vegetable box. Rather than just dropping down to the local supermarket.

So, what these customers are doing is partly a market transaction and partly a gift transaction. They're making an ethical consumer choice to get local produce, to get produce that's grown sustainably. Their gift also allows some workers to have control over daily production decisions. Taken as a whole, the arrangement creates a social link between customers and producers absent in the typical market context. Customers and farmers are associates working together to produce and consume food.

This is all very encouraging and a good example of a hybrid. It has worked for seven years now so even if it failed next week, it is still an important intervention. But what are the limitations of their practice? What market sanctions make an ethical practice of this kind difficult? The first one is that the eight members of the co-op are not paid well for their work. The cooperative is getting an average of £7,000 per week for their produce (in 2020). They must pay for inputs out of that income. The remainder must be divided between eight people. They are charging £40 to £60 for a box of veggies every week. That is cheap compared to typical supermarket prices for organic vegetables.

They must keep their prices low to compensate customers for the inconvenience of their product. Supermarket prices set the upper limit of their own pricing. The supermarket prices rely on the exploitation of labour from the global South (including Eastern Europe), along with the cheap price of farming land in the global South. So how is the cooperative dealing with that? They are paying their members very low wages. Twenty pounds for a six-hour day of work. Supplementing these low wages, the government gives each of their workers a £50 per week subsidy. A subsidy designed to prop up low wage work and keep people off welfare. The co-op members also get bed and board free of charge. Adding it up, they are typically ending up with about £150 pounds in money plus bed and board. The median wage in the UK at the time I did the interviews was £584 pounds a week.

On the one hand, this wage arrangement reveals the extent of their departure from normal market practice. They are *giving* away some of their capacity to earn income. What it also means is that participation in the cooperative is tenuous and comes with certain costs. Some members of the co-op cannot get by on their co-op income and are supplementing that with other work. One member is doing three days of building work per week. We can think of a hybrid as a prefiguring strategy, which is intended to undermine and replace capitalism. The low wage consequence of this departure from market practice reduces the number of people in the UK willing to do this. A market sanction. Low wages are a consequence of market competition with supermarkets—that are behaving perfectly rationally as market actors.

Obviously, you will get a small minority of people who are prepared to take these low wages because they're ethically committed. But it is unlikely that this kind of intervention will take over 90% of the UK food industry. The middle class are the people most psychologically equipped to take a risk with money like this. The options they close off through a long-term commitment to low wages are—for example—buying a house, sending their children to university, owning a car.

I asked Alice about these issues. I suggested they were charging a low price for their vegetables.

Probably, yeah, probably it depends. Like now some of the industrial organic farm movement is like ruining this shit. Same as they have in the states. So now Aldi have gone organic. All their vegetables are 'organic'. They're not local. Who knows really, how they're farmed. 'Organic' doesn't mean anything anymore. We need to relabel like 'fresh', 'local'.

Their low prices are forced upon them—because they're competing with Aldi. Aldi has declared all their vegetables 'organic'. In fact, those Aldi organic vegetables are grown on massive farms, in a low wage country, exploiting local people at dirt cheap wages, and then trucked all the way to the UK. Followed by refrigeration for months.

The next market sanction to consider is land ownership. Their land ownership is very insecure, as I have explained. They are in an extremely lucky position, having a parental loan of land. Their aim is to get crowd funding. To buy the farm from the parents. But it's now seven years into the co-op and they have not yet been able to do that. Zooming out to look at the prospects for this kind of intervention in the UK in general. Farming land in the UK is owned by a wealthy elite with a price well above its value for commercial farming. The cost of land is a barrier to small scale cooperative farms selling organic food locally—the most ethical form of food provision for the UK. As Alice explained, to make a farm commercially viable in competition with the supermarkets:

> Land workers and the products of the land have got to be ludicrously cheap. Land is so expensive. We need to get that land. They need to look at government programs for helping people to become tenant farmers, like the ecological land trust to set up farming situations for people. So, you don't have to have like a half a million quid to become a peasant. And they need to look at the price of food. They need to look at the way they subsidize farmers for doing environmental goods.

In other words, the only way to make an ethical intervention like this more common is to take strong state action and make more radical inroads into the capitalist economy. The government should buy land and give it to farmers at a subsidized rate—so that we can diversify ownership and allow more community control of food provision. While this (or something similar) might well happen in the context of system change, it's not likely in the immediate future.

The Mondragon collectives in Spain

I will consider the Mondragon collectives next because they're iconic.[3] People often refer to them as an example of an alternative that prefigures the 'solidarity economy'. A post-capitalist society in which the dominant economic form is collectives of workers operating in a market economy.[4] I will use the Mondragon collectives as an example through which to consider some of the problems with that vision.

The Mondragon collectives are in the north of Spain. Catholic priests initiated them in the fifties when Franco was in power. They manufacture white goods, like washing machines, fridges, ovens. The cooperative owns the factories, plant and equipment. To begin with, all workers were members of the cooperative and had voting rights to make decisions about how the cooperative would be run. So, this is a paradigm of the ideal leftist cooperative that people envisage. It's still operating today so it has been around for more than 70 years. Apparently showing that a workers' cooperative can be sustainable in a market economy. I will review this as a hybrid. The market aspects, the non-market aspects, the limitations of their practice.

The market aspects are as follows. They are selling white goods on an international market for white goods. They have private ownership of the means of production—their firm is owned privately. People who are not members have no rights. As with any market business, the workers are wage earners. They are members because they want a reliable wage. They depend on market success for their income. If their washing machines are not marketable, they just won't get an income. An income is proportional to the success of their market endeavour.

Let's look at some aspects of their practice that mark the cooperative as a hybrid of the gift economy and capitalism.

The factories are not owned by a capitalist or a suite of shareholders. People who sit back and receive profits from their shares. It is owned by the workers themselves. The money goes back to them or into improving their plant. It does not go to a separate exploiting group. They are making democratic decisions about the use of their profits. There is an analogy to a gift economy in this. A collective of workers owns their means of production and can make decisions about distribution. An example that shows this power to be quite real is their decision to cap wages as profits increase. Instead of increasing their wages, they have decided to allocate some earnings to community services such as buses and childcare centres. Another allocation is for the promotion of the cooperative movement. These allocations are clearly gifts. They are making a *gift* of some profits to the community, not expecting any monetary return. A completely non-market practice.

Let's look now at the limitations of their intervention. The level of wages is constrained by the labour market. They cannot pay substantially less than the going rate without endangering the cooperative. They cannot pay a lot more than the going rate without increasing the cost of their whitegoods and losing their market. One effect is that the cooperatives had to decide to pay a higher rate to professionals, such as engineers and accountants. The ordinary industrial workers are working just as hard and yet they're not being paid as much. This goes against the norms of a gift economy—in which distribution is allocated in relation to need. This unequal pay scale is a necessity in relation to market pressures. They would find it hard to recruit the professionals they need if pay was drastically different to that typical of the labour market. At the same time, there is some difference – professionals in the collectives are being paid slightly less than the going rate. A gift to the cooperative. But a gift limited by market constraint.

There is a more profound determination by the market economy here. Saito makes the point that capitalism as a system invades every detail of the production process. Setting it up to make the highest possible profit.[5] A pressure that is certainly applied to the Mondragon collectives—selling their whitegoods on the international market. One aspect is the separation between intellectual and manual work so entrenched in capitalist production. As Braverman[6] argued, decades ago, this separation removes daily control over production from the hands of ordinary workers and vests it in a 'paper' (now digital) determination of the production process. Organized by engineers, a privileged caste vis a vis production line workers. As Saito points out, to overthrow this capitalist technology, it would be necessary to demolish this hierarchical arrangement. Given the competitive pressures of the market, the Mondragon collectives have not been able to do this. Instead, they organize their production like any typical firm. They have set up production to achieve 'efficiency'—measured by money. That is what the market requires. However, this 'efficiency' is not necessarily what would make sense in a gift economy. If we were trying to maximize the enjoyment of work—as well as produce a useful product.

'Efficiency' in creating monetary value is also inevitably a political project. The separation of planning and execution. The monetary structures of reward accompanying this. These are designed to *control* ordinary workers who are alienated. Bored, not paying attention, not invested in the outcomes. In actual resistance, as in sabotage, going slow, stealing. The professional class are paid for their *loyalty* as much as for the fact that their *skills* command a higher price. How much this all applies in Mondragon is hard to determine. On the one hand, because they are working for a collective, all the workers of Mondragon would want to increase value, measured in money. That is where they get their income. On the other hand, as individual workers, they are caught up in a system of production alienating in its subordination to market demands. The structures of command linked to this exacerbate this problem.

There's a second thing. So obvious it feels strange to talk about it. Every worker in the collective is being paid in money and needs that money to live their life. They are doing that by buying goods and services produced by people around the world working for wages. Those people are doing what makes market sense. Often the opposite of enjoyable and useful work. They're most likely being ordered around by a boss—making decisions purely on a profit basis. A boss who does not care how unpleasant the work is. These workers feel humiliated, that they are being ordered around, that they are bored beyond belief.[7] Every time the workers of Mondragon spend money to live their *own* lives, they are complicit in this market economy.

An aspect of their location in the market economy is that the company needs income from sales. They cannot give what they produce free of charge. They may be aware that they are selling their white goods to affluent workers in the rich countries. They might know that many in the global South do not have access to fresh water. Rural villages could benefit from a pump for a tube well, from tanks and guttering to harvest water, from concrete and poly-pipe for small dams and water reticulation. But the hands of the Mondragon workers are tied. They cannot abandon the market in white goods that guarantees their incomes. They cannot start producing village water systems and donating them.

This discussion is leading to a telling example of the way their operations are confined by market processes. As readers of this book know, the capitalist class in the 1970s and 1980s worked out how to offshore production from the global North to the global South—where wages are much lower. Producing the same manufactured goods at much reduced prices. And incidentally destroying the political power of the working class in the global North.

As you can imagine, the Mondragon cooperatives were staring down the barrel of annihilation. They could not reduce wages for their workers in Spain—without losing their workforce. They had to reduce the price of their white goods to compete in the post globalisation marketplace. They made a fateful decision. They would supplement their cooperative workforce with cheaper labour. They employed people who were not members of their cooperatives and paid them 20% less. That's what they did in Spain. They also started setting up plants to make components in the global South—in Thailand, Brazil, India and China, to name some of the countries involved. At local wage rates. Now, nine per cent of what they sell is made in those overseas plants. The cooperative did not invite these new workers from the global South to be members. Now, of every ten employees working directly for the Mondragon cooperative, only four are *members* of the cooperative[8]. Mondragon has turned their *original members* into a labour aristocracy. Their other workers are disenfranchised.

My point is not to blame them for these decisions. They have accomplished a serious improvement on business-as-usual capitalism. At the same time, these compromises remind us just how difficult it is to implement gift economy ethics in a market economy.

Lessons from hybrids

What lessons can we draw from this discussion of hybrids? To begin, that there are barriers in the way of gift economy practices. These are not barriers set up by a conspiracy of capitalist elites—they're barriers implicit in the market economy. They come about through structures that everybody implements, in their daily life, without even thinking about it. Structures which make money and the market work as social institutions. My conclusion is that we need to get rid of the market and money. Hybrids are a useful step. But they do not go far enough in the long term.

Take an optimistic view. These hybrids start to dominate the economy. Their market aspects wither. Let's look at the Mondragon collectives. Assume they decide to continue to market some of their produce to rich people—at higher than standard prices. As well, they compact to *donate* other productions to African villages. Defying market logic. Add another assumption. While their work force is receiving some of their income as wages, they are also receiving gifts from other generous cooperatives. Providing the Mondragon workers with things they might need—sailing holidays around the Mediterranean, buses and bikes, free steel. The market aspects of their cooperative have less and less relevance. They can afford generous donations to an African village.

An avalanche of hybrids could bring about the gift economy. All hybrids reduce the power of the market to determine production and distribution. If a huge wave of hybrids took over the economy, the power of the market would fade to nothing. Clearly this is carrying things to extremes. A thought experiment. The more likely scenario is that hybrids take up more and more economic space and lead people to question the market. A prefiguring leading on to a revolutionary installation of the gift economy.

Why hybrids cannot constitute an 'alternative' market economy

I want to conclude this chapter by saying what I think are the practical perils of seeing hybrids as *alternative* market forms—that will come to dominate and eventually achieve a market-based post capitalism. This pro-market analysis is not just social theory. For example, in the permaculture movement people say, 'markets are not the problem', 'societies always have markets,' 'we need a cultural shift,' 'people must find right livelihoods and use their money ethically.'

There are practical problems associated with this. The market acts as a social force to punish departures from market principles. If you believe there is no problem with the market it is easy to think that an 'ethical business' is no more difficult than any other stock standard business. This can lead to terrible burnout and depression when market sanctions bites. When it is actually very difficult to live a reasonable life (however spartan) and earn the money you need. To avoid this burnout, understand that what you are doing goes against the grain of market practice—and will accordingly be difficult. That is not a reason to abandon the attempt, but it can help to engender a more pragmatic approach.

This optimistic 'alternative market' theory of hybrids can turn judgemental where most people's choices are concerned. If this is so easy, why are only a few die-hard permaculture people doing it? Answer. Most people have not seen the light and are seduced by capitalist culture. They are taking the easy way out—not realizing the desperate plight we are all in. The necessity to behave ethically where money is concerned.

Of course, this judgemental account is not entirely wrong. What it forgets is the class distribution of economic opportunities and cultural backgrounds. I remember the 'Global Gardener' video. Bill Mollison, one of the two founders of permaculture, stands on his veranda. He is looking over his lush food forest and intones. 'If people only realized that everything they needed is right outside their door. All you really need is sun, plants, and keep your eye on the soil'. The 'you' of this proclamation are members of the Australian middle class. Backed up by the wealth of their parents—with the cultural capital that comes with that. Useful for real estate deals, handling the welfare bureaucracy, applying for grants, setting up a website. With a childhood experience of economic security. Taking advantage of cheap land in remote parts of Australia.[9] The existing capitalist economy is the context for hybrids. Ethics cannot make this context go away. The next chapter will continue this discussion, giving more examples of how hybrid prefiguring works.

Endnotes

[1] Julie Katherine Gibson-Graham, *The End of Capitalism (As We Knew It)*, University of Minnesota Press, Minneapolis, 2006a; Julie Katherine Gibson-Graham, *Post-Capitalist Politics*, Minnesota, University of Minneapolis Press, 2006b; Eric Olin Wright, *Envisioning Real Utopias*, Verso, London, 2010.

[2] Terry Leahy, *The Politics of Permaculture*, London, Pluto, 2022.

[3] Anjel Mari Errasti, Inaki Heras, Baleren Bakaikoa and Pilar Elgoibar, 'The internationalisation of cooperatives: the case of the Mondragon cooperative corporation', *Annals of Public and Cooperative Economics*, vol. 74:4, 2003, pp. 553-684; Nick Romeo, 'How Mondragon became the world's largest co-op', *New Yorker*, 27 August 2022; Lynne Weiss, 'The Mondragon cooperatives', *What I'm Seeing and Hearing*, 21 September, 2022, viewed on 6 July 2023, https://lynneweisswriter. com; Gibson-Graham, *Post-Capitalist Politics*, pp. 101-126.

[4] Michael A. Lebowitz, *The Socialist Alternative: Real Human Development*, Monthly Review Press, New York, 2010.

[5] Saito, Kohei, *Marx in the Anthropocene: Towards the Idea of Degrowth Communism*, Cambridge, Cambridge University Press, 2023.

6 Harry Braverman, *Labor and Monopoly Capital: The degradation of work in the twentieth century*, Monthly Review Press, New York, 1999 [1974].

7 Terkel, Studs, *Working: People Talk About What They Do All Day and How They Feel About What They Do*, The New Press, New York, 1997.

8 Errasti, Anjel Mari, Inaki Heras, Baleren Bakaikoa and Pilar Elgoibar, 'The internationalisation of cooperatives: the case of the Mondragon cooperative corporation', *Annals of Public and Cooperative Economics*, vol. 74:4, 2003, pp. 553-684.

9 Julian Russell and Tony Galley, *Global Gardener: Permaculture with Bill Mollison*, Bullfrog Films, Oley, Philadelphia, 1991; Bill Mollison, *Permaculture: A Designers' Manual*, Tagari Publications, Tyalgum, Australia, 1988; Terry Leahy, *Permaculture*.

Chapter 11
Prefiguring the Gift Economy:
Second Bite

This is the second chapter on hybrids of the gift economy and capitalism. Taken as prefiguring strategies of a transition to the gift economy. I am adding this chapter to give more examples. One reason is to show just how ubiquitous these alternative economic organisations are. To point out that they are not necessarily conceived as 'political' or even as 'alternative' by the participants. The other is to see how the concept of 'hybrids' can be used to make sense of effective aid work in the global South.

Margaretta's Middle Eastern dance school

I will begin by outlining the operation of a Middle Eastern dancing school in an Australian city. I participated in this school as a drummer and this account is based on my memory of the school from 1996 to 2016. I will put this in the present tense to give a sense of how I experienced it at the time.

Margaretta is the choreographer and owner of the school. Choreographed performances are accompanied by a track from a Middle Eastern music CD, or with music for drummers that Margaretta composes. There are at least five Middle Eastern dance schools in the city. Some focus on Middle Eastern 'cabaret' dancing and some focus on a United States synthetic style called 'tribal'. Margaretta is keen to promote a more folkloric style with an emphasis on folkloric costumes and choreographed community dances. There are classes of about 12 women sorted into competence grades—

beginners, intermediate, advanced. For example, Monday, Wednesday and Thursday evening, with a rehearsal on Saturday afternoon for 'the troupe', the most competent dancers. The students are of mixed age, from 15 to 70. Performances are at school halls, community fetes, the studio itself. The school is running out of a rented studio, which used to be a squash court. There are two stories, rooms for storage, a kitchen, sewing room, workshop. The most important room in the studio is a large dance room with a wooden floor and with mirrors installed by Margaretta and her partner.

Market aspects

The following are the market aspects of the school. From the economic perspective, the school is a business. Margaretta and her partner are paying a mortgage on their house. They need income from the school, if only to pay the expenses incurred by the school itself. The students are paying customers, learning to dance in this style as a leisure pastime. So the school is in market competition with other providers of dancing lessons in the city, not just Middle Eastern dancing but also jazz ballet, classical, salsa and so on. The studio was the most recent of Margaretta's dancing venues and by far the best. It was however very expensive to rent. This is a constant source of stress. Margaretta must earn an income at least sufficient to cover the rent. Competing dance schools have two strategies that allow them to keep their fees down. One is to pay much less rent. Hire a much smaller and more run-down hall. In a more remote suburb, with little security of tenure. This is typical of the other Middle Eastern dance schools. The other is to concentrate the business on teenage and younger children. Offer classical, jazz and modern lessons, with preparation for national accreditation. Margaretta eschews both options, preferring her studio, despite the high rent. Security of tenure and sole occupancy allow Margaretta to instal dance training mirrors. She has complete control of her timetable, booking the studio for seven days a week. There is space to use for storage, sewing and a trade workshop. The location allows easy access for a middle-class clientele from the inner suburbs.

These advantages allow Margaretta a high level of artistic excellence in performance, but they augment the stress of market competition.

Gift economy aspects

Now let's look at the ways Margaretta's school differs from a typical capitalist firm. As a sole owner business, it is not 'Capitalist' with a capital 'C'—as described in Marx's *Capital*. Margaretta almost never pays anyone as an 'employee' of the business, extracting surplus value from their labour. Occasionally, she might pay one of her best dancers to help by running a class for her. This is the exception. For the most part, the school is a market business but not 'capitalist'. It is what Marxists call 'simple commodity production'.

There are numerous other ways that the operation of the school departs from market assumptions. The assumptions that make money, the market and capitalism possible. Margaretta has chosen a career in which she can express her creative passions—rather than making a choice to get the best paid employment. At work she has no boss telling her what to do. She donates her passion to the community. She is a devotee of Middle Eastern music and can express that through her teaching and performances. A degree of control over production and distribution. Her work is political. In the context of Islamophobia, she is promoting a dance form that comes from the Islamic heartland. She goes out of her way to educate her students and audiences about the origins of the styles that she favours. A syncretism of local village traditions, Romany culture, and Middle Eastern popular film and music. She sees this folkloric style as an expression of women's culture, both in its originating countries and in the global North, a celebration of women's bodies. She is meticulous in instructing students to perform the dance moves exactly as the tradition requires. In short, she lives her ethical values through her work. A gift to her community.

The students are not just Margaretta's paying customers – in a totally market relationship with the school. They are also volunteers. Their voluntary work makes the school possible. They volunteer for the public performances staged by the school and commit to the necessary work. The school's volunteer drummers also contribute their labour. Not just in performances but helping with the stage set up and bumping out. Of course, the public performances that these volunteers enable also recruit new students, contributing to the school as a business. These performances are almost always free to the public, a gift to the community. For example, at a school fete, a street fair organized by a council or a Middle Eastern dancing festival. The dancing is being performed as a labour of love by the dancers, who are also volunteering this service to the community. Students also cook and bring food to events, donating their time and ingredients. At end of term performances at the studio, students sell food they have prepared at home to help finance the school. The school hosts a network of emotional labour. For example, the students visited Margaretta when she was in hospital. Students constantly talk to each other about their lives and offer each other support and advice.

Tensions of a hybrid

Now I will discuss the tensions and limitations involved in trying to run a gift economy hybrid in the context of a capitalist market economy. The rent on the studio eats up all almost all the income from student fees. The market economy in rent drives this hybrid to the margins of viability. Margaretta's partner Andrew is working a lot of hours of paid work to provide the income the couple need. He is also working as unpaid help for the dance school, drumming, fixing things, helping sew the costumes, sourcing necessary machinery, running the sound system, and acting as an unpaid 'roadie'. The school cannot get out of these difficulties by increasing fees. It must compete on price with other dance schools. The typical students of this and other competing schools are women, on lower wages than their partners, working only part time to manage young children, or retired single women. In cases where the student is dependent on a male breadwinner, the dance fees can be seen as a burden on the family income. All of this puts a limit on fees. So, Margaretta is doing a very long week of work and just covering the rent on the studio. The structural context for the hybrid is the necessity of earning income in a market economy, and the precarious economic position of women in capitalist patriarchy.

Market competition is implied in the very real risk that Margaretta's choreographies will be plagiarized by competing schools. Because the music Margaretta used is readily available on CDs, one of her students can learn a choreography, leave the school, set up her own dance classes and use Margaretta's choreographies. Competing with Margaretta's business. This has in fact happened, and Margaretta is always concerned that it might happen again.

A shifting terrain of competing dance styles is played out in the market competition between schools. As mentioned above, a new dance style, 'American Tribal' became popular in the city by 2010. It drew on Middle Eastern and other folkloric styles. Some teachers of Middle Eastern dance became enthusiasts and converted their schools to 'tribal'. New schools teaching 'tribal' sprang up. These schools perform at the Middle Eastern dance festivals, competing with Margaretta to attract students. While she could trump this competition by running her own 'tribal' classes she refuses to do this— for political and aesthetic reasons. So, while Margaretta maintains a non-alienated creative expression through her work, the cost is a stressful economic vulnerability.

So, Margaretta is bearing a considerable financial burden to express herself through her work. While the school is performing very well as community art, it is not functioning well *as a business*. Economically, she would have been much better off with a more conventional option. She is trained as a school art teacher and gave that up to follow her dream. Likely she would have ended up as a senior teacher, with permanency, a good income and good superannuation. So Margaretta is to some extent *giving* her creative labour to the community. This is not without economic consequences for Margaretta as a 'proletarian'. Someone who needs an income to access the social product.

Members of the 'troupe', the featured dancers in public performances, are often the mothers of pre-school children or students in higher education when they first join the school. In either case, they do not have the pressure of a full-time job and their schedules are flexible. These options are short term. They might have children and add that workload to their student commitments. Later they graduate, get a professional job and are too busy. Their children start primary school. Those who try to stay and do everything are likely to burn out. In all these cases, market necessities encroach on the dance school. Margaretta finds all this very frustrating. She puts years of work into a student dancer, recruits them into the troupe and trains them in all the troupe dances, only to have them drop out. Patriarchy and the market economy combine to pull human resources from the school. For her students, the necessity to maintain a household income adds to gendered inequalities in housework and childcare.

There is a tension between the publicity needs of the school (as a business) and esteem issues for the dancers. For a public performance, Margaretta makes sure that only the best dancers perform the complicated choreographies. Other pieces involve everybody and are easier to perform. Margaretta allocates dancers into different groups based on their performance skills. Some students find it demeaning when Margaretta classifies their skills. They are not happy with her choices. For her, it is a business necessity to present the school in the best possible way. Also, an aesthetic choice to present her art as well as she can. But you cannot ignore the economic consequences of a different practice.

Margaretta has to abandon students who can no longer afford the fees. This happens quite frequently. Often the ones who must leave are very skilled dancers. She has spent many hours teaching them, with their performances improving year by year. They are a resource, as contributors to her aesthetic project. Yet, running a business, she must ignore these considerations.

Dancers would sometimes resent the amount of unpaid labour they are doing for the school. If the school manages to secure a set of performances in a major theatre, there is extra work required. Students can resist this voluntary commitment. Their family or work responsibilities prevent them from participating fully. Margaretta might scold them for their patchy participation—they had signed up for these performances.

Margaretta cannot afford a public presentation that is less than perfect. The dancers are limited by their market and family commitments. While dancers may have wanted to operate the studio more democratically, Margaretta needs to maintain control of her business. Members of the troupe met to set up a committee to help Margaretta run the studio, but she blocked this. A typical conflict was when one of the senior dancers started to advise newer dancers on the way to perform the moves. Margaretta saw this as an interruption to her teaching and a presumptuous attempt at aesthetic control. The conflict ended up with three dancers leaving the school—setting up their own dance collective, a voluntary club of friends.

An everyday hybrid

I have considered this example for several reasons. One is to point out that hybrids of the gift economy and capitalism are an everyday occurrence. In this case, people are expressing their creativity and sociability through a participation that in part expresses the economic logic of the gift economy. Such combinations are prefigurative in training people with the skills necessary to operate a non-market economy. Also, by fostering desires that the market cannot satisfy. We can also see how Margaretta's studio is constrained by the market economy. It does not float free of market pressures because there is no boss extracting surplus profit. Instead, various difficulties and limitations come from its market context. The constraints that a hybrid faces within a market economy.

The Chikukwa Project, Zimbabwe

The Chikukwa project, in Zimbabwe is my next example. I found out about this project while doing research on food security in Southern and South-Eastern African countries, starting in 2003. The field work for the Chikukwa project was from 2009 to 2014. With my sister I produced *The Chikukwa Project* documentary, released in 2013.[1]

This is an extremely successful food security and permaculture project. It was started in the early nineties. Participants are the villagers of the Chikukwa clan. There are about 7,000 people living on small farmsteads, linked together as six 'villages', extending over 15 kilometres. The villages are neighbourhoods of adjoining small farms, spread out through the landscape, a stretch of valleys, backed by hills, with a river on one edge. It is bound by a border with Mozambique, a national park, and a timber plantation.

By the nineties, factors both internal and external drove the villagers into an impossible situation. The original land of the clan had been cut down to about a quarter of their traditional lands, while their population had expanded. They were living, farming, and grazing their cattle on the hillside slopes. Soil erosion and compaction was severe. With almost all tree cover removed, the water poured down the slope in the rainy season, with silt covering fields and gardens. By the dry season the ground was dry and barren. They were losing topsoil every year. The springs they relied on for their water supply had dried up. They had to trek down to the river and carry water back up to their houses. A domestic labour nightmare. They did not have enough wood for cooking and building needs. Crop yields were woeful. Malnutrition was severe.

Their community permaculture project changed all this and is still operating today. I first met representatives from the project at a permaculture convergence in Malawi in 2009. I visited the site first in 2010 and then in 2014. I interviewed participants and saw the photos of the site taken in the nineties. They had completely transformed the landscape. To give some examples, they had established woodlots on the ridges to absorb the rainfall and release it gradually throughout the year. Also providing firewood and building timber. Parties of villagers put in contour bunds and swales, snaking across the hills and trapping water coming down the slope. They fenced off the gullies to prevent cattle destroying the creeks, re-establishing the original indigenous species. They put in check dams, slowing the flow of water, and spreading water into the landscape. As the springs returned, they made small dams and laid poly-pipe to village water tanks, constructed with mortar and local bricks. In turn these tanks piped water to taps in households.

Households have created permaculture gardens and cropping fields for a diverse diet. Field crops are maize, squash, beans, wheat, sorghum and millet. Surrounding the house will be an orchard with mixed fruit trees, avocadoes and nuts. A patch of bananas receives run off water from the yard. Poultry forage in the banana patch. Providing eggs and animal protein. Households may also keep other small livestock. Below the orchard and in full sun, a vegetable patch grows easy and prolific vegetables, a cabbage variety, amaranth, canola, tomatoes and so on. The small livestock produce manure that is used to make compost. A pit toilet ensures sanitation. A washing up rack in the open makes sure that crockery does not transmit infection. This household system has been massively successful in providing adequate food while maintaining soil quality.

Working together on all this has cemented social links. For example, parties of village volunteers used picks and spades to build the contour bunds. Families who were first adopters of the various permaculture technologies host visits from other villagers—and CELUCT pays them a small fee to thank them for their help. The project runs classes and workshops to teach these techniques and deal with problems that people are facing.

The central body of the project is the Chikukwa Ecological Land Use Community Trust – CELUCT. The villagers together built the centre which houses CELUCT. Including kitchens, meeting rooms, offices, and accommodation for trainees and visitors. The project works by establishing clubs in each village, like a permaculture club or women's discussion group or people living with HIV aids or a preschool committee. CELUCT refers to each of these aspects of community work as 'departments' of their organisation.

Market aspects

Let us now review the market aspects of the project.

One market aspect is that the farming land is owned individually by households. In theory, the hereditary chief of the clan owns all the land on behalf of the community. But in practice, each individual family uses their land as private property. CELUCT as a community NGO owns their centre and the land on which it stands.

CELUCT was initiated on a purely voluntary basis—but developed into an organisation that depended on monetary donations. Some neighbours invited two permaculture experts from the capital to run several workshops. Their 'Strong Bees' began transforming the landscape by calling on other villagers to help them. After about five years, they formalized their status as an NGO and accepted donations. With this funding, CELUCT (their new organisation) began paying its officers and recruiting from outside the villages. There is a core of 10 to 15 paid employees who rely on CELUCT for an income. Including kitchen staff and gardeners from the villages and the local officers of the project. The latter are former local teachers, villagers trained by the project, or former agriculture extension workers from outside the district. An accountant. CELUCT also pays villagers to host farm visits to demonstrate technologies, such as organic pest control, fishponds or similar. CELUCT and its manifestations in the villages depend on commodities from the wider market economy. For example, the CELUCT car, poly-pipe, concrete, fencing mesh. Villagers themselves depend on cash income for some needs. The Chikukwa villages are not a totally self-sufficient economy. For example, mobile phones, small solar panels, cooking utensils, agricultural tools, iron-framed windows. CELUCT also supports small market enterprises based in local agricultural production. For example, beekeeping and selling honey. So, all these are market aspects of the project.

Gift economy aspects

The non-market aspects of CELUCT are equally essential. CELUCT depends on donations from overseas. Mainly from a German Protestant organization, and a leftist British aid organization. These donations fund the paid employees and the CELUCT equipment. This is a gift from a section of the middle class of the rich countries. Also, this global North middle class are gaining some control over the global means of production—steering development away from typical market developments.

Mostly, the project is concerned with *subsistence* (non-market) production. Almost all CELUCT assistance is assistance to household food provision. For example, farmer to farmer training in small livestock, composting, organic pest solutions, fish farming. On their own farms, villagers are doing unpaid work. They're just growing food for their own family. A non-cash non-market transaction. The project depends on voluntary (non-market) community labour. For example, the voluntary work that constructed the CELUCT centre, built huge contour bunds, planted trees, fenced off the gullies and put in check dams and village water tanks. There is even a volunteer appointed to go around and monitor the use of the water. All this work takes place outside of the market economy.

Much of this implies community ownership and creation of means of production. Such as the check dams in the creeks and the fencing to protect the gullies. Using gifts from the global North along with their own labour to build community structures.

The organisation of CELUCT enables community control. CELUCT management committees include both the professional paid staff and also elected representatives from the villages. These committees make decisions about how to operate the project and use donor funds. CELUCT receives suggestions from the villages and these suggestions initiate their projects. Each village club is elected on an 'open day' by members of the whole village. In turn the local club sends representatives to CELUCT. If villagers have a problem, they approach their relevant village club. The club represents the issue to CELUCT and seeks support. For example, some villagers were worried that owners of a woodlot were overcutting their timber, causing erosion, and spoiling the gardens further down the slope. They approached their village permaculture club which presented the issue to CELUCT. CELUCT agreed to a project and sent a team to meet with villagers at a local household. Mediation began with an improvised dramatization of the problem, with staff playing the roles of the different parties involved. Discussion followed with separate meetings of the men and women from the village. They worked out a consensus solution and members of the CELUCT team joined the villagers to begin working on it. A ban on further timber cutting, re-planting, a check dam in the creek. Community processes like this reduce the effective rights of private property—to prioritize community control.

So, this example shows community control of the time and resources of the CELUCT NGO, along with community control of land use on household farms.

Kindness (the gift of care) is a key value of the project. For example, HIV/AIDS is a stigmatized condition in Africa. The project sets up self-help groups for people living with HIV, provides education to reduce stigma and organizes material support. CELUCT also sets up plots of land to grow food for the more marginal members of the community—orphans and people who have lost their partner through HIV. An economy of 'the gift' is also implied in CELUCT events. For example, for a village mediation CELUCT representatives arrived in the CELUCT car. At morning tea, the staff handed out drinks of cordial, apples and bread rolls. A ritual of the gift. CELUCT is coming and we are giving you something.

Limitations and tensions of a hybrid – the cattle project

Let's look at the limitations of CELUCT as a hybrid. Problems with their cattle project illustrate a conflict between the private market interests of some villagers and community interests. The conflict shows how the project must take these private interests into account to remain successful. The following account is not a critique of CELUCT. This was a temporary glitch, that has since been resolved. But it shows how market forces can interfere with the operation of a hybrid.

In the Chikukwa villages, individual households might own a small herd of cattle. As in all the community trust lands of this region of Africa, only a minority of families own cattle. All these Chikukwa cattle have access to the community grazing land above the villages. A treeless pasture on the hill tops. In the arrangement established before the cattle project got started, households appointed a young relative to take the cattle up to the community grazing area in the morning and then bring them back to the household kraal—their cattle enclosure in the village—at night. These young people got bed and board as their payment. An apprenticeship. Marking the individual household ownership of the cattle—despite the common ownership of the grazing lands. Each household had *their own* relative looking after *their own* cattle.

As these wealthier villagers expanded their herds, their cattle began to destroy the pasture. Overgrazing compacted the soil. The pasture quality suffered. Typical problems of community grazing in this part of Africa. By the time this project started, CELUCT had become an affiliated body of a community NGO that worked in the whole of the Chimanimani district - TSURO. TSURO, decided that in each local area of the district they would set up a cattle project to deal with such issues. On the Chikukwa lands, the project was run out of CELUCT.

The project used painted stones to mark the boundaries of different paddocks within the community grazing area. For two months, the cattle would be in the first paddock. Then the herders would move the cattle into the second paddock. And so on. Using this method of rotation, they would end up back in the first paddock at the beginning of the following year. This procedure is called 'holistic grazing management'. The aim is to let the grass recover between one bout of predation and the next, a year later. The method mimics the natural behaviour of herds on the African savannah. The grass gets deeper roots, more rainwater soaks into the soil and the cattle eat better. Improved infiltration on the hill tops means less erosion in the rainy season—and more ground water further down the hill in the dry season.

The plan was that four herders appointed by the CELUCT grazing committee would replace the household herders, the young relatives. A levy from the cattle owners would raise money to pay for the herders. These paid herders would receive training in holistic grazing management. Donor money had paid for a moveable kraal so the herders could stay overnight on the grazing area with all the cattle. A side benefit was to be keeping cattle out of the villages at night.

This planned strategy began well, with strong community support, but soon ran into severe problems.

As representatives from CELUCT explained these problems, they began with Paul. Paul had been in CELUCT from its very origins. He was one of the wealthier villagers and owned cattle. He also marketed coffee as a cash crop. CELUCT chose him to take training in holistic management. Paul was funded by CELUCT to spend a year learning this technique. When he came back from the training, he ended up in a dispute with the CELUCT management. He believed that CELUCT should extend his contract and give him a position as their holistic management expert. CELUCT claimed they had no funding for that. According to the CELUCT version, Paul expressed his frustration by sabotaging the project. He encouraged the cattle owners to refuse the levy. Grazing on the community land was their right, he said. The project had in fact received funding to pay the herders. But the CELUCT team had 'eaten' the money. The herders CELUCT had appointed were incompetent. They were not looking after the cattle properly.

Paul also encouraged the herders to demand higher wages, and to go on strike. Allowing the cattle to wreak havoc in the villages.

This sabotage was extremely effective. The only people whose cattle remained in the project were those who could not recruit a young relative for their herding. There are 91 households that own cattle in the Chikukwa villages. With about 1,000 households in the Chikukwa villages in total. In the beginning of the project 54 households joined up. But by 2014, there were only 27 households. Of the 972 cattle in the villages, only 152 were left in the program. Holistic management depends on *all* the cattle on the community grazing lands moving together from one paddock to the next—relieving the pressure on the pasture till the following year. But of course, this was now impossible.

What was the perspective of the cattle owners who left the program? They claimed that at the end of a grazing cycle, the cattle had chewed the grass down to nothing in the working paddock. Starving the cattle. Up to six had died. They objected to the project's commitment to herding the cattle together at night and keeping them on the grazing land—rather than taking them back to their household kraal in the village—as per previous practice. This new procedure transmitted infection. It was the design of the project and the incompetence of the paid herders that was causing the cattle deaths, they claimed.

The CELUCT cattle management team had a different interpretation of the deaths. That the owners of the cattle were not supervising them when they returned to the villages at night. They had eaten plastic waste on the side of the road and gummed up their digestion.

So CELUCT is trying to intensify the community ownership of resources through taking control of the community grazing area. A gift economy measure to deal with problems in a private market arrangement—by asserting community control. Saving the gardens of villagers, increasing infiltration of water, sustaining the grazing fields as a long-term community resource. The market economy context spoils this plan. Cattle owners worry that their valuable cattle may be in danger. The few families that own cattle have a background in migrant labour. Men migrate to work in mining, industry, or on commercial farms—when they are young. The women stay in the village, looking after the children and the household farm. The men save some money and buy cattle. A bank in retirement. For weddings and funerals, or emergency medical treatment. The households that own cattle are the lucky few. They do not want to trust their hard-won resource to community herders and an experimental system of cattle management. They do not want to pay for herding, using up their scarce cash resources. The dispute is kicked off by Paul when CELUCT does not grant him an extension on his contract, dashing his hopes for a paid job. He resents the CELUCT management team. Some on the team began in CELUCT as community volunteers when he was also a young community volunteer. Now this lucky few have a dependable cash income. He persuades the cattle owners that the management team has selfishly appropriated some of the community funds. A likely piece of market behaviour, even though a slander in this case.

Other challenges to the project

This is just one example of a clash between the market context of the program and its gift economy initiatives. Other more basic structural issues are also relevant.

There is a global context that limits and threatens CELUCT. A project like CELUCT is a very rare thing in NGO and rich country government aid in Africa—and in African government initiatives in the villages. Almost all projects are devoted to the pipe dream of entrepreneurial success. The idea that food security will come about when these smallholders sell a niche crop—and use that money to *buy* food and synthetic agricultural inputs. Such projects almost never work, but they express the hegemony of the capitalist cultural machine. That global market context makes a hybrid like CELUCT unusual. The pressure towards entrepreneurial solutions is a constant threat. The danger is that CELUCT will drop household food provision and be diverted to entrepreneurial projects—for the more well-educated families.

An entrepreneurial path is also very attractive to the Chikukwa villagers themselves. Subsistence household production is low status compared to a cash income. By 2014, the next generation (following the initiation of the CELUCT project) had finished high school. They had absorbed the skills their parents had learned from the project. Calculating yields, experimenting with different pest control solutions, cropping techniques, animal husbandry. A form of cultural capital with economic potential. Some young people from the villages grasped this opportunity. They re-opened fields owned by their clan 15 kilometres from the villages. Growing a crop of potatoes for the nearby town market. They were assisted by agricultural extension officers, advising them on inputs for a commercial crop. Following the logic of college agriculture training. Some of the most enthusiastic young people were now too busy to support the subsistence solutions that had been the hallmark of CELUCT. These potato growing households maintained their cereal cropping – with purchased inputs. But they neglected the household production of vegetables, fruit, and small livestock. They would *buy* these extras. In practice these purchased additions were patchy and insufficient. This commercial solution was only open to a minority, leaving the poorer villagers with their subsistence solutions—and without the help of the young shakers and movers.

This market context is also implied in charitable funding. Non-government donors are *giving* help rather than trying to make a profit. But their help reflects the hegemony of market ideology. They reach for entrepreneurial solutions. Quite often, local leaders also see these as the way forward. Charitable organisations from the global North fund some subsistence projects but rarely make a clear distinction between these 'household food provision' projects and entrepreneurial projects—tending to favour the latter. These aid-based entrepreneurial projects hardly ever work[2]. This setting was a pressure on CELUCT. Their German church donors (DEE) had provided them with most of their aid funding. After funding household food solutions for more than a decade, DEE turned to strategies closer to their Christian mission. Peace building and conflict resolution. CELUCT certainly had expertise in this field and were able to take up these funding options. DEE initiated a community mediation project for the whole district—organized by TSURO, the district organisation that grew out of CELUCT in the Chikukwa villages. This change in emphasis drained funds from the permaculture wing of CELUCT. There was little chance of any *other* international NGO reaching out to fund CELUCT's *non-market* interventions in the villages.

Perspectives on hybrids

This discussion of hybrids is not meant to sideline other transitional strategies. For example, 'direct action'—interfering with the capitalist machine. Forest blockades, mining blockades, occupations. Autonomous zones, trying to carve out social space outside the market.[3] Reformist strategies working through environmentalist or social democratic parties. My view is that it is very hard to predict what is going to work best to advance system change. Where the strategies mentioned above are concerned, the debate on the left treads a well-worn path. By contrast, 'hybrids of the gift economy and capitalism' are not understood well. The misunderstandings come from all parts of the political spectrum.

In the liberal imagination

In the liberal imagination these organisations are 'civil society'—a necessary counterbalance to the market. In civil society people are 'citizens' and not just 'employees' or 'consumers'. The combination of market capitalism and civil society enables representative democracy, the perfect solution to the world's problems.[4]

It is true that pure market capitalism is an impossibility. Capitalism always rests on non-market community action. What I reject in liberal analysis is the idea that 'civil society' unproblematically *supports* the market economy. These two chapters have shown how hybrids *challenge* the market economy. They can be prefiguring institutions that point the way to a post-capitalist system of gift exchange and community ownership.

Hybrids with rose-coloured spectacles

Many environmentalists are likely to see these hybrids as *just* market organisations. They are *alternative* market institutions because they are governed by ethical commitments. They prefigure a change to an alternative post-capitalist market economy where businesses will operate according to a 'triple bottom line'. System change will be change to an ethical market economy. I will call this 'the rose-coloured view of hybrids.'

The permaculture movement, following Mollison's writings describes this strategy as 'right livelihood.' Mollison writes:

> ... adoption of an ethical basis to action, to the placement of money and resources, and to the determination to act in accordance with one's beliefs. All of these can occur independently of political change ... when enough people change, then political systems (if they are to survive) may follow.[5]

Within social theory, geographers Julie and Katherine Gibson-Graham and the sociologist, Erik Olin Wright adopt a similar perspective.[6]

Summarising my analysis in these chapters.

- Alternative ethical businesses are limited by their market economy context. They may survive these pressures. But they may not—falling by the wayside or becoming just another standard business.
- It is misleading to see these businesses as simply 'market' businesses. What they do is *challenge* market logic in one way or another.
- The rose-coloured approach ignores the dangers of recuperation. As Anitra Nelson puts it, there is a monetary system out there that can 'fatally interfere with and damage non-capitalist models that attempt to persist alongside it.'.[7]
- The rose-coloured viewpoint sees alternative market institutions as first pieces in a post-capitalist market economy. My argument is that to get to post-capitalism, hybrids would have to change their spots. Linking up. Behaving less and less like market cooperatives today.
- Hybrids are just one part of a total transition strategy. Autonomous zones[8], confrontations, propaganda for system change and the revolution itself are also necessary.

Leftist purism and hybrids

Finally, there is another leftist approach to these hybrids, a 'left purist' critique of hybrids.

One approach of left purism is to argue that hybrids cannot be an authentic opposition to the system because they do not *challenge* the power of the capitalist class. The most useful leftist strategies are direct actions (blocking capitalism) and propaganda for the revolution (the only real solution). As John Jordan puts this view, it is a myth that capitalism can be transformed through the peaceful development of alternatives. We need resistance, 'confronting and dismantling unjust structures of power to make way for other cultures to flourish'.[9]

Another version of left purism argues that *real* prefigurative institutions reject all participation in the system. Hybrids cannot be *counted* as alternative. For example, they pay wages or sell commodities. Purist leftists see the writing on the wall when a community organisation starts to pay its executive officers. The slippery slope to recuperation. Next thing you know you will be cutting deals with evil magnates. The 'autonomous zone' is offered up as the only useful prefiguration for post-capitalism.

My argument is that confronting capitalism is not enough and can often be a waste of time. Prefigurative cultural change is a necessity for a successful revolution. This can come from hybrids—that often work when an autonomous zone would not. Investigating the gift economy in these organisations allows us to see what is prefigurative about them.

The purist attack on hybrids sets a high bar. We will never charge for anything, we will commit our time without payment, we will only use items that have been produced ethically. Taken literally, these goals are unattainable. The capitalist class owns the means of production. Almost every useful item has been produced to make money. Almost everyone needs a paying job. You will end up falling short one way or another. Activists can gloss over awkward realities, framing their practice in the best possible light. A leading organizer never worries about getting a job—their parents will help out if things get really dire. What we are using in our activism has all been produced at someone's expense—the phones, laptops, heaters, fridges, electric kettles, amplifiers, and projectors. Our prefiguring alternatives fold up when the volunteers get other commitments. Young people—who do not yet have a full-time job—do most of the voluntary work. We struggle to pay the rent on our community centres. These issues are hard to raise in groups dominated by purist leftism. Constant self-criticism drains energy. There is always something that we could be doing more correctly. It helps to recognize what we are doing as a *hybrid*—and to make it a success in its inevitable market context.

Purist leftists make 'the revolution' a measuring rod for current activism. I would be the first to agree that we need system change. But judging one's actions by that rubric is an open cheque for self-sacrifice. That does not make a lot of sense if we want a post-capitalism based on autonomous sociable creativity. People create hybrids to bring optimism to their lives. Using the market enables that in ways that purism forecloses. Margaretta could not have a full-time career in Middle Eastern dance without charging for tuition.

The next chapter will be a concluding discussion. Reviewing the argument of the book, taken as a whole. But also focussing in on some of the issues that get raised when you lay out a program of this kind. Is it colonialism to propose a utopia? What about population control in a gift economy? If science and technology have been shaped by a capitalist and Western hegemony, would we be better off doing without them? Or at least by looking to a pluriverse of very diverse localized alternatives rather than a global utopia? How can these questions be informed by a feminist critique? Or by an investigation into human societies as they were lived prior to the scientific revolution? What are the basic causes of class that may get revived in a post-capitalist aftermath?

Endnotes

[1] Terry Leahy, *Food Security for Rural Africa*, London, Routledge, 2019; Gillian Leahy and Terry Leahy, *The Chikukwa Project*, DVD, Black Dog Pictures, Australia, 2013.

[2] Terry Leahy, *Food Security*.

[3] Hakim Bey, *T.A.Z.: The Temporary Autonomous Zone, Ontological Anarchy, Poetic Terrorism*, 1985, viewed on November 22, 2023, https://theanarchistlibrary.org/library/hakim-bey-t-a-z-the-temporary-autonomous-zone-ontological-anarchy-poetic-terrorism.

[4] For example, Robert D. Putnam, *Bowling Alone: The Collapse and Revival of American Community*, Simon and Schuster, New York, 2000; Karl Polanyi, *The Great Transformation: The Political and Economic Origins of Our Time*, Beacon Press, Boston, 2001.

[5] Bill Mollison, *Designers' Manual*, Tagari Publications, Tyalgum, Australia, 1988, p. 50.

[6] Julie and Katherine Gibson-Graham, *The End of Capitalism (As We Knew It)*, University of Minnesota Press, Minneapolis, 2006a; Julie and Katherine Gibson-Graham, *Post-Capitalist Politics*, University of

Minnesota Press, Minneapolis, 2006b; Erik Olin Wright, *Envisioning Real Utopias*, Verso, New York, 2010.

7 Anitra Nelson, *Beyond Money: A Post-Capitalist Strategy*, Pluto Press, London, 2022, p. 98.

8 Bey, *The Temporary Autonomous Zone*.

9 John Jordan, 'Artivism: Injecting imagination into degrowth', in *Degrowth in Movement(s): Exploring Pathways for Transformation*, Corinna Burkhart, Matthias Schmelzer and Nina Treu (eds), Zero Press, London, 2020, p. 69.

Chapter 12
Conclusions

This book has been written to explain how system change to a liveable future could actually work. I have been outlining a feasible pathway to a gift economy post-capitalism. Showing how such a post-capitalism might be preferable to other options. But, of course, it would be fanciful to ignore the difficulties we might have. Class society has been around for at least six thousand years of human history. It seems like a mad dream to imagine a sustainable society that is also a long-term victory over class. Our environmental problems mean that system change is inevitable. But there is nothing to prevent a new class society rising from the ashes. Pushing the vast bulk of humanity into impoverished slavery. A new feudalism as it has been called[1]. Class society is a simple mechanism. Cereal agriculture permits an agricultural surplus. A ruling class takes control of the surplus. It pays an army, either in kind or with money. They manage the subordinate class and stave off attacks from other states. What is thoroughly depressing is this. It is unlikely that any of the key requirements of this mechanism will go away, however dire the current crisis. We are unlikely to forget how to do cereal agriculture!

Beyond money

Doing without money is a huge part of the gift economy utopia that has been explained here. A new social mechanism to end class and live sustainably cannot use money. Money is not accidentally connected to class society. A class society may operate without money – like the Incas. But money is a useful tool of class societies. It is no accident that the class societies of Eurasia used money. Also, no accident that capitalism, a social order premised on money, is yet another class society. Continuing the use of money is guaranteed to re-start class society, whatever the good intentions.

The usefulness of money and markets is premised on alienated labour. Money makes it easy to provision an army and raise taxes. An economy based on money sidelines other values – social and environmental. The failure of so many revolutions is partly down to the continuation of money into the post-revolutionary settlement. Monetary economies allowed aspiring elites to take control again. Destroying attempts to do things differently.

In a market every player must make sure that they win monetary exchanges as often as possible. To fail in this is to fail to get the resources you need to make your operation work, to secure your standard of living, your place in market competition—within a hierarchical order defined by money. Money inevitably claims priority.

Money implies a state. A universal system of valuation requires a centralized enforcement—to make sure the value of money is protected and maintained.

Money creates inequality. The lesson of the Monopoly game. There are winners and losers in every monetary exchange. Winners are given leverage to win more.

The market and colonialism go hand in hand. Market competition tempts players to the easy leg up provided by primitive accumulation. Turning nonmarket resources into capital.

The earth cannot afford this system. Money looks past the environment. It cannot do otherwise. The gift economy is the way to combine autonomous creative work, distribution by the producers, high-tech production, care of the environment, gender equality, cultural diversity, and participatory governance.

Utopias

One of the common objections to a project like this book is that we have had enough of utopias. Utopias make a mad assumption that all humans are basically the same and that a one size fits all solution can work. There is an implied imperialism, crushing diversity.[2] An argument that goes back to Foucault's essays on the Enlightenment and grand narratives. I have a few comments on that.[3]

It is money that imposes a uniformity on societies. Competition between producers tends to produce a universal price on commodities, as Amin points out.[4] The market imperative drives companies to globalize similar products, even when there are local variations. Cars, apartments, pop music styles.[5] At the same time the market imposes a uniform system of social ranking. A gradation of ownership and income, quantified through a global monetary system. The gift economy is the opposite of all this. A global society that encourages and permits diversity. People are producing goods and services that fit their own cultural understandings and distributing them with a regard to need—in a way that makes sense to them.

My view is that you cannot get away from 'utopias' by rejecting them as imperialist. Any set of ethical critiques adds up to a list of recommendations. Even when couched as not this, not that, not the other. It still ends up as – well instead this, well instead that and so on.[6] It is all very well to promise the world that you do not intend to impose your utopia on other people. But just *having* an ethical perspective is to contradict some other perspective, you cannot avoid that.

We are naïve if we think we can tell people we need system change without explaining our utopia. You think the present system is a catastrophe. No argument with that. Well, what do you propose to replace it? A perfectly reasonable question. A very unsatisfying answer is to say, we want diversity. That different people will come up with different answers. Anti-utopianism masks a very real problem for those wanting to replace capitalism. We do not agree about what that replacement might be. This sends a message that we do not know what we are doing. And a lot of our suggested solutions are not very convincing.

This book has identified the gift economy as one approach and recommended that. I have identified two other left approaches. One is democratic socialism. Most everyday punters understand that idea perfectly well and do not like it. The other is radical reformism. The default for leftists who reject socialism. But hardly a popular solution for most people. If they liked it, they would be voting for the Greens parties. They see it as the nanny state. Life run by interfering, moralising middle class bullies—who cannot be trusted. In this book I have been more concerned with why it cannot work, even if people wanted it.

My last point on this. I do not really take these anti-utopian relativist raves seriously. Do these critics of utopias really want a diverse global future—with half of humanity living as serfs in a theocratic ethno-state? Well no. Scratch the surface and you will find one of three things.

1. Anarcho-primitivism a la John Zerzan and Derrick Jensen. A diversity of horticultural egalitarian societies with a pre-class toolkit.[7]

2. The gift economy as metaphor. Moral ideologies about caring and looking after each other—but not much about how that looks—*as an economy*. Money is not explained as a system of social organisation. Critical asides about exchange value and commodities. But never anything you can get your teeth into.[8]

3. Our old friend radical reformism. A la Herman Daly with a post-colonialist gloss tacked on.[9]

I am sorry to be so caustic. These are lovely people. But really?

Population

Population is the topic that you always get when you lay out an alternative economic system before an audience. Don't we need to reduce population to relieve the pressure on the planet? How can you do that in a gift economy? The people raising these issues imagine that a strong central government—with a police force and army—is the only thing that can control population pressure. Yes and no.

Within current capitalism, some governments have done a much better job at this than others. Which points to the fact that it is a social and cultural problem. Not an innate evolution-based drive of the human species. The governments that have done nothing are usually beholden to some mad version of Christian fundamentalism. Posing as traditional. Backed up by a version of masculinity that sees offspring as a proof of manly vigour and economic status.[10]

Social scientists know quite a lot about this issue. It is surprising so many global North environmentalists are ignorant.[11] First up, birth rates are in fact falling. With this, global population will peak and then start to fall later this century.[12] Second, environmental problems are very much connected to one's position in the global economy. Australian per capita consumption is four times what the earth can bear while the global *average* is 1.5 times. The old slogan I = P×A×T (Impact equals Population × Affluence × Technology) applies. Third, even in poor countries today, the level of education of women is a key to population pressure. Increase the education and independence of women and you see a decline in fertility rates. This suggestion is not meant to let men off the hook where population is concerned. To treat it as 'a woman's problem'. It is about tactics that may work where patriarchy is well entrenched. Where men want children as a token of masculine achievement. Finally, the bleeding obvious. People have more children when they worry some will die. They are depending on their children to look after them in their old age – because society won't.[13]

The gift economy is the ideal social structure to deal with all these issues. A safety net of community material support, security in all basic necessities, equality for women, a reduction in unnecessary consumption. A largely local bioregional economy. Where people know how they depend on adequate land and forests for future generations. An economy where you do not have to destroy the environment to get access to necessities.

Tech and the gift economy

Whenever you introduce the idea of a gift economy, a typical reaction is to assume that you are talking about a low-tech Hobbit village society, with feudal technologies. I have explained why I do not make this assumption. A complex technological society could function without money. I envisage quite a bit of use of high tech. Nevertheless, I would make the following comments. We need to massively cut down our use of non-renewable resources. By using less high-tech things made from metals. By rigorously recycling everything we can't grow. We need technologies that well-informed people can understand and fix – Illich's concept of convivial technology.[14]

We could make do with a lot less high tech than we think. I go ballistic when I hear people say that the starving global South needs fossil fuels to rescue them from poverty. In my experience in African rural villages, a huge improvement could be made to people's lives by composting toilets, and a local version of permaculture agriculture. The technological requirements are all very low tech—chicken wire, fencing wire, nails, garden tools, poly-pipe, a bit of cement, mosquito nets, some guttering and that is about it. The problems in those villages are not an absence of high tech. In fact, they are usually awash with mobile phones. Their problems are based in social structure, local politics, and the dominance of the capitalist imaginary.[15] Yes, I would like to maintain a high-tech solution for serious medical problems and pandemics. For example, vaccination treatments. I think good contraception and safe childbirth is essential to save us from patriarchy. But I would hate to think that we are scared of getting rid of class society—because we are worried about losing our high-tech. There is too much at stake.

Anarcho Primitivism

I would like to take a look at 'anarcho-primitivism'. It is not a strong contender in the left at the present time. Nevertheless, I get the feeling that the more current postcolonial critiques of modernity end up with similar implications.[16] Recent attacks on high technology as inherently alienating—and environmentally destructive—tread the same path.[17]

Anarcho-primitivism starts from the recognition that societies throughout most of human history were stateless. Using anthropological terminology, these were hunting and gathering societies. Even after the invention of agriculture, agricultural polities in a very large part of the globe were still stateless. Usually called 'horticultural' by anthropologists. Anarcho-primitivists suggest that we could do well by abandoning the technologies developed by class societies. Doing this, they argue, we could go back to this kind of stateless culture. In a recent formulation, we would do much better by restricting ourselves to tools powered by human muscles.[18] In a suggestion for post-capitalism, Skrbina and Kordie recommend going back to tools that do not use fossil fuel energy and do not use electricity.[19] Through a gradual process of increasing divestment away from high technology over a hundred years. They do not explain the rationale for eliminating electrical technology—except to note it as a part of our problem now. But we can certainly think of reasons. The question mark hanging over whether it really is possible to replace fossil fuels as an energy source for electricity. Going right back to mining the ores without using fossil fuels. The damage caused by 'extractivism', when the minerals needed for renewable energy are sourced by mining. The shortage of minerals if any whole scale renewables solution attempted to replace electricity powered with fossil fuels.

I am not entirely unsympathetic to this perspective. The stateless societies that anarcho-primitivists extol were egalitarian, at least as far as men were concerned. Within the partially separate community of women, there was also a rough equality. Though some people had more influence, no one had the authority to command obedience. These societies looked after their environments and had an enviable connection to the natural world. They had a rich cultural and creative life. Their work, if you could call it that, was not alienated. They chose what to do with their time and how they might want to distribute what they produced. Much of this is identical to what I have described as the gift economy.

What could be wrong with the anarcho-primitivist solution? Maybe this is the end point of collapse anyway and not a bad thing at that. I would certainly like a gift economy to be set up that has the scope to enable this—for those who want it. But I have a few qualms if it is conceived as a one size fits all solution for post-capitalism.

One issue is that there is no way we can forget our agricultural knowledge. The whole process of class society would surely start up again as soon as one of these horticultural societies, the offspring of collapse, re-invented class. Using an agricultural stored surplus to back up a ruling elite.

I do not find this solution particularly utopian where gender is concerned. My reading of these societies—as they have been in the past—suggests the following unpleasant aspects. Patriarchy, competitive masculinity, raids and small wars, cruel initiations, domestic violence. More intense in horticultural societies, but also present in hunting and gathering societies. Personally, as a long-term defector from all this toxic rubbish, I would not want to live there.[20] Also, as I have argued in this book, all these patriarchal aspects provide a grounding for the next roll out of class society. I do not think an act of will—and a cultural resolve carried over from the present—could eliminate all this from an anarcho-primitivism in practice. This time it *will* be different is not a convincing program.

Then there is the low-tech aspiration of anarcho-primitivists. Technology got us into this mess so let's abandon it. In a classic statement of the technological determinist position, Ellul claims that technologies determine social relationships.

> Technique [i.e. technology] elicits and conditions social, political, and economic change. It is the prime mover of all the rest, in spite of any appearance to the contrary and in spite of human pride … External necessities no longer determine technique. Technique's own internal necessities are determinative.[21]

This being the case, we must look at modern technology as responsible for the catastrophic crisis we are facing.

I doubt this supposed relationship. For example, maize was the staple crop of horticultural egalitarian Americans before Columbus. But also, the staple crop and a fundamental pillar of the class civilisations of the Americas. The Aztecs, Mayans, Incans, Cahokia. Far from maize, as a technology, shaping society in its image, it was a staple in two radically different social regimes.

The cutting edge of our environmental crisis is always technology. As Pineault demonstrates, technologies that use prodigious amounts of non-renewable resources and fossil fuel energy. But I see this damaging technology as being put in place because it serves the needs of particular capitalist firms, countries and entrepreneurs. The decision to go with these damaging technologies is a decision made to increase profits in a competitive market environment. Along with a political context that permits firms to externalize environmental and social damage when making technological decisions. As argued in other chapters, I see a much-reduced use of electricity as a reasonable target for post-capitalism. A level of use of renewables that would enable the cultural options coming out of digital communication.

In the community at large (north and south) there is really no appetite for this anti-technology solution. Most people view collapse to a low-tech world as a disaster. Without the knowledge that informs current technology, we would lose much of our useful understanding of the world. Along with the technological options that go with that. For example, our medical science, our current understanding of the cosmos, our agricultural science, our chemistry, the many sciences of the natural world—including those telling us where we are going seriously wrong. Our complex digital archiving and communication of cultural products. It is unlikely that we could maintain a global tolerant pluriverse without digital communication.

I use the 'our' here intentionally. I am of course aware that we have this knowledge now, at least in part, as a by-product of vicious global exploitation. Also, that this knowledge is spread very thin in some quarters. And finally, that this knowledge is used to much ill effect in the context of capitalism. Nevertheless, our understanding of all this science is very much a global resource by now. Do we have to lose all this to get rid of class society?

I mean if this is truly the only answer that will save the planet, I am all for it. Modern science be gone. But is it? I think that this thinking is based on a false analysis of why we are in the present pickle. It is not modernity/colonialism/science/the enlightenment/humanism—as a de novo package of *cultural invention* from Europe—that have caused the disasters of class society and its latest capitalist version.[22] Instead, I see it like this. The prime mover of the modern world is the ghost in the machine, the capitalist imaginary. That cultural invention has informed a social machine. The developments mentioned above have taken shape in the context of *that* social machine. Capitalism has made them serve it.[23] On the other hand, a lot of these developments have their own sources, they are not just side effects of capitalism. Likewise, these cultural inventions are not necessarily and forever tied to the capitalist machine.[24] What we might make of this flotsam and jetsam, washed up after the demise of capitalism, it is hard to tell.

Patriarchy, class and technology

What anarcho-primitivists overlook is the link between patriarchy and class. And the link between feminism and technology. It is no accident that anarcho-primitivism sounds like a very macho vision. A warrior fantasy.

As discussed in other chapters, patriarchy is well-nigh universal in human societies.[25] It depends on the advantage men have in political conflicts with women. While it is a wonderful thing to be responsible for childbirth and breast feeding, the gendered division of labour coming out of this allows men to take control of political life. The first significant feminist movement, in the late Victorian period, comes about as the size of the family drops, as reliable contraception is introduced, as death in childbirth is reduced. It gets another boost in the seventies with even more reliable contraception.

It is not technological determinism to say this. Women mobilized to attack patriarchy. A choice, a cultural invention. Yet at the same time a cultural invention enabled by a change in the material conditions. To wrap this argument up. Some version of our current medical understanding and our low birth rate are the preconditions for a successful feminist movement. In other words, a medical high technology to enable women to take equal power.

So, what is the link between patriarchy and class? As explained in this book, class society depends on patriarchy as a necessary precondition. Patriarchy is not enough in itself to cause class. But it is a vital plank. In patriarchy, men are largely absent from the daily care of infants. They have other fish to fry. The emotional links that come out of caring for infants tie you down. Boys growing up are anxious and uncertain about what it is 'to be a man'. They solve this problem by rejecting femininity and proving their masculinity in competition with other men – sorting the men from the boys, cutting the mother's apron strings. Some version of 'toxic' masculinity is a central element of patriarchy, reinforcing that power structure as men deny their nurturing side. The other key effect of the patriarchal family is the way it trains us all in the psychology of hierarchy and willing subordination. Through the experience of early childhood in the patriarchal household.[26]

These psychological characteristics are of great assistance to any class society. They inform the oppressive hierarchy of class and the wars that are necessary to maintain elite power. Without a technology that makes feminism possible, an anarcho-primitivism cannot remain egalitarian and horticultural for very long. The elements necessary to re-start class are all present—cereal agriculture and patriarchal masculinity.

While anarcho-primitivists benchmark horticultural egalitarian societies, some recent authors reference feudal and tributary societies of the ancient world. I find their defence of the glories of mediaeval cathedrals and Athenian philosophy unconvincing. If you look beyond these glories to everything else going on at the same time.[27] It seems more than a bit odd to insist on the determination of modern society by modern technology. While assuming that feudal technology has no similar determining power. That we could have a benign egalitarian sustainable society using feudal technologies.

My take is that technological knowledge provides options. Given those options, the social game, the ghost in the machine, is fundamental. Looking at all this, we must ask how far we might want to push an anti-modernist agenda. At any rate, that is how I look at it.

Winding up

I worry a bit that this book is a fairy tale. An escapist romp. We are facing a collapse. We are likely to destroy a large part of biodiversity before things settle down. With a warming of two degrees, people could only live south of Melbourne or north of London.[28] A superhuman effort in social reform and material construction would be necessary to re-locate the world's people. Even if that was in fact possible. That we could feed this number on that amount of land. We need some solutions that are politically possible in the short run. What to say about this. This book does not reject the reformist initiatives that seem more feasible in current times. But I have also pointed to their problems. Working on blocking the worst effects of capitalism—while developing a program to get rid of it—makes sense. Capitalism is the root of our worries. Even as disasters pile up, we can be aiming at the gift economy as the long-term solution. I don't know about anyone else. I look back at six thousand years of class society and think about the everyday people of those worlds. The ruin of their lives. And now we face extinction. There must be some way to end all this. That there will come a time when we look back on class societies as a great mistake, thankfully a thing of the past.

Endnotes

[1] For example, Yanis Varoufakis, *Technofeudalism: What Killed Capitalism*, New York, Vintage 2023; Thomas Piketty and Arthur Goldhammer, *Capital in the Twenty-First Century*, New York, Belknap Press, 2017; Wolfgang Streeck, *How Will Capitalism End?: Essays on a Failing System*, London, Verso 2016.

[2] Go, Julian, *Postcolonial Thought and Social Theory*, OUP, Oxford, 2016; Vanessa Machado De Oliveira, *Hospicing Modernity: Facing*

Humanity's Wrongs and the Implications for Social Activism, North Atlantic Books, Berkeley, California, 2021; Arturo Escobar, *Encountering Development: The Making and Unmaking of the Third World: 1*, Princeton Unversity Press, 2012; Ashish Khothari,, Ariel Salleh, Arturo Escobar, Federico Demaria, Alberto Acosta (eds), *Pluriverse: A Post-Development Dictionary*, Tulika Books, New Delhi, 2019; Michel Foucault, *The Foucault Reader*, ed. Paul Rabinow, Penguin, Harmondsworth, Middlessex, 1984.

[3] Foucault, *The Foucault Reader*.

[4] Samir Amin, *Global History: A View from the South*. Pambazuka, Capetown, 2011.

[5] Pamela Nilan and Yekti Maunati, *Decolonizing Social Science Research in Southeast Asia*, Palgrave, Singapore, 2025.

[6] Terry Leahy, *Humanist Realism for Sociologists*, Routledge, London, 2017.

[7] For example, Tyson Yunkaporta, *Sand Talk: How indigenous thinking can save the world*, Text Publishing, Melbourne, 2019; De Oliveira, *Hospicing Modernity*; Derrick Jensen, *Endgame: Vol 2: Resistance*, Seven Stories Press, New York, New York: 2006; John Zerzan, *Future Primitive and Other Essays*, Autonomedia, New York, 1994; Zerzan, John, *Running on Emptiness: The Pathology of Civilisation*, Feral House, Los Angeles, 2002.

[8] Kimmerer, Robin Wall, *The Serviceberry: An economy of gifts and abundance*, Penguin, Random House, 2024; Genevieve Vaughan, *For-Giving: A feminist criticism of exchange*, Plain View Press, Austin, Texas, 1997; Frank Adloff, *Politics of the Gift: Towards a Convivial Society*, Bristol University Press, 2022.

[9] Go, *Postcolonial Thought*; Kimmerer, *Serviceberry*; Tim Hollo, *Living Democracy: An Ecological Manifesto for the End of the World as We Know It*, University of New South Wales, Sydney, 2022.

[10] Terry Leahy, *Food Security for Rural Africa*, Routledge, London, 2019.

[11] William E. Rees, 'The Human Ecology of Overshoot: Why a Major 'Population Correction' Is Inevitable', *World* 2023, 4, pp. 509–527.

[12] Hannah Ritchie, Lucas Rodés-Guirao, Edouard Mathieu, Marcel Gerber, Esteban Ortiz-Ospina, Joe Hasell and Max

Roser, 'Population growth', *Our World in Data*, viewed on 26 November 2023, https://ourworldindata.org/population-growth?insight=population-growth-is-no-longer-exponential-it-peaked-decades-ago#key-insights; Kim Jungho, 'Female education and its impact on fertility: The relationship is more complex than one may think', *IZA World of Labor*, viewed on 26 November 2023. https://wol.iza.org/uploads/articles/228/pdfs/female-education-and-its-impact-on-fertility.pdf; Leahy, Terry, *Food Security for Rural Africa: Feeding the Farmers First*, Routledge, London, 2019.

[13] Ruth Dixon-Mueller, *Population Policy & Women's Rights: Transforming Reproductive Choice*, Westport, Connecticut, Praeger, 1993.

[14] Ivan Illich, *Tools for Conviviality*, Marion Boyars, London, 2001.

[15] Leahy, *Food Security for Rural Africa*.

[16] Yunkaporta, *Sand Talk*; De Oiveira, *Hospicing Modernity*; Jensen, *Endgame.*; Zerzan, *Future Primitive*; Zerzan, John, *Running on Emptiness*; Rees, *Overshoot*.

[17] Pasi Heikkurinen, Toni Ruuska (eds), *Sustainability Beyond Technology: Philosophy, Critique, and Implications for Human Organization*, Oxford Uni Press, 2021; Jean Baptiste Frezzos, *Happy Apocalypse, A History of Technological Risk*, Verso, London 2024; Jathan Sadowski, *The Mechanic and the Luddite: A Ruthless Criticism of Technology and Capitalism*, Oakland, CA, University of California, 2025.

[18] Toni Ruuska, 'Conditions for Alienation Technological Development and Capital Accumulation,' in Heikkurinen, *Sustainability*, p. 157.

[19] David Skrbina and Renee Kordie 'Creative Reconstruction of the Technological Society: A Path to Sustainability' in Heikkurinen, *Sustainability*, pp. 254-276.

[20] Yolanda Murphy and Robert Francis Murphy, *Women of the Forest*, Columbia University Press, New York, 2004; Colin M. Turnbull, *The Forest People*, Macmillan, London, 1993; Marvin Harris, *Cows, Pigs, Wars and Witches: The Riddles of Culture*, Hutchinson, London, 1975; Phyllis M. Kaberry, *Aboriginal Woman Sacred and Profane*, Taylor and Francis, London, 2004 [1939]; Ernestine Friedl, *Women and Men: An Anthropological View*, Holt, Rinehart and Winston,

New York, 1975; Baldwin Spencer, and Frederick J. Gillen, *The Native Tribes of Central Australia*, Macmillan, London, 1938; Pierre Clastres, *Archaeology of Violence*, Semiotext(e), Los Angeles, 2010; Kenneth Maddock, *The Australian Aborigines*, 2nd ed., Penguin, Ringwood, Victoria, 1982.

21 Cited in David Skrbina and Renee Kordie 'Creative Reconstruction of theTechnological SocietyA Path to Sustainability' in Heikkurinen, *Sustainability*, pp. 254-276; p. 264.

22 As argued by Go, *Postcolonial Though*; De Oliveira, *Hospicing Modernity*; Yunkaporta, *Sand Talk*.

23 Rachel Carson, *Silent Spring*, Houghton-Mifflin, Boston, 1962; Pineault; Luddites; Inventions; edited collection.

24 Michel Foucault, *The Birth of the Clinic*, A.M. Sheridan (trans), London. Routledge, 2003; Arthur Koestler, *The Sleepwalkers: A History of Man's Changing Vision of the Universe*, Hutchinson, London, 1959; Thomas S. Kuhn, *The Structure of Scientific Revolutions*, University of Chicago Press, Chicago, 1962.

25 Michelle Z. Rosaldo and Louise Lamphere (eds), *Woman, Culture and Society*, Stanford University Press, Stanford, 1974; Friedl, *Women and Men*.

26 Nancy Chodorow, 'Family Structure and Feminine Personality', in *Woman, Culture and Society*, Michelle. Z. Rosaldo and Louise Lamphere (eds), Stanford University Press, Stanford, 1974, pp. 43-66; Firestone Shulamith, *The Dialectic of Sex: The Case for Feminist Revolution*, Paladin, New York, 1972; Ti-Grace Atkinson, *Amazon Odyssey*, Link, New York, 1974; Wilhelm Reich, *The Mass Psychology of Fascism*, V.R. Carfagno (trans), Penguin, Harmondsworth, 1970.

27 Skrbina and Kordie 'Creative Reconstruction, pp. 269-270, also David Holmgren, *Future Scenarios: How Communities Can Adapt to Peak Oil and Climate Change*, Vermont: Chelsea Green, 2009; for accounts of feudal life, see for example Peter Laslett, *The World We Have Lost*. London: Methuen, 1965; Gideon Sjoberg, *The pre-industrial city: Past and present*. New York: Free Press,1965.

28 James Hansen, *Storms of My Grandchildren*, Bloomsbury, New York, 2009.

Appendix A – Capitalist Patriarchy

In feudal society

To understand the gender regime of capitalist patriarchy, let us begin with Europe. The source region for global capitalism. Let's consider its previous society—European feudalism.[1] Patriarchy was hegemonic as a cultural force. For example, religion was patriarchal. God and his son conceived as men. Men officiating as priests, bishops, popes. A bible that told women to obey their husbands. Accompanying folk viewpoints. The term 'scold' stigmatized women who tried to control their husbands in any way. A woman who talked back and made decisions. A husband who was 'hen pecked' could suffer a demeaning ritual. Made to ride backwards on a donkey while being insulted by the other villagers. It was expected that men would control their wives with violent beatings. An unequal division of labour—with women doing more hours of work than men. Men were more likely to travel away from home on work trips. When men and women were working together, men had authority. Random misogynists harassed prostitutes and state pogroms persecuted them. Parties of bachelors would rape servant women, claiming them to be prostitutes. Men had a right to the 'conjugal service' of their wives. Rape in war was ubiquitous.

Yet in comparison to the Victorian ideals that developed with capitalism, there were surprising expressions of women's power. If a husband died, the wife could take over the business as the widow. Women had recognized professional roles—as midwives or herbalists. Even the role of nuns as independent women, to some extent running their own show. With some female religious leaders canonized as saints. There was no expectation that women would be uninterested in sex, as developed in Victorian Europe. Theoretically, wives could also exercise the right to conjugal service. All these elements of women's power were built into feudal society.[2]

In feudal society, the division between men's work, as part of 'the economy' and women's work as 'private' and domestic, did not apply. Most production, including agriculture, was organized by the household with complementary roles for men and women. For example, women making the cheese while the men were ploughing. As a result, there was no clear economic distinction between domestic work and production. In the early feudal period, most people did not depend on a job paying money. They produced for their own use. Buying things with money was only a small part of daily life. The feudal ruling class would get a surplus when their peasants supplied a tribute in kind. Like looking after the lord's dog pack. Providing a portion of the crop. Making the lord's bed.

As we have seen, despite this complementarity in the economy, men dominated in families and in the broader political structures. Religion, the political system, the use of armed force. In the transition to capitalism, men used the leverage they had in feudal patriarchy to institute a new gender regime—capitalist patriarchy.

The transition to capitalism

So, let's look now at how this feudal patriarchy came to an end in the transition to capitalist patriarchy. Eli Zaretsky was a New Left author on these topics in the seventies.[3] Followed by the work of dual systems theorists such as Batya Weinbaum and Heidi Hartmann by the end of that decade.[4] Starting with Marx and Weber, Zaretsky points out that capitalism separates paid work outside the home from unpaid domestic work. In the capitalist economy, you make money out of the means of production by producing more stuff and selling it. Making a profit through that and extracting surplus value. To facilitate this, in the first stage of industrialisation, entrepreneurs brought weaving looms together in factories. Replacing cottage weavers (in their homes) with factory workers (in factories). The capitalist class did this because they wanted complete control over the paid work.

The work that was left over in the home suddenly became separated from 'production'. In fact, all this domestic work is also productive. But the work that was paid and directly benefited the capitalist owner was the work outside the home. This paid work ended up being called 'productive' work—as opposed to unpaid domestic labour. Federici traces the gender impact of these developments to the very earliest moments of capitalist wage labour. Urban guilds maintained the differential rates of pay between their male members and new female employees. After enclosure, it was easier for men to leave their villages and get work in towns, while women were tied down with family responsibilities.[5]

Nevertheless, the transition to wage labour posed a challenge to the patriarchal regime of the feudal period. In the feudal household the patriarch exercised direct and sometimes violent authority. As Weinbaum and Hartmann point out, the post-feudal economy of wage labour meant that it was perfectly possible for women, and adult children, to slip away from this authority and to live on a wage paid out by a capitalist boss.[6]

As these authors document, in England, the leading industrial country, several strategic interventions closed off this option. There was a cross-class alliance. Upper-class male philanthropists—alarmed at the 'moral' effects of industrial work on women—joined working-class male unionists—demanding exclusive access to higher paid positions. The factory acts restricted the hours women could work and excluded children from factory work—forcing women to return home to look after them. Along with this, men made demands to define their work as 'skilled' and to be paid at a higher rate than women. These strategies consolidated the link between women and domesticity. Ensuring that men achieved economic power through the wage.

In parliament, where the factory acts were enacted, the changes were introduced to 'protect' women from the immorality supposedly connected to factory work and mining. For example, drawings of half-naked women—towing carts in coal mines—created a scandal. Patriarchy masked as chivalry.

The moral economy of capitalist patriarchy

These changes were also early steps in the developing moral economy of capitalist patriarchy. In that cultural landscape, women take the role of 'God's police' as Ann Summers dubs it.[7] The historian Ruth Bloch talks about the rise of 'the moral mother'. The role of the moral mother is to institute an early moral discipline. To embody Victorian and puritanical moral ideals in her own conduct and to socialize children in those values. Values that back up the regime of the capitalist economy. Most fundamentally the work ethic, but also the allied puritan values—sobriety, punctuality, honesty, respect for property rights, sexual propriety. This moral landscape became the justification for the down grading of women's participation in the labour market. The stay-at-home mother as the acme of feminine virtue. As the working class gained income, working class women in rich countries left the labour market. Women who had to work could be paid a pittance because paid work was never a woman's true calling. The effect of this myth was to paint the home as a refuge of innocence from the dangerous public world. Implying that adult men had to be tough to survive this realm of nastiness and competition. As Ellen Willis pointed out, the social landscape becomes populated with good cops and bad cops. The good cops are husbands protecting their families from the nasty world out there. The bad cops are violent and dangerous men.[8]

The ideal of the moral mother started off in the upper class and was gradually implemented lower down the class hierarchy. By the 1920s, in the rich countries, many working- and middle-class women were staying home, unpaid. At least while the children were young. Government action cemented this ideal. In Australia the Harvester judgement of 1907 established a basic wage for men—premised on the idea that their wage would support their family. There were rules to exclude married women from the public service. And so on.[9]

Ann Cranny Francis unpicks the Red Riding Hood story in relation to the 'good cop'—'bad cop' duality that Willis describes. Red Riding Hood gets into trouble when she strays from the path that her mother has set for her. The Hunter is the good cop. He looks after Red Riding Hood by coming to her rescue. Killing the evil wolf, the bad cop, with his axe. This folk narrative reflects the construction of hegemonic masculinity in current capitalism. Men's sexuality is conceived as innately dangerous and problematic. It must be controlled. The good man controls their sexuality and looks after women, protecting them from the evil men out there—who act like wild beasts.[10]

The Red Riding Hood myth is a metaphor for the economy of capitalist patriarchy. Women are dependent on men economically. In the whole life course, they get only half the income of men of their own class.[11] So, husbands perform the role of the good cop, bringing home the income and protecting their families through that. Meanwhile men in general, men as a political and economic sex-class are the bad cops. Unless you're attached to a husband don't expect any help from us. Society will not come to your assistance. We will hang on to our control of income—rather than see women get a fair share. There will be no way to bring up a child comfortably—without the support of a husband. These dynamics still operate, after decades of feminist activism. These controls on money are part of the furniture of capitalist society. They are rarely seen clearly as foundational to a gender regime.[12]

As the terms, 'good cop' and 'bad cop' indicate, women are also in danger from the men in their families. Men who have the economic power. Ranging from exploitation in domestic labour to violence.

Capitalist patriarchy as a circle of causes and effects

This economic structure operates as a circle. Start at any point and go round the circle to get back to where you came from. So, let's start at women's low income. The higher income men get through their wages gives them power in the family. They use that power to force a division of labour that advantages them. Their wives do more hours of obligatory work for the couple. Considering both paid work and domestic work. This means that men have free time in their lives to organize politically to maintain patriarchy. This can take the form of men's leisure pursuits with other men. A site where men collude in consolidating patriarchy. Through participation in public and political life. From the local football club to parliament and company management. This political power enables men to maintain their economic domination, their higher incomes relative to women. We are back where we started.

Capitalist patriarchy comes to the Global South

As capitalist imperial power comes out of Europe, colonizing the rest of the world, it is facing up to very different patriarchal gender regimes. Some of these allowed powers to women analogous to the power options of medieval women in Europe.[13] The early response of colonial governments is to enslave or kill off the local population without regard to gender. Beyond this, capitalism begins to institute a regime of paid labour. Like the regime of the home countries. The colonial authorities and commercial interests are most likely to attract the most powerful gender in the local population by offering them paid work. Access to the monetary economy. In mining, landed estates or manufacturing. Doing this, they are making assumptions about money and gender that are already entrenched in the rich countries. Treating men as breadwinners. On the other hand, to maintain the colonial advantage of super exploitation they are not actually paying these men a living wage. They are assuming that women will supplement the family's cash income with some subsistence production. Tying women to their villages—further closing off their options to move to urban cash employment. Leading rural women to spearhead resistance to new capitalist accumulations in the countryside.[14] As Federici mentions, this new patriarchal development is not just a *cultural* phenomenon of capitalist patriarchy coming out of Europe. Women's role in reproduction enables it. It is harder for women to achieve the mobility necessary to chase new opportunities in paid employment—opened up by capitalism in the global South. As in Europe, a patriarchal gender order advantages men—relative to women—in the subordinate classes.[15]

Be that as it may, a contrary tendency also operates in the global South in recent decades. Young women are preferentially recruited in factory work, in urban work, in tourism and as temporary migrants working in other countries. Because of their cheap cost as workers and the opportunity to move away from the family before marriage. This counter tendency empowers women through the wage, however minimal. In the middle classes of much of the global South, dual income families are common and education for women is entrenched. These phenomena illustrate the point made by dual systems theorists for the European context. Capitalism allows various challenges to feudal patriarchal regimes.

Endnotes

[1] Jean- Louis Flandrin, *Families in Former Times*, Cambridge University Press, London, 1979; Rodney Hilton, *Class Conflict and the Crisis of Feudalism*, Verso, London, 1990; Eileen Power, *Medieval Women*, Cambridge University Press, 1975; Janet L. Nelson, *The Frankish World 750-900*, Hambledon Press, London, 1996; Marc Bloch, *Feudal Society*, Vols 1 & 2, Routledge, London; Peter Laslett, *The World We Have Lost*, Methuen, London, 1965.

[2] Sylvia Federici, *Caliban and the Witch: Women, the Body and Primitive Accumulation*. Autonomedia, New York, 2004.

[3] Eli Zaretsky, *Capitalism, the Family and Personal Life*, Harper Collins, New York, 1986;

[4] Heidi Hartmann, 'Capitalism, Patriarchy and Job Segregation by Sex', in *Capitalist Patriarchy and the Case for Socialist Feminism*, (ed) Z. Eisenstein, Monthly Review Press, New York, pp. 206-247, 1979; Batya Weinbaum, *The Curious Courtship of Socialism and Feminism*, Monthly Review Press, New York, 1978.

[5] Federici, *Caliban and the Witch*.

[6] Weinbaum *op cit*; Hartmann *op cit*.

[7] Ann Summers, *Damned Whores and God's Police*, UNSW Press, Sydney, 2016; Ruth H Bloch, 'American feminine ideals in transition: the rise of the moral mother, 1785-1815', *Feminist Studies* 4 (2) pp.101-126, 1978; Phillipe Aries, *Centuries of Childhood*, Pimlico, London, 1996.

[8] Ellen Willis, 'Feminism, Moralism and Pornography', *New York Law School Review*, 38 (1), 1993.

[9] Ann Summers, *op cit*.

[10] Anne Cranny-Francis, *Engendered Fiction: Analysing Gender In The Production And Reception Of Texts*, NSWU Press, Kensington, NSW, 1992.

[11] Hugh Davies, and Heather Joshi, 'Gender and Income Inequality in the UK 1968-1990: the feminization of earnings or poverty?', *Journal of the Royal Statistical Society*, 161(1): 33-61, 1998.

[12] Christine Delphy and Diane Leonard, *Familiar exploitation: a new analysis of marriage in contemporary Western societies*, Polity Press, Cambridge MA, 1992.

[13] Pam Nilan and Yekti Maunati, *Decolonizing Social Science Research in Southeast Asia: New ways of knowing*, Palgrave, Singapore, 2025.

[14] Nilan and Maunati, *Decolonizing Social Science Research*; Federici, Caliban and the Witch; Terry Leahy, *The Riddles of History and System Change*.

[15] Federici, *Caliban and the Witch*; Terry Leahy, *The Riddles of History and System Change*, http://gifteconomy.au/feminism-and-ecofeminism/ 2025; Terry Leahy, 2019, *Food Security for Rural Africa: Feeding the farmers first*, Routledge, London, 2019.

[16] Nilan and Maunati, *Decolonizing Social Science Research*.

Appendix B – The Gift Economy and the Anthropologists

As mentioned in chapter four, the Situationists of the late sixties were the first to use the term 'gift economy' in the sense meant in this book. Doing this, they borrowed the term from the anthropological theorist, Marcel Mauss. Mauss did not envisage the term as referring to a mode of production—a concept to describe a whole society. A society may have a variety of 'economies' including both gift economies and trading economies.[1] On the other hand, it makes sense to see our current economy as dominated by capitalism. The term 'capitalist mode of production' makes sense. Likewise, many of the stateless societies studied by anthropologists have no money, most exchanges are gifts, and a calculative trading economy is a small part of economic life—if it exists at all. It is not completely silly to see these as 'gift economies.'

In a grand overview statement, Mauss makes a declaration that must inspire optimism for the post-capitalist gift economy.

> Thus, we see that a part of mankind, wealthy, hard-working and creating large surpluses, exchanges vast amounts in ways and for reasons other than those which we are familiar from our own societies.[2]

Chris Gregory defines the 'gift economy' as a system of production and consumption where the 'circulation [of gifts] creates relationships of a particular type, namely a qualitative relationship between the parties to the exchange. This makes them reciprocally dependent on one another'.[3] By contrast, commodity economies set up *quantitative* relationships between objects, expressed as money value.[4]

Mauss looks at several societies as paradigmatic for this concept.

The Northwest Native American tribes are famous for the *potlatch* ceremony. For example, the Tlingit and the Haida. These are societies in which hereditary rank systems create some men as chiefs or nobles. These chiefs hold large ceremonies in which their village hosts chiefs from other villages and their communities. There are festivities, ritual events and feasting. The host chief and his community entertain their guests. The chief gives away items that are valuable—decorated blankets, coppers. The chief may burn some of these items as a sign of his wealth. These ceremonies are competitive. The rival chief invited is obliged to hold a similar ceremony down the track and invite the first chief and his community. 'The obligation of worthy return is imperative. Face is lost forever if it is not made'.[5] Prestige goes to the chief who most recently hosted the biggest potlatch. The 'remarkable thing about these tribes is the spirit of rivalry and antagonism that dominates all their activities'.[6]

> The agonistic character of the prestation is pronounced. Essentially usurious and extravagant, it is above all a struggle among nobles to determine their position in the hierarchy to the ultimate benefit, if they are successful, of their own clans.[7]

Malinowski is an anthropologist who studied the Trobriand Islands societies. Mauss draws on his account. Here, a set of islands communicate with each other through a particular kind of gift exchange. The key players are chiefs who represent their communities. There are two key prestige items. One is armbands made from a shell, normally worn by men on special occasions. The other are necklaces of red spondylus shells worn by women. Along with these special ritual gifts, expeditions in sea going canoes carry more prosaic and everyday useful gifts such as stone axes. The chief or their representative leads an expedition to another island.[8] When they arrive, they meet their trading partners. Men who do not yet have a partner tempt them with gifts. The host chiefs and important men from the island community hold festivals and feasting. Ultimately, they 'loan' the special armbands or shell necklaces to their partners. The obligation on the partner when they return from their expedition is to hold the gift for a time. Then to mount another expedition to pass it on to yet another island community in a similar visit. While the precious object is resting the community holding it gloats over the gift that their chief has obtained.[9] There is a complex play of shells and armbands. Armbands move from island to island, west to east. Shell necklaces move east to west. Like the potlatch, these ceremonies are competitive. There is a circular motion that links up these transactions so that the cycle can be completed. The chief and his cohort from island A who visit island B are repaid by a visit to A from island B. The aim of the chief and his cohort from island B is to outdo the original gift. The one that came with the previous visit from island A to their island.

The underlying motives are competition, rivalry, show, and a desire for greatness and wealth.[10]

The third gift exchange that Mauss describes is that of the Maori. In this, the donor A gives a prestige gift to B. The obligation on B is to pass the gift on to a third party, C. C is then obliged to give a gift back to A. These gifts can be different items but are regarded as having similar value. There is prestige in being the donor and in giving, if possible, a larger gift. Mauss interprets this exchange in terms of the Maori concept of the *hau* of a gift. Translated as the 'spirit of the gift'. The gift has a spirit that is attached to its place of origin and its original owner. As it is passed on, it is still 'owned' by the donor. Leant to the recipient. The obligation on the recipient is to pass that spirit on to C through a gift to C. In turn, the *hau* of the gift demands that the gift, which can be a different item altogether, is returned to A. The *hau* wants to 'return to the place of its birth, to its sanctuary of forest and clan and to its owner'.[11] So C then returns a gift to A to achieve this completion. The gift constrains the recipient to return some kind of gift. Not necessarily the same as the original gift. It could be some property, merchandise, labour, feasts, entertainments or gifts—of equivalent or superior value. This return will give the new donor power over the donor of the first gift.[12]

Mauss draws a general conclusion from this case, which he applies to all examples. In a gift economy, the gift never totally leaves the possession of its original owner.[13] It is as though this object continues to be a part of its original owner.[14] As such, the only way to repay the gift and cancel the debt and obligation, is to return it to its original owner in some form or another. By giving a bigger return gift, the recipient obligates the original owner. In a commodity economy, the commodity is an object that can be alienated completely from its original owner and the person who produced it through an exchange. For example, by trade, replacing the first object with another of the same value. Or sale, replacing the traded object with money. This can never happen in a gift economy. The gift remains an extension of the personality of the donor. In the case of the Siane, the object is the property of the producer by virtue of the work done to create it. It is likened to their shadow, a part of their person.[15]

As Chris Gregory points out, this argument relates to a similar claim made by Marx.[16] In societies where everything is owned in common, trade in commodities is impossible. The person who owns a commodity owns it individually. Because of that they can pass this ownership on to someone else—through the sale of the object for money. But if everyone in your community has some claim to ownership of all things—the common wealth of the community—you cannot do this. Instead, gifts in such societies are to an extent loans. A change in use rights that does not obliterate the original ownership of the donor community and its representative in the donor.

Later anthropologists have added a fourth example. These are exchanges from Papua New Guinea.[17] The *moka* gifts of the Kawelka and other tribes. In these, big men aim to enhance their prestige by holding a feast and donating pigs, yams and other valuables to another residential community. They encourage their community to raise up the pigs required. A burden for the women of the community, who must grow the sweet potatoes to feed the pigs.[18] These events are competitive. The big man from the recipient community is obliged to hold a similar feast and gift back. To become the big man is to outdo the original host community. 'For example, if A gives 100 pigs to B, and the latter replies with a counter-gift of 150 pigs which A cannot repay, then B is the "big-man" because he gave the last gift.'[19]

As the above examples make clear, prestige gifts often have no obvious economic utility. They can be the same item, returned later.

Pigs replace pigs. Necklaces replace armbands—that replace necklaces. So, what is the point? Mauss and later writers see the main point as creating alliances and making friends.[20] The rivalry between these chiefs and big men is often expressed as warfare. But in the gift exchanges, this warfare is replaced by events signifying alliance and friendship.[21] Even if there is a competitive logic to the exchanges. Competition by means of gifts rather than war. Alongside these showy prestige gift events are exchanges with a more obvious pragmatic value. For example, yams exchanged for fish, stone axes exchanged for ornamental feathers.

Mauss and later writers also talk about forms of gift in stateless societies that are not so regulated or calculated. That are not part of prestige competition between important men. Gregory refers to these as systems of *generalized exchange*.[22] Another term is *generalized reciprocity*.[23] In the economic mode of generalized exchange, participants in a community provide others in their community with goods and services in response to need or in response to a request. The principle that the giver is superior in prestige to the recipient does not operate.[24] The obligation is to look after the members of your community. This can be informal and ad hoc. Like helping someone looking after a child. Or it can be quite formalized, with the obligation specified in detail. For example, it is very typical in clan-based societies to distribute meat from a hunt according to specified kinship ties. For the Thonga of southern Africa, the hind leg goes to the younger brother, the tail and rump to the in laws, a piece of the loin to the maternal uncle.[25] The key fact is that there is a general expectation of reciprocity. You expect the person you helped to help you at some future time. But there is nothing specific about reciprocating. Also, no definite idea about when the reciprocating might happen. Finally, reciprocity may take the form of a gift from another member of the clan, not the recipient of your gift. The exchanges are not just about providing necessities to other people in your clan. They also represent 'an important symbol of clan solidarity and identity'.[26] Gifts of food and cooperative work parties are common forms of generalized exchange. As Yan points out, in many cases like this the concept of reciprocity does not really capture what is happening. It is a gift without any obligation to reciprocate or any expectation of reciprocity.[27]

By contrast to *generalized exchange*, the four paradigmatic 'gift economies' described above (*potlatch, kula, hau, moka*) are referred to as systems of *balanced exchange*, or *balanced reciprocity*. In a balanced exchange there are definite expectations that the recipient will reciprocate with an equivalent or better gift—within a time frame that is also quite precise.

A third kind of exchange, *trading exchange* is referred to as *negative reciprocity*. These are based on the hope of making a good deal—a calculative exchange.[28] Negative in the sense that you want to give *less* than you get back. For example, barter or commodity exchange.

Sahlins, the author of *Stone Age Economics*, develops a formula to sum up where the three different kinds of exchange are most likely. Those who are closest in kinship ties and closest in space—living in the same residential community—are most likely to have relationships based in generalized exchange. Those at more distance—like members of the same clan or tribe in another village—are more likely to exchange goods via balanced exchange. People at the margins of your cultural milieu— like those from another tribe—are more likely to exchange goods with you through calculative trading. Where the aim of the partners is to get the best deal possible. By getting *more* goods in exchange for what you have to offer. The opposite of a balanced exchange, where the aim is to *give* more goods and services to enhance prestige.

> Reciprocity accordingly inclines toward balance and chicane in proportion to sectoral distance ... generalized modes are dominant in the narrowest spheres and play out in wider spheres, balanced reciprocity is characteristic of intermediate sectors, chicane of the most peripheral spheres.[29]

Gregory claims this generalization is backed up by a wealth of anthropological evidence.[30]

Relevance to the Post-Capitalist Gift Economy?

So, is this anthropology in any way relevant to the idea of the gift economy as a post-capitalism? Chris Gregory, in a suggestive comment, indicates that the classic gift economy and its alternative, the commodity economy, may just be *two* economic systems. There might be others that political economy could also describe. So, the post-capitalist gift economy promoted in this work may be yet a third option, different from either of these.[31]

These systems are analogous to the gift economy of post-capitalism in relation to the dichotomy—obligated or voluntary. The usual dichotomy operating today holds economic contracts as obligatory and gifts as voluntary. In fact, economic contracts can be upheld through a legal process that specifies coercive compulsions. By contrast, gifts are voluntary.[32] No one can compel you to give your uncle a Christmas present! The balanced exchanges of stateless societies defy that dichotomy. The gift is conceived as voluntary, as a generous act of good will. The donors retain their right to refuse a return gift 'and it is this which lends an appearance of generosity to the circulation of goods.'[33] As Gregory reminds us, a clan-based economy is relatively egalitarian—'there does not exist one group of people who live off the surplus product of another group.' The distribution of land tends to be equal. There is no way to coerce people by threatening their basic livelihood.[34] Yet there is a *social obligation* to return an equivalent gift. To pass on the gift. Ultimately, the failure of these balanced exchanges may end up with a tribal war. So, these gifts are neither purely 'free and gratuitous presentations' nor are they 'purely utilitarian production and exchange', they are a 'kind of hybrid.'[35]

The gift economy of post-capitalism is a bit like this. Compacts are promises to provide gifts. They are formal and written down with specified dates. But at the end of the day, the decision to make such a promise is a decision of the donor community and its workers. The end of alienated labour implies that workers have a right to determine distribution. What is more, the obligation to fulfil the term of a compact is enforced through the court of public opinion.

It does not come with coercive sanctions. It is only to be expected that there are cases where the compact cannot be met for quite valid reasons. Nevertheless, there are limits to what people can do *without* encountering a coercive sanction. A community that hoards a valuable resource may end up being taken over by angry neighbouring communities. That is the logic of the revolution itself. A community that released a toxic gift on its recipients would be compelled to desist. For example, nuclear waste that is a peril for future generations.

The idea that the prestige gift is never really alienated from the original donor finds an echo in the post-capitalist gift economy. The key principle is this. The person doing the labour has the right to distribute the fruits of their labour. Perhaps that is not an absolute right. The community of origin and the community of the recipients also have an input into these distributions. It is expected that workers will tailor their work to expressed needs. That compacts will detail these expectations. Yet the workers can review their options and decide to give their product to another recipient. It is not like a commodity economy, where the work is available to anyone with money to pay the price. With possession passing completely to the new owner. Instead, in the post-capitalist gift economy, as in these stateless societies, the spirit of the original owner passes on with the gift. This debt to the workers would follow the gift and be expressed through festive celebrations.

Let us look at balanced reciprocity. The post-capitalist gift economy could well host some exchanges that looked like balanced reciprocity. One village might provide another with fencing mesh. While the receiving village provided the donor village with chairs. These could be regarded as equivalents. On the other hand, a complex technological economy could hardly function if such reciprocal arrangements were compulsory for exchange. A train service must give its services to a great number of customers. Train workers would not want an avalanche of small gifts to provide recompense. In most cases the gift economy of post-capitalism would function more like the exchanges of the Maori that Mauss describes. A gives to B who gives to C who gives to D and D gives to A. But without any expectation of equivalence.

The only equivalence would come from the aim of all players to see *everyone* living enjoyable and interesting lives. Looking after the planet and its living beings.

Sahlin's theory of reciprocity can be stated as a general theory of human nature and economic structures. In stateless societies, it makes sense to look after your own local community (generalized reciprocity)—engaging in competitive prestige games (balanced reciprocity) with neighbouring communities. Avoiding war through that. At the extreme, friendly relationships are neither advantageous nor practical with remote strangers. Accordingly, calculative trade contacts are how you gain the best deal. Ultimately, the capitalist commodity economy which treats every person as a stranger and potential enemy—and uses money to create equivalences.[36]

I am somewhat sceptical of this reading of the anthropology. As the reader may have worked out, the post-capitalist gift economy seems most to resemble *generalized exchange*. Most anthropologists claim that this form of exchange is restricted to the local units of stateless communities. In one reading of this theory, generalized exchange is impossible in a large complex society.

Let us begin with the anthropology itself. The empirical generalisation Sahlins discovers may reflect the conditions of anthropology. A science linked to colonization coming from a commodity economy. It is no surprise that clan-based societies trade and barter at the border between their clan world and the commodity world. For example, the hunting and gathering !Kung —surrounded by Bantu farmers and pastoralists.

Another concern is the meaning of 'balance' in balanced relationships—and the meaning of 'equivalence' in trading relationships. As these concepts are found *in practice*. A small army of caveats undermines the concepts of balance and equivalence informing Sahlins' theory. Gifts may not always be the same. How they are rendered as equivalent, when a common measure of exchange value is absent, is a mystery. The quantity of goods that are regarded as *equivalent*, even with 'trading' between remote communities, is a very variable matter, changing from year to year.[37] The *time delay* in balanced exchanges varies. The return gift may never even happen. The nature of the return gift is so variable as to empty equivalence of any real content. It may just be prestige or a feast in honour of the donor. Consequently, the anthropologist, Graeber questions the very concept of 'balanced reciprocity'. It is more of a theory about how things *should* proceed than a description of what in fact happens.[38]

Lastly, in stateless societies, what has been called 'trading' between communities is not always seen as such. For example, the two trading partners become 'as kin'. They are 'friends', even if they are from distant communities.[39] At their meeting place, one lays out their offerings on the ground as a gift. Later, the other one returns and offers a gift of different items. This reciprocation is intended to go higher than the first offering.[40] Is this a calculative trading exchange—or a gift exchange? Different from the balanced competitive prestige exchange studied by Mauss. But all the same, a form of gift exchange? Sahlins describes the relationships between 'trading kinsmen' of the Huon.

> All goods are handed over as free gifts offered from motives of sentiment. Discussion of value is avoided, and the donor does the best he can to convey the impression that no thought of a counter gift has entered his head.'[41]

Alongside these questions about the anthropology, we can question whether these studies reveal the full extent of what may be possible for a post-capitalist economy.

1. Such societies do not have at their fingertips the technological resources that enable us to build global communities. These global communities can function through friendship and solidarity between remote partners. The internet and digital cultural artefacts enable an empathetic understanding of people who are geographically remote. Modern transport options (even the sustainable ones) allow travel and face to

face contact. The complexity of the gift economy, as I envisage it, requires *some* international cooperation. Though not on the scale of our current capitalist globalism. We have an interest in making this work. In a gift economy, these chains of production would function through partnerships quite like the trade partnerships of the stateless societies studied by anthropologists. But arranged by compacts, facilitated by digital communications, with goods transported in trains, airships and sailing ships. The basic unit would be international clubs of enthusiasts for a particular technology, science or cultural form. Cooperating to bring their expertise to the whole world.

2. The societies studied by anthropologists cannot be separated from their context in patriarchy. The toxic masculinity that goes with that and that *also* informs class societies. The demand for equivalence, the competitive striving for prestige, the constant danger of warfare, gift cycles as a substitute for war.[42] All these make sense for a masculinity that is fragile. With men striving to prove manhood by defeating rival men in gifting competitions. We could hope to get rid of all that in a future gift economy. To make use of aspects of human nature that are revealed in the generalized reciprocity also found in stateless societies. The pleasure and status to be found in looking after other people— expecting they will do the same for us. Rather than a demand for equivalence. To shore up an insecure psyche, damaged by the patriarchal family.

Endnotes

[1] Marcel Mauss, *The Gift: Forms and functions of exchange in archaic societies*, Trans. Ian Cunnison, Routledge and Kegan Paul, London, 1970, p. 20; Andrew Strathern and Pamela J. Stewart, 'Ceremonial Exchange: Debates and comparisons', in James G. Carrier (ed), *A Handbook of Economic Anthropology*, Second edition, Edward Elgar, Cheltenham UK, 2012, p. 245, 246.

[2] Mauss, p. 31.

[3] Chris A. Gregory, *Gifts and Commodities*, Hau Books, Chicago, 2015, p.xxvii.

[4] Gregory, *Gifts and Commodities*, pp. lxi, 4, 6.

[5] Mauss, p. 41.

[6] Mauss, p. 4.

[7] Mauss, p. 4.

[8] Mauss, p. 20.

[9] Mauss. p22.

[10] Mauss, p.26.

[11] Mauss. p. 9

[12] Mauss, p. 10.

[13] Mauss, p. 62, 42.

[14] Mauss, p. 10.

[15] Gregory, *Gifts and Commodities*, p. 43.

[16] Gregory, *Gifts and Commodities*, pp. 6, 12.

[17] Gregory, *Gifts and Commodities*; Strathern and Stewart, 'Ceremonial Exchange'.

[18] Gregory, *Gifts and Commodities*, p. xxv.

[19] Gregory, *Gifts and Commodities*, p.lviii.

[20] Marshall Sahlins, *Stone Age Economics*, Tavistock, London 1974, p. 220; Yungxian Yan, 'The Gift and the Gift Economy', in James A. Carrier (ed), *A Handbook of Economic Anthropology*, Second Edition, Edward Elgar, Cheltenham, UK, p. 277.

[21] Mauss, p. 18.

[22] Gregory, *Gifts and Commodities*, p. 16; Yan, pp. 292-296.

[23] Susana Narotsky, *New Directions in Economic Anthropology*, Pluto Press, London, 1997, Locs 974-986.

[24] Gregory, *Gifts and Commodities*, p. 50.

[25] Gregory, *Gifts and Commodities*, p. 51.

[26] Gregory, *Gifts and Commodities*, p. 51.

[27] Yan, *The Gift*, pp. 292-302.

[28] Yan, *The Gift*, p. 280.

[29] Sahlins, *Stone Age Economics*, p. 198.

[30] Gregory, *Gifts and Commodities*, p. 18.

[31] Gregory, *Gifts and Commodities*, p. lxii.

[32] Yan, p. 286, 287; Strathern and Stewart, *Ceremonial Exchange*, p. 240.

[33] Mauss, p.71.

[34] Gregory, *Gifts and Commodities*, pp. 14, 33, 34.

[35] Mauss, p. 70.

[36] Gregory, *Gifts and Commodities*, p. 41.

[37] Sahlins, p. 279.

[38] As noted by Gregory, p. xxxv.

[39] Sahlins, p. 198.

[40] Sahlins, p. 198.

[41] Sahlins, p. 303.

[42] Narotsky, *New Directions*, Loc 1337.

Acknowledgements

In writing this book I have been helped considerably by my friends and relatives. Ageing hippy and intellectual muse Pam Nilan encouraged me to face up to the concerns people have with utopias, plans for a stateless society, the likelihood of a successful anti-capitalist revolution and the like. Pam's research is always a background to my writings on related topics. Her commitment to ethnography is something I share. My long-time friend and colleague in my approach to system change is Anitra Nelson, who I met in 2010. We both have an intense commitment to a non-monetary way forward and to degrowth in the rich countries. I am always borrowing ideas from her writings. In joint presentations, we get to see how these ideas are received. Discussing such sessions has informed much of what is in this book. Eden Shadow is another close friend. We have been talking about this stuff for decades now. Eden came along to a set of presentations at Black Spark—where I workshopped these chapters with the Melbourne Degrowth group. Then Eden read the whole draft—giving me lots of useful editing suggestions and alerting me to points that needed more treatment.

Beyond this, I must acknowledge my other close friends and relations. My wonderful children who are always up for a discussion. Lily has had a particular role, helping me with several key chapters as a consultant and informant. My other housemate, Lena, the doyenne of 'Tarot Down Under', a humorous take on the Trump madness. As a result, I know more about this than most Australians. My male age peer mates, Dhirendra, Colin, Hans, Gary. My great array of amazing cousins. Always a strong support base. My sister, Gillian, one of the early organizers of women's liberation in Australia. An encounter with feminism that has been central to how I conceive system change. My long-standing involvement in permaculture is very evident in the book. Most of the issues I address come from years of hanging out at permaculture events. My best friend in the movement is April.

The groups I have been involved with since coming to Melbourne have provided the motive and opportunity to write these ideas up—from their first incarnations as a YouTube channel and podcast. Riff Raff radical marching band performs at left rallies of every description. They are great people and generous and kind activists. Black Spark and Catalyst are the two anarchist centres that host every kind of radical activity. I have been lucky to present ideas and get invites to seminars, zine fairs and night-time Solstice ceremonies. New International Book Shop organized a reading group that covered many books referred to here. I like their inclusive take on political action. Most recently I have joined a choir. Typical of inner Melbourne, choristers presume you will share a leftist politics. Likewise, the people who regularly meet at the local dog park. Where dog owners discuss political and personal events while the dogs frolic. Most directly relevant to this book is the Degrowth group that Anisa got going several years ago. We meet once a month face to face and then the following week on zoom for the Australia wide group.

In Newcastle, from 1990 to 2016, I got a lot from the Uni colleagues and from my teaching. Most of the undergrads were first in family. Newcastle gave me a way to understand Australian working-class perspectives—that I would never have had if I had stayed in Sydney. The feral environmentalist movement that mutated from anti-logging to climate change. The Middle Eastern dance school with Margaretta and Andrew, featured in one of the chapters here. The gay community and queer activists.

This book has been informed by face-to-face encounters with people from the global South. My friends, students, interviewees, and random strangers. In the mid-nineties, the university of Newcastle was an enthusiastic recruiter of overseas students. One cohort were academics and public service workers from Indonesia, taking PhDs on scholarships. Nazrina became my student with a thesis on North Bali farmers. I became friends with her and her partner Jean—while they were in Newcastle for the candidature. I travelled to stay in the villages she was looking at. Mere's thesis was on an environmentalist campaign in Bandung. I met Doni, another one of the students on scholarships, and a worker from IDEP, the peak permaculture body in Indonesia. At the Uni, we set up the Master of Social Change and Development in the mid-nineties. By 2003 we had recruited a team of students from Africa and other countries. They had a background in extension work in the rural villages, or work in local councils. This led to visits—where I stayed in villages with local people. Margaret, a primary teacher in a Limpopo village. Thoko, a health worker in a rural Northwest Province village. An international permaculture convergence in Malawi introduced me to people leading rural projects in Uganda and Zimbabwe. The CELUCT Chikukwa project in Zimbabwe was and is amazing. I stayed there three times. Making a documentary film about it with my sister in 2010. Getting to know the team running the project with their community. Eli and Ulli, Zeddy, Patience, Baba and Mai Matsekete, Phineas, Julious, Sam and others. In these years, I also stayed in Port St John, South Africa, and visited rural villages with the Is'Baya project officers, especially Peter.

A book on a post-capitalist system is inevitably in dialogue with the experiences of Indigenous people. I am also a white person whose lucky life has been premised on settler colonialism. I have been fortunate to have had some deep conversations with Aboriginal people in Australia. Helping me to understand the dire and ongoing effects of colonisation. In the eighties, my housemate Ned was the director of 'Wrong Side of the Road'. A fictionalized but ethnographic account of contemporary Aboriginal life. Auntie Veronica and her sister, from a community in South Australia, came to stay at our house—while the filming went on in Sydney. Lots of cups of tea and discussions. The daily narratives of harassment by the police, tragic young deaths and health problems. Later in Armidale I took on some Aboriginal tutoring that introduced me to the community there.

There are many more people that I could acknowledge but this is a good start. As always, the faults in this book are all mine. I cannot thank these supportive people enough for what they have contributed.